BIBLICAL GREEK
MADE SIMPLE

BIBLICAL GREEK MADE SIMPLE

All the Basics in One Semester

H. Daniel Zacharias

LEXHAM PRESS

Biblical Greek Made Simple: All the Basics in One Semester

Copyright 2018 H. Daniel Zacharias

Lexham Press, 1313 Commercial St., Bellingham, WA 98225
LexhamPress.com

Print ISBN 9781683591009
Digital ISBN 9781683591016

Lexham Editorial: Derek R. Brown, Thom Blair, James Spinti
Cover Design: Brittany Schrock
Typesetting: Scribe, Abigail Stocker

This book is a labor of love borne from necessity for my Greek students at Acadia Divinity College. I want to thank all of those students over many years who pushed me to be creative and innovative in my teaching of Greek. Thanks also to my colleagues and the leadership of Acadia Divinity College, particularly Dr. Harry Gardner, for their support and encouragement in my life.

Table of Contents

CHAPTER 3

Case Functions Made Simple 39

CHAPTER 4

Greek Indicative Verbs Made Simple 63

CHAPTER 5

Principal Parts and Alternative-Pattern Indicative Verbs Made Simple

CHAPTER 6

The Article, Adjectives, Pronouns, and Numbers Made Simple

CHAPTER 7

Adverbs, Prepositions, Phrases, and Clauses Made Simple. 153

Infinitives Made Simple 243

Where Do I Go From Here? 271

List of Tables

Abbreviations

acc.	accusative
adj.	adjective
adv.	adverb
aor.	aorist
conj.	conjunction
dat.	dative
decl.	declension
fem.	feminine
freq.	frequency
gen.	genitive
indecl.	indeclinable
inter.	interjection
interj.	interjection
masc.	masculine
mid.	middle
mid/pass	middle/passive
m/p	middle/passive
neut.	neuter
nom.	nominative
partic.	particle
pl.	plural
prep.	preposition
pr.noun	proper noun
pron.	pronoun
sg.	singular
voc.	vocative
w/	with

Texts and Resources

DBL Greek	*Dictionary of Biblical Languages with Semantic Domains*
EDNT	Exegetical Dictionary of the New Testament
LALGNT	*Lexham Analytical Lexicon of the Greek New Testament*
LN	Louw-Nida
LXX	Septuagint
NIDNTTE	New International Dictionary of New Testament Theology and Exegesis
NT	New Testament
TDNT	Theological Dictionary of the New Testament

Introducing *Biblical Greek Made Simple*

L earning the biblical languages is a worthy endeavor that can bear much fruit in the life of the faithful student of God's Word. Yet many students are apprehensive about learning Greek. They may question its usefulness or are even downright hostile toward the idea. This short introduction is intended to give you some encouragement for the journey as well as to explain why many Bible colleges and seminaries today are still committed to teaching future ministers how to engage with the biblical text in its original language. I want to tell you why I believe that Greek is worth the effort.

I have gone through the challenging process of learning Greek, and so has your professor. You need to recognize that not only has your teacher been right where you are, but you are probably in a classroom of students in the same boat as you. It is tempting to think, "no one is suffering with this as much as me!" You are wrong. There are many other believers around the globe who are engaging in the study of Greek. If you are like I was, Greek was the first language beyond English you learned. However, you have many brothers and sisters in Christ throughout the world who are learning Greek as their third or fourth language. Remember, countless thousands have already trod this path. Fathers in church history, spiritual giants in the faith, and pastors have trod this path. They did it because they believed it was worth the effort to be able to study of God's word it its original languages.

Another important point of encouragement you need in this process is about learning a language in general. Learning a language often makes you feel like a kid again. That is okay! You'll forget things; you'll mispronounce things; and you'll ask questions about things you learned only 30 seconds before you asked it. This is normal, so

ENCOURAGEMENT

don't feel discouraged. The rest of your classmates are likely feeling the same way. The nature of learning a language, especially the grammatical portions, is that you will often not feel like you really "get" it. You will not feel like you understand chapter 3 until you are finishing chapter 5—particularly those of you in a classroom setting. This is normal, and it is why repetition is so important for learning a language.

I assure you that God's word is worth the investment of your time and worthy of engagement in its primary languages. We live in a culture of instant gratification, but that is not God's way, and it certainly will not be your experience when learning Greek. It will require hard work, a lot of time, patience with yourself, and a good attitude. As you work through this grammar, keep in mind these words of encouragement:

> The main point is, with all and above all, study the Greek and Hebrew Bible, and the love of Christ.—*John Wesley*

> I have firmly decided to study Greek. Nobody except God can prevent it. It is not a matter of personal ambition, but one of understanding the most Sacred Writings.—*Ulrich Zwingli*

> The more a theologian detaches himself from the basic Hebrew and Greek text of Holy Scripture, the more he detaches himself from the source of real theology! And real theology is the foundation of a fruitful and blessed ministry.—*Heinrich Bitzer*

KEEPING THE END IN MIND

God has designed our body in a curious (and wonderful) way: the more we exercise, the stronger we get. Our brains are no different. They get stronger with more use and exercise. Learning Greek will be difficult, as will your education in general. This is a good thing—have high expectations set for yourself! As the apostle Paul says, "Make every effort to present yourself before God as a proven worker who does not need to be ashamed, teaching the message of truth accurately." (2 Tim 2:15 NET).

Gaining knowledge and confidence in the study of Biblical Greek will elevate your understanding of the text and will equip you to read in high definition, enabling you to read the Bible in a more faithful and accurate way. This is because engaging with God's word in the original language causes you to *slow down* and see with greater perception than you ever have before. If ever there is a spot to slow down and delay the instant gratification mentality of modern society, your time with God and the Bible is that time. Equipping yourself with the skills to study the Bible in its original languages enables you to slow down and observe. You will be thankful that you did.

A word of caution: the ability to read the Bible in its original languages is not a mystical portal to secret knowledge. Read the following from Moisés Silva about what competence in Greek means:

> The kind of competence in view here does not necessarily lead to a display of linguistic fireworks. In fact, such knowledge often does not even rise to the surface, but that does not mean it has been unproductive. Language students, to be sure, typically feel cheated if as a result of their hard work they cannot come up with exegetical razzle-dazzle . . . It is not the primary purpose of language study to provide the means for reaching astounding exegetical conclusions, although sound linguistic training can at least prevent students from adopting inadmissible interpretations. The true goal of learning New Testament Greek is rather to build a much broader base of knowledge and understanding than the student would otherwise have . . . what matters most is the newly acquired ability to interpret texts responsibly on the basis of comprehensive rather than fragmented (and therefore distorted) information.[1]

---

1. Moisés Silva, Introduction to *New Testament Greek for Beginners* by J. Gresham Machen and Dan G. McCartney (Prentice Hall, 2003), 10–11. I'm indebted to Rodney Decker for alerting me to Silva's discussion (http://ntresources.com/blog/).

WHY AND HOW THIS GRAMMAR IS DIFFERENT

The approach of *Biblical Greek Made Simple* is unique. It is different from other grammars not only in layout, but its distinct pedagogical approach and breakdown.

1. *Biblical Greek Made Simple* is designed for a 12-week (or so) class or self-learner. That is why there are only 11 chapters in this book. Most (not all) Greek textbooks, certainly all of the popular ones used in seminaries today, are designed for a full year (i.e., two semester) course and span from 20 to 35 chapters or more.

2. *Biblical Greek Made Simple* teaches you to work with Logos Bible Software. Although some Greek professors want you to avoid Bible software because it is a crutch (and it certainly can be!), it is increasingly a reality that students, pastors and laypersons are using Bible software to aid their study of the Bible. Instead of fighting that trend, I am embracing it and trying to equip you to use Logos Bible Software to its full potential. If you are about to embark on learning Greek with this grammar, purchase of a Logos Bible Software base package is highly encouraged. If you are a student, Logos is generous with student discounts, so be sure to sign up for their academic discount.

3. Because of the above two realities, *Biblical Greek Made Simple* employs a conceptual, or wide-angle approach to teaching you Greek. It is by no means a dumbing down of Greek—there is still plenty of memorization work to be done. But the questions asked are different from a typical grammar. For instance, a typical grammar would ask a student "what is the parsing of λύομαι?" To which your answer would be "present, middle/passive, indicative, first-person, singular, from λύω." Instead, this grammar will say, "Your Bible software tells you that λύομαι is present, middle/passive, indicative, first-person, singular, from λύω. How does Logos know that? What does it mean

to be present? What does it mean to be middle/passive? What does it mean to be indicative? And how good of a job did your English translation do in translating that word?" This textbook will strive to give you a solid overview of the entire NT Greek system, and challenge you to answer questions relevant to meaning and translation, while still helping you understand the basics of how Greek works and how Greek words are formed.

4. *Biblical Greek Made Simple* accommodates those who want to go on to further Greek studies, in particular those who want to spend another 12 or so weeks to increase their competency in Greek such that they are at the level of other students using a traditional full-year grammar. This is done by going through the book twice. At the end of each chapter, there is a *Second Time Around* section for those who are doing their second pass through the grammar, to suggest some things to focus on and any applicable additional information.

Are you ready? Here we go!

Signs and Sounds of Greek Made Simple

What's the Point: Here is a statistic for you—100 percent of the New Testament was written using Greek letters. How else can you learn how to read and speak a language than by learning the alphabet? Learning this chapter thoroughly will equip you for proper reading, recognition, and pronunciation of the Greek New Testament.

1.1 THE GREEK ALPHABET

The first building block of any language is the alphabet. While the primary goal for most students of New Testament Greek is to learn to read and interpret, being able to read Greek aloud with proper pronunciation is very valuable—after all how many of you want to go through months of Greek and not even be able to read it aloud! Take the time right from the beginning to *read all the Greek you see aloud*, even if you don't understand it yet.[1]

Scholars are not entirely certain how ancients pronounced Greek, but there are several popular options. Most introductory grammars, including this one, choose what is called the Erasmian method.

The following table of the Greek alphabet shows you the regular and capital letters,[2] as well as the transliteration letter used, and finally a pronunciation example. Transliteration is the English letters used to write Greek words to replicate the sound. While it is not critical that you know how to transliterate, it is good to know because many books, articles, and commentaries employ transliteration when discussing Greek.

---

1. How to access the audio of the Greek New Testament in Logos will be explained at a later point.

2. Greek capital letters are called majuscules and the small letters are called minuscules. In your Greek New Testament you will encounter mostly minuscules. Capital letters will occur at the beginning of paragraphs (but not sentences), at the beginning of quotations, and as the first letter of proper names.

Table 1: Greek Alphabet

majuscule	minuscule	name	transliteration	pronunciation
A	α	alpha	a	**f**ather
B	β	beta	b	**b**est
Γ	γ	gamma	g, n[1]	**g**ame
Δ	δ	delta	d	**d**irty
E	ε	epsilon	e	**e**stablish
Z	ζ	zeta	z, dz[2]	**z**oo, ad**ds**
H	η	eta	e	pr**ey**
Θ	θ	theta	th	**th**ought
I	ι, ᾳ[3]	iota	i, y[4]	id**i**ot, **i**gnite (short)
K	κ	kappa	k (or c)	**k**ite
Λ	λ	lambda	l	**l**augh
M	μ	mu	m	**m**ark
N	ν	nu	n	**n**ice
Ξ	ξ	xi	x	bo**x**
O	ο	omicron	o	**o**xen
Π	π	pi	p	**p**aint
P	ρ	rho	r	**r**ight
Σ	σ, ς[5]	sigma	s	**s**ound
T	τ	tau	t	**t**ight
Υ	υ	upsilon	y, u[6]	s**u**per, **u**sher (short)
Φ	φ	phi	ph	**ph**ilosophy
X	χ	chi	ch	**ch**iropractor
Ψ	ψ	psi	ps	li**ps**
Ω	ω	omega	ō	**o**dor

1. A *gamma* (γ) is pronounced "n" sound when it comes before γ, κ, ξ, and χ.

2. A *zeta* (ζ) is pronounced "dz" sound when it is in the middle of a word.

3. The little mark underneath the *alpha* is called an iota subscript. It appears under *alphas* (ᾳ), *etas* (ῃ), and *omegas* (ῳ). When it is a subscript it is still transliterated, but it IS NOT pronounced.

4. An *iota* (ι) is transliterated with a "y" when followed immediately by another vowel.

5. This second form of the *sigma* is called a final *sigma*, and is used only when the *sigma* is on the end of a word.

6. A "u" is used in transliteration when an *upsilon* (υ) follows another vowel.

1.2

GREEK VOWELS

Like English, some vowels are always short, some are always long, some can be both, and they can form a tag-team to make a new sound combination called a diphthong. Work especially on identifying diphthongs in words and pronouncing them correctly.

Table 2: Greek Vowels and Diphthongs

Short	Long	Pronunciation
ε, ο		see above
	η, ω	see above
α, ι, υ or α, ι, υ		see above
	αι[1]	**ais**le
	αυ	**ou**t
	ει	**eigh**t
	ευ	**feu**d
	οι	**oi**l
	ου	gr**ou**p
	υι	s**ui**te
	ηυ	**ayoo**
	ωυ	s**ou**l

1.2.1

Vowel Contraction

Another important thing to know is that vowels can lengthen or change. There are a few in particular to be most aware of. *Alphas* (α) and *epsilons* (ε), when they come into contact with another vowel (like another α or ε), will often lengthen to an *eta* (η). Under similar circumstances, *omicrons* (ο) lengthen to *omegas* (ω). Vowels can also contract together to become diphthongs. You do not need to know how or why, just know that it does happen *a lot* when vowels come into contact with one another.

◣ Watch the video at ◥
http://youtu.be/S8842oS0CtU to solidify the previous section.

---

1. Students will most often mispronounce this diphthong because ai in English says "ay" not "eye."

1.3
GREEK
CONSONANTS

The Greek consonants are grouped into different categories based on the way they are pronounced with our mouths. Sibilants have an "s" sound, liquid letters keep the air flowing through your mouth, and stop letters stop the air in your mouth at some point. Stop letters are further subdivided into labials (you stop the air with your lips), palatals (you stop the air by touching the roof of your mouth), and dentals (you stop the air by touching your teeth). Try reading through the alphabet in the previous section again and pay attention to what your mouth does.

Table 3: Consonant Categories

Sibilants		σ (ς) ζ ξ ψ		
Liquids		λ μ ν ρ		
Stops[1]		smooth	→→→[2]	rough
	labials	π	β	φ
	palatals	κ	γ	χ
	dentals	τ	δ	θ

1.3.1
The Sigma with a
Liquid

Of all of the letters, you will learn to treat the *sigma* with the most fear and trepidation because it causes the most problems. The first thing you need to know is that a *sigma* has an invisibility cloak. When it follows a liquid letter, it will often disappear completely (more on this in future chapters)—I like to say that it "slips on the liquid." *Theta* (θ) also can do this after liquid letters.

1.3.2
The Sigma with the
Stops

The second thing about *sigma* (σ, ς) is that it is a bully. When it comes after a labial stop, the two combine to become a ψ. If the *sigma* comes after a palatal it becomes a ξ. The *sigma* is most sinister after a dental, I like to say that the dental loses its teeth because the dental will disappear all together. Dentals are also weaklings in that they do not like to end a word. If they do, they disappear.

---

1. The darkened portion of the table is often referred to as the "square of stops" or "table of stops."

2. There are times when a smooth stop consonant will change to a rough stop.

Although *sigma* is the biggest bully, *kappa* (κ) and *theta* also interact with the stop letters in similar ways—they are *sigma*-wannabees. When a *kappa* follows a labial, it prefers the rough stop and will cause a *pi* (π) or a *beta* (β) to become a *phi* (φ), but this change will make the *kappa* disappear. *Kappa* changes smooth palatals to the rough palatal as well. It acts like a *sigma* with dentals, making them disappear altogether, while it sticks around. A *theta* causes the same changes as a *kappa*, but it doesn't disappear. The *sigma* rears its ugly head once more when a *theta* follows a dental. The dental disappears, and a *sigma* takes its place!

Table 4: Stop Interactions

	smooth		rough		+ σ¹			+ κ			+ θ	
labials	π	β	φ	+ σ	= ψ	+ κ	= φ	+ θ	= φθ
palatals	κ	γ	χ	+ σ	= ξ	+ κ	= χ	+ θ	= χθ
dentals	τ²	δ	θ	+ σ	= σ	+ κ	= κ	+ θ	= σθ

▲ Watch the video at ◣
http://youtu.be/7R4AXepe5p4 to solidify the previous section.

There are three sets of marks that are important to know in Greek: breathing marks, accent marks, and punctuation. The first two sets are related to pronunciation. Greek punctuation was not part of the original text but were added by later editors.

1.4
JOTS AND TITTLES IN GREEK

Every Greek word that begins with a vowel (or ρ) has a breathing mark. You may have noticed in the alphabet table that there is no letter that makes an "h" sound. Greek rough breathing makes the "h" sound. A smooth breathing mark makes no difference in pronunciation. Breathing marks are written: (1) above the first letter of any word beginning with a vowel or ρ, (2) above the second letter if the word begins with a diphthong, or (3) in front of the letter if it is a capital letter.

1.4.1
Breathing Marks

---

1. This section shows what happens when a *sigma* is added to any of the consonants in that row. With the following sections showing the interactions when a *kappa* or *theta* is added.

2. Sometimes, not always, when a τ is preceded by a *nu* (ν), the *sigma* bully may kick them both out.

Table 5: Breathing Marks

Name	Mark	Above letter	With capital	With diphthong
smooth breathing (no pronunciation)	’	ἐστιν (estin)	Ἰησοῦς (Yesous)	εἰμί (eimi)
rough breathing ("h" sound)	‘	ὑμῶν (humōn)	Ῥαββί (rhabbi)	εἰς (heis)

1.4.2

Accent Marks

Although English does not write accents, most readers have seen accents—on French words, for instance. Accents alert the reader where to place emphasis in the word. Do not worry too much about memorizing the accents, just learn to see them and work on emphasizing the syllable that they are on when reading aloud. There are a few times when accents help to identify otherwise identical words; these will be pointed out when the time comes.

An accent's quantity means it will sit over short or long vowels or diphthongs. Finally, you will only ever see an accent over the last three syllables of a word, and only the last three syllables of a Greek word are named. These three syllables are:

Antepenult	Penult	Ultima
ἄν	θρω	πος
ἐ	αυ	τοῦ
	αὐ	τοῦ
		ὅ

Table 6: Accent Marks

Name	Mark	Quantity	Syllable position	Example	W/breathing mark	
acute	´	short or long	antepenult/ penult/ultima	βάλε	ὅτι	ἤδη
circumflex	~	long	penult/ultima	σῶμα	ἦν	ὧδε
grave	`	short or long	ultima	μὴ	ὃν	ἂν

Punctuation marks are not original to the writing of the scriptures, but nonetheless are important parts of our current Greek text. People that know Greek much better than you (or I!) added punctuation, so in general you can trust them. These punctuation marks will help you recognize sentence divisions, clause divisions, and questions.

1.4.3
Punctuation Marks

Table 7: Punctuation Marks

Name	Mark	Example
period	.	ταῦτα γράφω ὑμῖν ἵνα μὴ ἁμάρτητε.
comma	,	Τεκνία μου,
question	;	τί ἐστιν ἀλήθεια;
semicolon or colon	·	λέγει αὐτῷ ὁ Πιλᾶτος·
quotation mark[1]	capital letter	καὶ λέγει, Οὐκ εἰμί.
	ὅτι	λέγουσιν αὐτῷ· ὅτι οὐδεὶς ἡμᾶς ἐμισθώσατο.

Diaeresis occurs over the second vowel of what looks like a diphthong. Essentially, diaeresis tells you *not* to treat those two vowels as a diphthong, but to pronounce them separately.

1.4.4
Diaeresis, Crasis, and Elision

Both crasis and elision are indicators that something odd has happened. What represents these two things is a *coronis*, which looks like our English apostrophe. Crasis is when two words are smashed together. The result is one word, with a coronis placed over the word to represent the change. Elision happens in English too, with words like "can't" and "don't." The apostrophe in English represents a dropped vowel. Elision in Greek also represents a dropped vowel.

---

1. Marks of a quotation are not considered punctuation marks, but are important markers to recognize in sentences for divisions.

Table 8: Diaeresis, Crasis, Elision

Name	Mark	Example
Diaeresis	¨	Μωϋσῆς
Crasis	᾽	κἀγώ (καὶ + ἐγώ)
Elision	᾽	ἐπ᾽ αὐτήν (ἐπὶ + αὐτήν)

1.4.5
Greek Syllables

Greek syllables function with one main rule just like English syllables: only one vowel (or diphthong) per syllable. There is also another rule that governs syllables, again like English: certain consonants always stick together. Consider in English: sh, ch, st, ck, etc. You would not divide English syllables between these consonants because they form a unit. In Greek many consonants also stick together: βλ, κλ, θλ, πλ, μν, πν, γρ, θρ, κρ, πρ, τρ, χρ, πτ, σκ, σπ, στ, σμ, σχ, _μ, and _ν. Syllabification is not important for meaning, but does help as you learn to pronounce Greek correctly.

1.5
THE LEAST YOU NEED TO KNOW

Each chapter in this book will end with a section called *The Least You Need to Know*. It will be a bullet point list of questions you should understand and be able to answer with a brief explanation (if your teacher is on the ball, they will also regularly appear on tests). It may be at times that you will be able to answer these questions but don't fully understand the words coming out of your mouth—that's okay! Repetition and exposure will bring understanding.

◢ Use the online flashcards at ◣
http://quizlet.com/_7teo4 to memorize the answers:[1]

- What is a majuscule?

- What is a minuscule?

- What is a diphthong?

- What is vowel contraction? When does it occur?

---

1. Quizlet offers a variety of ways to test yourself. Take the time to learn how to use this online flashcard site.

- What is a liquid consonant?

- What is a sibilant consonant?

- What is a labial stop consonant?

- What is a palatal stop consonant?

- What is a dental stop consonant?

- What happens when a *sigma* follows a liquid?

- What happens when a *sigma* follows a labial?

- What happens when a *sigma* follows a palatal?

- What happens when a *sigma* follows a dental?

- What happens when a *kappa* follows a labial?

- What happens when a *kappa* follows a palatal?

- What happens when a *kappa* follows a dental?

- What happens when a *theta* follows a labial?

- What happens when a *theta* follows a palatal?

- What happens when a *theta* follows a dental?

- What is a rough breathing mark?

- What does an accent do?

- What is the one major governing principle for Greek syllables?

1.6 GREEK@LOGOS

Throughout the textbook chapters you will be learning how to work with Logos Bible Software. If you haven't already, go purchase the Logos Bible Software base package.[1]

For this first chapter, learn the basics of Logos. To do this, please visit https://support.logos.com and watch *all* of the videos specific to your platform (Mac or PC). Watch them over until you get all the

---

1. Logos gives great discounts to students, so be sure to sign up for academic pricing before you make your purchase (http://logos.com/academic-discount) if this applies to you.

basics down. While you are watching the videos, mimic what you see in your own version of Logos. Through the rest of this book, you will learn additional skills that assume you know the basics taught in these Logos videos.

1.7
VOCABULARY

Great news! You already know hundreds of Greek words because of the influence of Greek upon English and your knowledge of the Bible as well. Through the following chapters, you will be asked to memorize the 180 highest frequency words in the New Testament. By the time you are done, you will know all words that occur 100 times or more.

Vocabulary will always be presented in a table, to give you information on the word, including: (1) the type of word, (2) the frequency of the word in the NT, and (3) an applicable English derivative (when available) to aid in memorization. For the type of word:

adj. = adjective

adv. = adverb

conj. = conjunction

inter. = interjection

partic. = particle

pron. = pronoun

pr.noun = proper noun

This first list contains the 14 most used proper nouns in the Greek New Testament. You should be able to easily remember these, as they sound so similar to their English counterparts. The second list has the 14 highest-frequency words in the NT. For those which have numerous glosses, try to memorize as many as you can.

Flash card programs can be highly useful for learning and retaining Greek words. For example:

- *FlashGreek Pro* is an iOS and Android flashcard application that is compatible with this grammar by being keyed to each chapter. It also includes multimedia components like audio, image mnemonics, and contextual examples. Visit www.Danny Zacharias.net.

- Logos Bible Software also produces a flashcard app (*Flashcards for Greek and Hebrew*) that is useful for vocabulary memorization.

Word	Gloss	Type	Freq.	Derivatives
Ἀβραάμ, ὁ[1]	Abraham	pr.noun	73	
Γαλιλαία, -ας, ἡ	Galilee	pr.noun	61	
Δαυίδ, ὁ	David[2]	pr.noun	59	
Ἱεροσόλυμα, τά or ἡ	Jerusalem[3]	pr.noun	62	
Ἱερουσαλήμ, ἡ	Jerusalem	pr.noun	77	
Ἰησοῦς, -οῦ, ὁ	Jesus, Joshua	pr.noun	917	
Ἰωάννης, -ου, ὁ	John	pr.noun	135	
Μωϋσῆς, -έως, ὁ	Moses	pr.noun	80	
Παῦλος, ὁ	Paul	pr.noun	158	
Πέτρος, ὁ	Peter	pr.noun	156	
Πιλᾶτος, ὁ	Pilate	pr.noun	55	
Σίμων, -ωνος, ὁ	Simon	pr.noun	75	
Φαρισαῖος, -ου, ὁ	Pharisee	pr.noun	98	
Χριστός, ὁ	Christ	pr.noun	529	

ὁ, ἡ, τό	the	article	19867	

γάρ	for, so, then	conj.	1041	
δέ	but, and	conj.	2792	
καί	and, even, also	conj.	9161	
ὅτι	because, that, since	conj.	1296	

1. Right now, do not worry about the gray font in these lists, it will be explained in §3.6.

2. There is no "v" sound in Greek.

3. The following eight names all begin with "J" in English. There is no J sound in Greek (or Hebrew). When you hear a "J" sound in a name in the NT (or LXX), it is usually representing an *iota*, which makes an "ee" sound.

Word	Gloss	Type	Freq.	Derivatives
θεός, -οῦ, ὁ	God, god	noun	1317	*theocracy, theology*
κύριος, -ου, ὁ	lord, Lord	noun	717	

μή	not, no; lest	partic.	1042	
οὐ, οὐκ, οὐχ	not	partic.	1606	

ἐν	(+dat.)[1] in, on, by	prep.	2752	endemic
εἰς	(+acc.) into, in; to, toward; among	prep.	1767	eisegesis
ἐκ (ἐξ)[2]	(+gen.) from, out of, of, by	prep.	914	exegesis
ἐπί (ἐπ', ἐφ')	(+gen.) on, over, when; (+dat.) on the basis of, at; (+acc.) on, to, against, for	prep.	890	epicenter
πρός	(+gen.) for; (+dat.) at; (+acc.) to, against	prep.	700	proselyte

1. Prepositions can mean different things when paired with different types of nouns. You will learn more about this in ch. 7. Just memorize what you see for now.

2. This is an alternative way this word may appear. You will learn more about this in ch. 7.

Chapter 1 Exercises

LEARNING ACTIVITY 1: VOCABULARY (1 HOUR)
Some students are able to memorize vocabulary easily, others may take hours. Because this is a wildcard in terms of time, an amount of 1 hour will be assumed for each chapter's vocabulary.

LEARNING ACTIVITY 2: READING (1 HOUR)
Read chapter 1 of the textbook.

Completed: _____Yes _____No

LEARNING ACTIVITY 3: ALPHABET (1–1.5 HOURS)
Learn the alphabet inside-out. Say it out loud many times. A great way to learn it is to sing it (use the resource below).

◢ Recommended for learning the alphabet: ◣
The Singing Grammarian: The Alphabet Song.
(https://youtu.be/3gaeIUsPJ-Y)

Completed: _____Yes _____No

LEARNING ACTIVITY 4: SYLLABLES AND ACCENTS (1–1.5 HOURS)
For the following paragraph: (1) circle diphthongs, (2) split syllables in all words, (3) transliterate the words below. Identify all of the accents, and find each coronis. Be sure your transliteration is correct, and practice reading the paragraph over and over.

οὕτως γὰρ ἠγάπησεν ὁ θεὸς τὸν κόσμον, ὥστε τὸν υἱὸν

_____

_____

_____

τὸν μονογενῆ ἔδωκεν, ἵνα πᾶς ὁ πιστεύων εἰς αὐτὸν μὴ

_____

_____

_____

ἀπόληται ἀλλ' ἔχῃ ζωὴν αἰώνιον. οὐ γὰρ ἀπέστειλεν ὁ

_____

_____

_____

θεὸς τὸν υἱὸν εἰς τὸν κόσμον ἵνα κρίνῃ τὸν κόσμον, ἀλλ'

_____

_____

_____

ἵνα σωθῇ ὁ κόσμος δι' αὐτοῦ. (John 3:16–17)

_____

_____

_____

LEARNING ACTIVITY 5: WRITING (1 HOUR)

Practice writing the alphabet. For help, see the following video:
http://youtu.be/MKDT1R9T45g

α   =   _____

β   =   _____

γ   =   _____

δ   =   _____

ε   =   _____

ζ   =   _____

η   =   _____

θ   =   _____

ι   =   _____

κ   =   _____

λ   =   _____

μ   =   _____

ν   =   _____

ξ   =   _____

ο   =   _____

π   =   _____

ρ   =   _____

σ, ς   =   _____

τ   =   _____

υ   =   _____

φ   =   _____

χ   =   _____

ψ   =   _____

ω   =   _____

LEARNING ACTIVITY 6: READING PRACTICE (2 HOURS)

Proper pronunciation will make your learning experience much more enjoyable. You can, with a good amount of practice time, learn how to read and pronounce Greek. There are two ways you should practice. First, open a Greek New Testament to whatever page you want and start reading. If you need to, transliterate the words. Second, read along with someone else who can already read it well. Finally, read along with the Greek audio Bible that comes with your Logos base package.

Completed: _____ Yes _____ No

LEARNING ACTIVITY 7: REVIEW (30–60 MINUTES RECOMMENDED)

You've just spent a good amount of time learning a lot of new things. Take 30 minutes to do one final look through the chapter to solidify the knowledge, and make sure you can answer all of the questions in *The Least You Need to Know* section. Use the online flashcards link in *The Least You Need to Know* section of the chapter to quiz yourself on the questions.

Completed: _____ Yes _____ No

LEARNING ACTIVITY 8: LOGOS (30–60 MINUTES RECOMMENDED)

In the Greek@Logos section of chapter 1, several videos are pointed out for learning the basics of Logos Bible Software. Please go through these.

Completed: _____ Yes _____ No

1.8
THE SECOND
TIME AROUND

The Second Time Around section will be the very last section of each chapter. This section will inform readers who are using the grammar for a second semester on what they should focus. When necessary, it will also provide additional information that is pertinent for students going beyond one semester. For this chapter, no additional information is necessary.

CHAPTER 2

Greek Nouns Made Simple

What's the Point: 20 percent of the New Testament is nouns; all of the people, places, and things mentioned in the New Testament are nouns. They are one of the primary parts of any language and thus essential to understand.

The English language relies on word order to tell you what nouns are doing in the sentence. We place the subject in the sentence first, followed by the verb, followed by the object. But if you speak or are familiar with another language, you know that not every language works this way. Greek does not care as much about word order;[1] it will tell you what the subject is or what the object is with something called inflection. Inflection is a way of tagging words to indicate their role in the sentence. Take a look at the following sentence:

2.1

GREEK INFLECTION

The father of Jack threw the ball in the house.

Now, I'm going to color code the same sentence to indicate the functions of the different nouns. The subject will be blue, the noun that is indicating possession will be green, an indirect object will be orange, the object will be red, and we will leave the verb black. The small words that work with the nouns (like the word "the" which always goes in front of the noun) will be color-coded with the noun that they are with.

The father of Jack threw the ball in the house.

Now if we pretend this sentence is Greek (or if you are Yoda from Star Wars®) we can mix up this sentence however we want.

1. Word order does matter for some things and will be pointed out when appropriate.

Threw in the house the father of Jack the ball.

The ball in the house the father of Jack threw.

In the house the ball threw the father of Jack.

Now, knowing that I have tagged the nouns by color, you can make sense of the sentence by reordering the words to conform to English word order. Instead of using color, Greek will inflect (i.e., tag) nouns by changing the end of the word. Here is a Greek example of a made up sentence "the son of man teaches people in a house."

ὁ υἱὸς	→	ἀνθρώπου	→	διδάσκει	→	λαὸν	→	οἴκῳ.
the son	→	of man	→	teaches	→	people	→	in a house.

Because of the inflection (i.e., tag) on the end of the nouns, the Greek words can be reordered any way the author wants to and we can still understand the sentence because the inflection tells us what the nouns are doing in the sentence:

λαὸν	→	οἴκῳ	→	ὁ υἱὸς	→	ἀνθρώπου	→	διδάσκει.
People	→	in a house	→	the son	→	of man	→	teaches.
οἴκῳ	→	διδάσκει	→	λαὸν	→	ὁ υἱὸς	→	ἀνθρώπου.
in a house	→	teaches	→	people	→	the son	→	of man.
διδάσκει	→	ὁ υἱὸς	→	ἀνθρώπου	→	οἴκῳ	→	λαόν.
teaches	→	the son	→	of man	→	in a house	→	people.

◣ Watch the video at ◢
http://youtu.be/upH6DmOZlgw to solidify the previous section.

2.2
NOUN CASES

Greek inflection tags indicate three things about the noun they are attached to: case, gender, and number—we'll focus on case first. There are four main cases, and one more used only occasionally.

1. NOMINATIVE:[1] A noun is inflected as a nominative mostly to indicate what the *subject* is in the sentence. The blue

1. Abbreviated "nom."

tag in the above Greek sentence is in the nominative case, indicating the subject.

2. GENITIVE:[1] A noun is inflected as a genitive to indicate things like *possession, comparison, origin, or an attribute.* When it comes to translating a genitive, it has several "built-in" prepositions that can be used in translation: "of," "from," or "by."[2] So, when you see a genitive noun translated, or when you translate a noun inflected as a genitive, one of these prepositions is often used.[3] We also indicate possession in English with apostrophe + s, so this is also used in translation. The green tag in the above Greek sentence is in the genitive case—notice how "of" is being used in the translation. Sometimes, the Greek author does not want to use one of the "built-in" prepositions. In this case, Greek will give you a different preposition prior to the genitive noun to use instead. You will learn more about prepositions in chapter 7.

One more thing about genitive nouns. The genitive noun will most often directly follow the noun that it is connected to. Notice in both the English and Greek examples above that the genitive noun followed the nominative because the genitive noun is indicating possession of the nominative. If the genitive were indicating possession of the object, it would have followed the red-tagged word.

3. DATIVE:[4] A noun is inflected as a dative to indicate things like *indirect object, to specify a location, or to specify agency.* When it comes to translating a dative, it has several "built-in" prepositions that can be used in translation: "to," "in," "with," "on," "for" or "by."[5] So, when you see a dative translated or when you translate a dative, use one of these

---

1. Abbreviated "gen."

2. I've listed these roughly in order of use. In other words, "of" is used most often.

3. Prepositions will be covered in more detail in a later chapter (chapter 7).

4. Abbreviated "dat."

5. These are listed roughly in order of use.

words, unless the sentence gives you a better preposition to use immediately before the dative noun. The orange tag in the above Greek sentence is in the dative case—notice how "in" is being used in the translation.

4. ACCUSATIVE:[1] A noun is inflected as an accusative to indicate the *direct object*[2] in the sentence. The red tag in the above Greek sentence is in the accusative case, indicating the object.

5. VOCATIVE:[3] A noun is inflected as a vocative to indicate *direct address*. It is a formal method of addressing someone, used in direct speech. Most vocatives in the NT are identical to the nominative and would be parsed as such. The only exception is second declension masculine singular nouns (see below). Because this case does not occur that frequently in the NT, it will not be focused on.

2.3 NOUN GENDER

In Greek, as well as English, nouns have gender. We tend to think of inanimate objects as being "it," not a "him" or "her." But even English speakers sometimes call their boat or car a "her." In Greek, the inflection (those colored parts above) often, but not always, help to indicate the gender of the noun (more on this below).

2.4 NOUN NUMBER

English makes a noun plural most often by adding an "s" after the noun—dogs, cats, humans. Occasionally, though, English will change how a word is spelled to make it a plural. So, "mouse" is singular, but "mice" is plural; "goose" is singular, but "geese" is plural.

Once again, it is the inflection of a Greek noun (the colored tags) that indicate whether it is singular or plural. A noun's number will dictate how it is translated, singular or plural.

2.5 NOUN LEXICAL FORM

What about the beginning of a Greek noun (i.e., all of the black letters before those colored tags)? Every noun is built upon its stem—the

---

1. Abbreviated "acc."
2. Some verbs prefer to take a genitive or a dative as their direct object rather than an accusative.
3. Abbreviated "voc."

part that actually carries the meaning. A lexical form is the word
as it appears in a lexicon (i.e., a dictionary). Consider English—if
I asked you to look up the word "houses" in a dictionary, it would
tell you it is the plural of "house." To know what the word actually
means, you need to look up "house" in the dictionary. The following
table takes the Greek word "God" and shows you all the ways it can
appear once tagged:

Table 9: Example of Inflected Forms

case	singular		plural	
	Inflected form	*Translation*	*Inflected form*	*Translation*
nominative	θεός	"God"	θεοί	"gods"
genitive	θεοῦ	"of God"	θεῶν	"of gods"
dative	θεῷ	"to/in God"	θεοῖς	"to/in gods"
accusative	θεόν	"God"	θεούς	"gods"

On the end of each of these Greek forms of "God" is the inflection. But "God" only occurs once in a Greek lexicon (dictionary). To
look up a Greek noun in a lexicon, the nominative singular form (the
blackest box) is what you need to find. So for all eight forms of God
in the table above, the lexical form is the nominative singular form,
θεός. This is the form of the word you would learn when learning it
as new vocabulary.

2.6 NOUN DECLENSIONS

One last item needs to be put into place to understand how Greek
nouns are formed. Greek nouns are categorized into three big groups.
What determines which category a word goes into is the last letter
on the word's stem. If the noun stem ends in *alpha* (α) or *eta* (η), it is
placed in a category called "first declension." If the noun stem ends in
omicron (ο), it is placed in a category called "second declension." If the
noun stem ends in anything else (usually consonants), it is placed in
a category called "third declension." Why does this matter? Because
each declension has its own set of inflection tags to add to the end of
the Greek nouns that are in its category.

2.7

NOUN CASE

ENDINGS

The following are the declension endings for Greek nouns. Do not be intimidated by the amount of forms—your task is to be able to recognize noun forms and understand why they look the way they do. In the next chapter the meaning and function of the Greek noun cases will be discussed in more detail. As you begin to work with Bible software, lexicons, and related tools, work on recognizing the endings from the tables below.

2.7.1

First Declension

As previously mentioned, first declension nouns have an *alpha* (α) or an *eta* (η) as the last letter of the words stem. In one particular group of first declension nouns, the *alpha* (α) or *eta* (η) is the second-to-last letter. The majority of first declension nouns are feminine in gender. However, the second group that has an *alpha* (α) or *eta* (η) as the second-to-last letter in the lexical form are masculine in gender.[1]

Table 10: First Declension Endings (normal)

	singular				plural		
	end of stem	*inflection*	**final form(s)**		*end of stem*	*inflection*	**final form**
nominative	α/η	+	-	=	α η	α/η	+	ι	=	αι
genitive	α/η	+	ς	=	ας ης	α/η	+	ων[2]	=	ων
dative	α/η	+	ι[3]	=	ᾳ ῃ	α/η	+	ις	=	αις
accusative	α/η	+	ν	=	αν ην	α/η	+	ς	=	ας

Table 11: First Declension Endings (second type)

	singular				plural		
	end of stem	*inflection*	**final form(s)**		*end of stem*	*inflection*	**final form**
nominative	α/η	+	ς	=	ας ης	α/η	+	ι	=	αι
genitive	α/η	+	υ	=	ου ου	α/η	+	ων	=	ων
dative	α/η	+	ι	=	ᾳ ῃ	α/η	+	ις	=	αις
accusative	α/η	+	ν	=	αν ην	α/η	+	ς	=	ας

---

1. There are no neuter nouns in the first declension.
2. The *omega* will absorb the *alpha* or *eta*. This process occurs in the genitive plural of the second type as well.

3. The *iota* will subscript. This process occurs in the dative singular of the second type as well.

Second declension nouns are stems that end in an *omicron*. Nouns that take the first set of endings below are mostly masculine in gender (though sometimes feminine). Nouns that take the second set of endings are neuter in gender. Notice also the similarities with first declension.

2.7.2

Second Declension

Table 12: Second Declension Endings (mostly masculine)

	singular[1]				plural				
	end of stem		*inflection*		*final form(s)*	*end of stem*		*inflection*		*final form*
nominative	ο	+	ς	=	ος	ο	+	ι	=	οι
genitive	ο	+	υ[2]	=	ου	ο	+	ων[3]	=	ων
dative	ο	+	ι[4]	=	ῳ	ο	+	ις	=	οις
accusative	ο	+	ν	=	ον	ο	+	υς	=	ους

Table 13: Second Declension Endings (neuter)

	singular				plural				
	end of stem		*inflection*		*final form(s)*	*end of stem*		*inflection*		*final form*
nominative	ο	+	ν	=	ον	ο	+	α	=	α
genitive	ο	+	υ	=	ου	ο	+	ων	=	ων
dative	ο	+	ι	=	ῳ	ο	+	ις	=	οις
accusative	ο	+	ν	=	ον	ο	+	α	=	α

Third declension nouns are stems that end in consonants. These nouns are the most difficult to identify because consonants will interact and change (remind yourself of the changes, particularly labials, palatals, and dentals, from §1.3.1 and §1.3.2). Whereas first declension nouns are mostly feminine and second declension nouns are mostly masculine or neuter, third declension nouns can be any gender.

2.7.3

Third Declension

1. The masculine singular vocative is the only vocative form that isn't identical to the nominative; its ending is an ε.

2. The inflection here and in table 13 is actually an *omicron*, and ο + ο = ου.

3. The *omega* will absorb the *omicron*.

4. The *iota* wants to subscript, but before it happens the *omicron* will end up being lengthened to an *omega*, because an *iota* cannot subscript under on *omicron*.

While the stem of first and second declension nouns are relatively easy to recognize because of a consistent last letter on the end of the stem, third declension nouns are not as easy because a stem can end with any consonant. Furthermore, the lexical form of a first or a second declension noun clearly shows you the stem: θεός is nominative masculine singular (second declension), ἔργον is nominative neuter singular (second declension), ἡμέρα is nominative feminine singular (first declension). In third declension, though, you cannot trust the nominative singular to show you the stem of the word because the nominative singular can: (1) change the final letter of the stem, (2) cause the final letter to drop off, (3) cause the final letter to disappear and then change the second-to-last letter, or (4) cause the final letter to drop off and lengthen the last vowel in the word.[1] *It is the genitive singular form of a third declension noun that will present the stem.*

You will see the the complexity of third declension nouns in the table below—but truth be told it gets even more complicated. There are numerous patterns of third declension nouns, but the core inflection is in the table below. You don't need to worry memorizing all of this, just understand the inflection and letter interactions.

Table 14: Third Declension Endings (masculine or feminine)

	singular			plural		
	end of stem	*inflection*	**final form(s)**	*end of stem*	*inflection*	**final form**
nominative	[labial] +	ς, -	=	ψ[2]/-	[labial] +	ες	=	[π]ες
	[palatal] +		=	ξ[3]/-	[palatal] +		=	[κ]ες
	[dental] +		=	ς[4]/-[5]	[dental] +		=	[δ]ες
	(ο)ντ +		=	ων[6]	(ο)ντ +		=	οντες
	κτ +		=	ξ[7]	κτ +		=	κτες

1. Other things can happen as well, but these are the main changes.

2. When a *sigma* follows a labial it transforms to a ψ (§1.3.2). This happens in the dative plural as well.

3. When a *sigma* follows a palatal it transforms to a ξ (§1.3.2). This happens in the dative plural as well.

4. A *sigma* kicks out a dental (§1.3.2). This happens in the dative plural.

5. If a Greek noun ends in a τ, and no ending (-) is added, the *tau* (τ) will drop out.

6. This type of word adds a *sigma*, resulting in 2 reactions: (1) dental + ς = ς, (2) the *sigma* slips on the liquid letter ν. This results in (3) the ο prior to the *nu* (ν) lengthening to *omega* (ω).

7. This type of word adds the *sigma* (ς), with the two typical reactions of a *sigma*: (1) Dental+*sigma* = ς, and then palatal+*sigma* = ξ.

	singular			plural		
	end of stem	inflection	final form(s)	end of stem	inflection	final form
genitive	[labial] +	ος	= [π]ος	[labial] +	ων	= [π]ων
	[palatal] +		= [κ]ος	[palatal] +		= [κ]ων
	[dental] +		= [δ]ος	[dental] +		= [δ]ων
	(ο)ντ +		= οντος	(ο)ντ +		= οντων
	κτ +		= κτος	κτ +		= κτων
dative	[labial] +	ι	= [π]ι	[labial] +	σι	= ψι(ν)[1]
	[palatal] +		= [κ]ι	[palatal] +		= ξι(ν)
	[dental] +		= [δ]ι	[dental] +		= σι(ν)
	(ο)ντ +		= οντι	(ο)ντ +		= ουσι(ν)[2]
	κτ +		= κτι	κτ +		= ξι(ν)
accusative	[labial] +	α, ν[3]	= [π]α	[labial] +	ας	= [π]ας
	[palatal] +		= [κ]α	[palatal] +		= [κ]ας
	[dental] +		= [δ]α	[dental] +		= [δ]ας
	(ο)ντ +		= οντα	(ο)ντ +		= οντας
	κτ +		= κτα	κτ +		= κτας

Table 15: Third Declension Endings (neuter)

	singular			plural		
	end of stem	inflection	final form(s)	end of stem	inflection	final form
nominative	[labial] +	-	= -	[labial] +	α	= [π]α
	[palatal] +		= -	[palatal] +		= [κ]α
	[dental] +		= -[4]	[dental] +		= [δ]α
	(ο)ντ +		= ων[5]	(ο)ντ +		= οντα
	κτ +		= κ[6]	κτ +		= κτα

(continued)

1. The *nu* (ν) here is called a moveable, or energic, *nu*. It is often added after a word that ends with a vowel.

2. The *sigma* (ς) of the inflection does real damage here, expelling the ντ and causing the ο to lengthen to ου.

3. This *nu* (ν) inflection occurs only on a few third declension nouns that end in *iota* (ι) or *upsilon* (υ).

4. If a Greek noun ends in a dental, and no ending (-) is added, the dental will drop out, because dentals do not like to sit on the end of a word.

5. This type of word adds no ending (-). This results in two reactions: (1) The *tau* (τ) does not like to be on the end and drops out and (2) the *omicron* (ο) prior to the *nu* (ν) lengthens to *omega* (ω).

6. Remember, dentals will drop off the end of a word.

Table 15: Third Declension Endings (neuter) *(continued)*

	singular			plural		
	end of stem		*inflection*	*final form(s)*	*end of stem*	*inflection*	*final form*
genitive	[labial]	+	oς	=	[π]oς	[labial]	+	ων	=	[π]ων
	[palatal]	+		=	[x]oς	[palatal]	+		=	[x]ων
	[dental]	+		=	[δ]oς	[dental]	+		=	[δ]ων
	(o)ντ	+		=	οντος	(o)ντ	+		=	οντων
	xτ	+		=	xτος	xτ	+		=	xτων
dative	[labial]	+	ι	=	[π]ι	[labial]	+	σι	=	ψι(ν)[4]
	[palatal]	+		=	[x]ι	[palatal]	+		=	ξι(ν)
	[dental]	+		=	[δ]ι	[dental]	+		=	σι(ν)
	(o)ντ	+		=	οντι	(o)ντ	+		=	ουσι(ν)[5]
	xτ	+		=	xτι	xτ	+		=	ξι(ν)
accusative	[labial]	+	-	=	-	[labial]	+	α	=	[π]α
	[palatal]	+		=	-	[palatal]	+		=	[x]α
	[dental]	+		=	-[6]	[dental]	+		=	[δ]α
	(o)ντ	+		=	ων[7]	(o)ντ	+		=	οντα
	xτ	+		=	x[8]	xτ	+		=	xτα

◣ Watch the video at ◤
http://youtu.be/RMqZd-NsUJo to solidify the previous section.

2.8
NOUN PARSING

When we come to any noun in the New Testament, we need to identify four essential elements of the noun: *case, gender, number, and lexical form.* The first three elements come from the inflection, and the
lexical form is the nominative singular form of the word. All of these
are essential in the translation of the word:

- *Case* indicates the function of the noun in the sentence.

- *Gender* is not always crucial in the translation, but will be important when we come to discuss items we will learn in chapter 6.

1. The *nu* (ν) here is called a moveable, or energic, *nu.*
It is often added after a word that ends with a vowel.

2. The *sigma* of the inflection does real damage here,
expelling the ντ and causing the o to lengthen to ου.

3. If a Greek noun ends in a dental, and no ending (-)
is added, the dental will drop out, because dental's do not

like to sit on the end of a word.

4. This type of word adds no ending (-). This results
in two reactions: (1) The *tau* (τ) does not like to be on the
end of a word and drops out and (2) the *omicron* (o) prior to the *nu*
(ν) lengthens to *omega* (ω).

5. Remember, dentals will drop off the end of a word.

- *Number* tells you whether or not to translate something as singular or plural.

- The *lexical form* carries the meaning of the word.

You should be able to clearly and accurately answer these questions. Use the online flashcards at http://quizlet.com/_7tft3 to memorize the answers:

2.9
THE LEAST YOU
NEED TO KNOW

- What is inflection?

- What does the nominative case signify?

- What does the genitive case signify?

- What does the dative case signify?

- What does the accusative case signify?

- What does the vocative case signify?

- What does noun gender signify?

- What does noun number signify?

- What are noun declensions and what is the parameter for deciding which declension a noun falls into?

- What genders are *most* first declension nouns?

- What genders are *most* second declension nouns?

- Why is the third declension so troublesome?

- What are the four essential elements of noun parsing?

- How do you identify the stem of a noun?

In the remainder of the chapters you will be encouraged to learn how to use Logos Bible Software. There are numerous helps available from Logos and its community. Logos Bible Software provides links to internal help files, which are indexed and searchable. In addition,

2.10
GREEK@LOGOS

links are provided to the Logos forums and the Logos user-edited wiki. In each of the *Greek@Logos* sections, a list of Logos features will be listed that users should learn how to use. When available, links to applicable YouTube videos will be given.

Users should take the time in this chapter to learn:

- How to put your Greek Bible and English Bible side by side so they scroll together using link sets

  □ See the article on Parallel Resources at https://support.logos.com

- How to access Logos's reverse interlinear Bibles

  □ See the article on Interlinear Bibles at https://support.logos.com

- How to turn on Logos's corresponding selection

  □ See the article on Corresponding Words at https://support.logos.com

- How to search for Greek nouns with specific tags (i.e., inflection) when searching for nouns

  □ See the article on Morph Search at https://support.logos.com

2.11
VOCABULARY

Word	Meaning	Type	Freq.	Derivatives
ἀλλά (ἀλλ᾽)	but, yet, except	conj.	638	
ἵνα	in order that, that	conj.	663	
οὖν	therefore, then, accordingly	conj.	499	
ὡς	as, while	conj.	504	

ἀδελφός, -οῦ, ὁ	brother	noun	343	Philadelphia
ἄνθρωπος, -ου, ὁ	man, person	noun	550	anthropology
ἡμέρα, -ας, ἡ	day	noun	389	
λόγος, -ου, ὁ	word, matter	noun	330	dialogue
οὐρανός, -οῦ, ὁ	heaven, sky	noun	273	Uranus

Word	Meaning	Type	Freq.	Derivatives
πατήρ, -τρός, ὁ	father	noun	413	*patriarch*
πνεῦμα, -ματος, τό	wind, spirit	noun	379	*pneumatics*
υἱός, -οῦ, ὁ	son, descendant; child	noun	377	

εἰ	if	partic.	502	

ἀπό (ἀπ', ἀφ')	[+gen.] (away) from	prep.	646	*apostle*
διά (δι')	(+gen.) through (+acc.) because of	prep.	667	*diameter*

Chapter 2 Exercises

LEARNING ACTIVITY 1: VOCABULARY (1 HOUR)
Be sure to review previous vocabulary as well as learn the new.

LEARNING ACTIVITY 2: READING (1 HOUR)
Read chapter 2 of the textbook.
Completed: _____ Yes _____ No

LEARNING ACTIVITY 3: READING PRACTICE (30–45 MINUTES)
Take 1 hour to practice your Greek reading using the Greek audio Bible resource in Logos. Remember, it is okay not to understand what you are reading. Work on pronunciation.
Completed: _____ Yes _____ No

LEARNING ACTIVITY 4: DECLENSION ENDINGS (60–90 MINUTES)
Take some time to become as familiar as possible with all of the declension endings. Sing along with the songs below over and over until you have memorized them.

◢ Recommended for learning declension endings: ◣
The Singing Grammarian:
(1) First Declension (https://youtu.be/UEyns65Zf8s),
(2) Second Declension (https://youtu.be/EBYeerWcB9c), and
(3) Third Declension Songs (https://youtu.be/45Q6qWHWP6o).

Completed: _____ Yes _____ No

LEARNING ACTIVITY 5: PARSING (2.5–3 HOURS)

(1) Find each word in Logos to determine its meaning and gender.	θεοί, θεόν, θεός, θεοῦ, θεῷ, θεοὺς, θεοῖς, θεῶν
(2) *Using just this textbook and your memory*, take the forms of each word from column 2, identify their endings, and write them into the appropriate slot (thus parsing them). Do it at least twice (not at the same time!) during your week. *note* Underlined forms are identical forms so they will appear in **two** different slots. second declension, lexical form θεός: meaning and gender: _____	
second declension, lexical form ἔργον: meaning and gender: _____	<u>ἔργα</u>, ἔργοις, ἔργον, ἔργου, ἔργῳ, ἔργων, ἔργον
first declension, lexical form ἁμαρτία: meaning and gender: _____	ἁμαρτία, ἁμαρτίᾳ, ἁμαρτίαι, ἁμαρτιῶν, ἁμαρτίαις, ἁμαρτίαν, <u>ἁμαρτίας</u>,
first declension, lexical form μαθητής: meaning and gender: _____	μαθητῇ, μαθηταί, μαθηταῖς, μαθητὴν, μαθητής, μαθητοῦ, μαθητῶν, μαθητάς
third declension, lexical form πνεῦμα: meaning and gender: _____	πνεύμασι(ν) πνεύματι πνεύματος πνεῦμα πνευμάτων πνεύματα
third declension, lexical form γυνή: meaning and gender: _____	γυναῖκα γυναῖκες γυναικί γυναικός γυναῖκας γυναιξί(ν) γυνή γυναικῶν

		masculine	*feminine*	*neuter*
sg	*nom*			
	gen			
	dat			
	acc			
pl	*nom*			
	gen			
	dat			
	acc			

LEARNING ACTIVITY 6: BIBLE SOFTWARE (1.5–2 HOURS)

Take time to understand your Bible software (you should have done so last chapter) and <u>clearly</u> answer the following questions:

1. How can you find out the parsing of a word with your Bible software? (Explain all possible ways to do this.)

   _____

   _____

   _____

   _____

   _____

2. How do you search for the lexical form of a noun in the NT, such that the results show you every time that word occurs no matter the inflection? (Explain all possible ways to do this.)

   _____

   _____

   _____

   _____

   _____

   _____

3. Logos provides statistics and information whenever you make a search. Open a search window and do a morph search. Ensure that you are searching the entire Greek New Testament. Search for "lemma:λόγος". ("Lemma" means the lexical form.)

   a. How many times does it occur in the NT?_____

   b. Click on the "Graph results" button in the top right. How many times does the word occur in the book of Acts?_____

   c. Close the graph pane, and in the search results click on "Analysis" in the search window. This displays the information of the search in columns (you can choose which columns to display). How many times does the word occur in the plural? (Click the header to sort by column.)_____

    d. How do you confine your search of λόγος to the book of Mark?

_____

_____

_____

    e. How many times does it occur in Mark? _____

4. How do you search for <u>a specific inflected form</u> (e.g., genitive plural of λόγος) of a noun in the NT? (Explain all possible ways to do this.)

_____

_____

_____

How many times does λόγος occur as a genitive plural in the NT?

_____

5. How do you search for any noun ONLY in 3 John?

_____

_____

How many nouns are in 3 John? _____

6. Search for βασιλεύς as a genitive, masculine, singular, and answer the following questions:

    a. What is the genitive, masculine, singular form of the word?

_____

    b. How many times does this inflected form occur? _____

    c. What books of the NT does it occur in? _____

7. What is the fastest way to look up a word from anywhere in your Logos Greek New Testament in your software's lexicon(s)?

_____

_____

_____

8. If you have finished this section in a short amount of time, then fill the remainder of the suggested 3 hours learning how to do other things (anything you want) with your Logos Bible Software.

LEARNING ACTIVITY 7: REVIEW (30 MINUTES)

You've just spent a good amount of time learning a lot of new things. Take 30 minutes to do one final read through of the chapter to solidify the knowledge, and make sure you can answer all of the questions in the *Least You Need to Know* section. Use the online flashcards link in the chapter to quiz yourself on the questions.

Completed: _____ Yes _____ No

2.12
THE SECOND
TIME AROUND

It is recommended that students who are passing through this chapter the second time around concentrate on the memorization of the case endings of each declension. Use *The Singing Grammarian* to assist you with this and test yourself with ParseGreek. This chapter should also be paired with the next chapter, with the bulk of your energy devoted to the memorization of the case endings and parsing nouns.

ADVANCED EXERCISES (CH. 2)

Learning Activity 1: Vocabulary (1 hour)

Learn your assigned vocabulary list from Appendix A. Be sure to review previous vocabulary as well as learn the new. Knowledge of this new vocabulary is assumed in the translation work.

Learning Activity 2: Reading (1 hour)

Read chapter 2 of the textbook again. (If you feel it necessary, read chapter 1 as well).

Completed: _____ Yes _____ No

Learning Activity 3: Memorize Declension Endings (2 hours)

Memorize the first, second, and third declension endings. Use *The Singing Grammarian* as help, and practice filling in the paradigms from memory using the practice tables.

Completed: _____ Yes _____ No

Learning Activity 4: Parsing Practice (1.5 hours)

Drill yourself using either ParseGreek or Paradigms Master Pro.

- For ParseGreek, choose any learned vocabulary range in conjunction with chapter 2 grammar concepts.

- For Paradigms Master Pro, work on first and second declension nouns.

note The program gives you the lexical form in the parsing. Take time to practice recognizing the lexical form on your own, as you will be responsible for providing the lexical form in testing.
Completed: _____ Yes _____No

Learning Activity 5: Parsing Work: First and Second Declension Focus (2 hours)

Parse the following nouns (case, gender, number, lexical form) and provide a translation.

1. θεοῦ _____

2. Χριστοῦ _____

3. θεῷ _____

4. γῆς_____

5. λόγον _____

6. ἀνθρώπου _____

7. ἡμέρας _____

8. κύριε _____

9. ἀδελφοί _____

10. ἀνθρώπων _____

11. μαθηταί _____

12. οὐρανοῦ _____

13. ἡμέρᾳ _____

14. γῆν _____

15. θεόν _____

16. κόσμου _____

17. ἔργα _____

18. δόξαν _____

19. καρδίας _____

20. ἐξουσίαν _____

Learning Activity 6: Translation (3.5 hours)

Translate the following sentences. Be ready to parse any nouns that appear in the sentences. The following sentences assume knowledge of all words occurring up to 90 times (chs. 1–11 and list 1). For difficult forms, consult the morphological information in Logos Bible Software.

ἐγὼ δὲ ὅτι τὴν ἀλήθειαν λέγω (I say), οὐ πιστεύετέ (y'all believe) μοι (John 8:45)

_____

_____

_____

λέγει (he says) αὐτῷ [ὁ] Ἰησοῦς· ἐγώ εἰμι ἡ ὁδὸς καὶ ἡ ἀλήθεια καὶ ἡ ζωή· οὐδεὶς ἔρχεται (he comes) πρὸς τὸν πατέρα εἰ μὴ δι' ἐμοῦ (me). (John 14:6)

_____

_____

_____

ὃς ἐποίησεν (he made) τὸν οὐρανὸν καὶ τὴν γῆν καὶ τὴν θάλασσαν (Acts 14:15)

_____

_____

_____

ἐγὼ δὲ λέγω (I say) εἰς Χριστὸν καὶ εἰς τὴν ἐκκλησίαν (Eph 5:32)

_____

_____

_____

Ἐν ἀρχῇ (beginning) ἦν (was) ὁ λόγος, καὶ ὁ λόγος ἦν πρὸς τὸν θεόν, καὶ θεὸς ἦν ὁ λόγος (John 1:1)

_____

_____

_____

λέγει (he says) αὐτοῖς ὁ Ἰησοῦς· εἰ τέκνα τοῦ Ἀβραάμ ἐστε (are), τὰ ἔργα τοῦ Ἀβραὰμ ἐποιεῖτε (y'all do) (John 8:39)

_____

_____

_____

οὐ δικαιοῦται (he is justified) ἄνθρωπος ἐξ ἔργων νόμου (Gal 2:16)

_____

_____

_____

Case Functions Made Simple

What's the Point: While the focus on morphology in the previous chapter is a lot to take in, the reality is that the more important question to ask about a noun is, "What are you doing in the sentence?" The previous chapter gave you the base uses of the four cases, but this chapter will introduce you to the myriad of ways Greek nouns can function in a sentence.

I n the previous chapter you learned about the base definitions of the four Greek cases. The truth is that the Greek cases can do much more than what their base definition implies. This is no different than English, and as you look at Greek cases always evaluate them alongside your preferred English translation. In the following examples, the noun case in question will be in bold, with any verbs underlined.

3.1

INTRODUCTION

Before you begin—please remind yourself of a few things:

1. You do *not* need to memorize all of this!

2. When understanding the functions of nouns in the examples below and the NT in the future, *always* evaluate alongside the English translation of your choice.

3. These types of questions are not solely unique to Greek— these types of functions are present in our own language as well. We just rarely take the time to put English under the microscope.

Finally, the truth of the matter is that even the many examples I give you below are still only a sampling. For a full view of all of the functions of Greek cases, see an advanced grammar like Daniel Wallace, *Greek Grammar Beyond the Basics*.[1]

3.2
NOMINATIVE

The nominative is the most straightforward of the cases, almost always indicating the subject of the sentence.

3.2.1
Simple Subject

The simple subject is the most basic and frequent function of a nominative noun.

- ἠγάπησεν ὁ θεός τὸν κόσμον (John 3:16)

- **God** loved the world. . . .

3.2.2
Predicate Nominative

The word "predicate" means *a verb and all of its modifiers*. You will learn later about equative verbs—these types of verbs do not tell about action, but tell you more about the subject. For example, "Jerry *is* the teacher." Notice how the subject Jerry is not doing anything, but the verb "is" tells us more about Jerry—the object is renaming the subject. Because the subject is being renamed, Greek uses another nominative as the object. We call this the *predicate nominative*. In the following verse, we have two nominative nouns: one is the subject and the other is the object (predicate nominative).

- κύριός ἐστιν ὁ υἱὸς τοῦ ἀνθρώπου καὶ [even] τοῦ σαββάτου (Mark 2:28)

- the **son** of man is **lord** even of the sabbath.

3.2.3
Apposition

Apposition is a common grammatical function of nouns in both Greek and English. A noun in apposition is a noun in parallel with another noun, giving you more information about the noun in parallel.

- παραγίνεται Ἰωάννης ὁ βαπτιστὴς κηρύσσων (Matt 3:1)

- **John** the **baptizer** came preaching.

1. The substance of this chapter draws on Wallace's fine work.

The genitive is the most versatile of all of the cases. If you recall from the last chapter, the "built-in" word to use for the genitive is "of." Consider these sentences:

3.3 GENITIVE

- The husband *of* Maria.

- Please take care *of* my cat.

- That is the dog *of* my next door neighbor.

All three of these sentences use the word "of" and yet none of the nouns that follow it are doing the same type of things. The first is expressing a relationship, the second is expressing the object, the third is indicating possession. Greek genitive nouns are also versatile. Do not be intimidated by this! In the approach of this book, you are looking at Greek right alongside English.

Many genitives indicate possession. So the noun in the genitive case possesses the noun it is connected to. The word "of," or apostrophe + s is what is most often used to translate the function into English.

3.3.1 Possessive

- τὸν δοῦλον τοῦ ἀρχιερέως (Matt 26:51)

- The slave **of the high priest**

The genitive is used in Greek to indicate relationship, particularly family relationship. Sometimes translation even warrants adding a word to indicate the relationship.

3.3.2 Genitive of Relationship

- Σίμων Ἰωάννου (John 21:15)

- Simon, [son] **of John**

An attributive genitive is much like an adjective in that it is describing an attribute of the noun it is connected to. Using "of," or translating the genitive immediately prior to the other noun, is how these types of genitives are often translated.

3.3.3 Attributive Genitive

- ὁ κριτὴς τῆς ἀδικίας (Luke 18:6)

- Judge **of unrighteousness** [or **unrighteous** judge]

3.3.4
Apposition

Apposition is a category already introduced under the nominative. The apposition function occurs in all of the cases. Remember that apposition is restating the noun it is connected to, often shedding a little more light.

- σωτῆρος ἡμῶν Ἰησοῦ Χριστοῦ (Titus 2:13)

- Our savior, **Jesus Christ**

3.3.5
Genitive of
Comparison

A genitive will often be coupled with a comparative adjective (see §6.2.1). The word "than" is the word that often needs to be added to best translate the function.

- ὁ ἄλλος μαθητὴς προέδραμεν τάχιον τοῦ Πέτρου (John 20:4)

- The other disciple ran **more** quickly **than Peter.**

3.3.6
Subjective Genitive

Sometimes a noun has a verbal idea baked right in, like love. In these cases a genitive that follows one of these nouns-with-a-verbal-idea-baked-in is the subject of that noun's baked-in action. The word "of," or apostrophe+s is what is most often used to translate the function into English.

- τίς ἡμᾶς χωρίσει ἀπὸ τῆς ἀγάπης τοῦ Χριστοῦ; (Rom 8:35)

- Who shall separate us from **the love of Christ**?

- (or Who shall separate us from **Christ's love** for us?)

3.3.7
Objective Genitive

Like the subjective genitive, a noun-with-a-verbal-idea-baked-in may indicate the object of the baked-in verbal idea with a genitive. The word "of," or apostrophe+s is what is most often used to translate the function into English.

- ἡ δὲ τοῦ πνεύματος βλασφημία οὐκ ἀφεθήσεται (Matt 12:31)

- But the blasphemy **of the Spirit** shall not be forgiven (or "blasphemy against the Spirit")

A genitive noun can be used when talking about time. In these instances a word like "during," "act," or "a" are used to translate the function into English.

3.3.8
Genitive of Time

- ἦλθεν πρὸς αὐτὸν νυκτός (John 3:2)

- He came to him **during the night**

Certain verbs, in both English and Greek, require a genitive as their object. In particular, they need the word "of."

3.3.9
Genitive as Direct Object

- ἐπιμελήθητι αὐτοῦ (Luke 10:35)

- Take care **of him**

A descriptive genitive gives some general description of the noun it is connected to. This category is a bit of a general category for when a noun doesn't fall into any of the other categories.

3.3.10
Descriptive

- Ἰωάννης . . . κηρύσσων βάπτισμα μετανοίας (Mark 1:4)

- John . . . [was] preaching a baptism **of repentance**

A dative noun indicating an indirect object is a common function of the dative case.

3.4
DATIVE
3.4.1
Indirect Object

- καὶ ἔδωκεν ἄν σοι ὕδωρ ζῶν (John 4:10)

- And he would have given **to you** living water

A dative of interest specifies the noun that is interested in the action of the sentence. The words "to" or "for" are often used when translating this type of dative noun.

3.4.2
Dative of Interest

- ἥτις ἐστὶν αὐτοῖς ἔνδειξις ἀπωλείας (Phil 1:28)

- which is a sign of destruction **to them**

3.4.3
Dative of Reference

A dative of reference noun is providing a frame of reference for the sentence. Often the words "with reference to" could be added before this type of noun. Typically, the words "to," "concerning," or "about" are used when translating this type of function into English.

- λογίζεσθε ἑαυτοὺς εἶναι νεκροὺς μὲν τῇ ἁμαρτίᾳ (Rom 6:11)

- Consider yourselves to be dead [with reference] **to sin**

3.4.4
Apposition

Like the other noun cases, the dative can also function in apposition.

- παρέδωκαν Πιλάτῳ τῷ ἡγεμόνι (Matt 27:2)

- they handed [him] over to Pilate, **the governor**

3.4.5
Dative of Sphere

The dative of sphere describes the location in which the word or action takes place or exists. Typically the word "in" is used to translate this function into English.

- ἐκκλησίαι ἐστερεοῦντο τῇ πίστει (Acts 16:5)

- the churches grew **in faith**

3.4.6
Dative of Time

The dative of time indicates the time when the action of the verb in the sentence happens. Typically the words "in" or "on" are used to translate this function into English.

- τῇ τρίτῃ ἡμέρᾳ ἐγερθήσεται (Matt 17:23)

- **on the third day** he will be raised

3.4.7
Dative of Association

The dative of association indicates an association between one noun and another. Typically the word "with" is used to translate this function into English.

- οἱ δὲ ἄνδρες οἱ συνοδεύοντες αὐτῷ (Acts 9:7)

- the men who were traveling **with him**

The dative of means indicates the instrument with which the action in the sentence happens. Typically the words "with," "by," or "by means of" are used to translate this function into English.

3.4.8

Dative of Means (Instrumental)

- ἐξέβαλεν τὰ πνεύματα λόγῳ (Matt 8:16)

- he cast out the spirits **by** [means of] **a word**

The dative of cause indicates the cause or reason for the action in the sentence. Typically the words "because of" are used to translate this function into English.

3.4.9

Dative of Cause

- ἵνα τῷ σταυρῷ τοῦ Χριστοῦ μὴ διώκωνται (Gal 6:12)

- only that they might not be persecuted **because of the cross** of Christ

The most common use of an accusative is to indicate the direct object.

3.5

ACCUSATIVE

3.5.1

Direct Object

- ἠγάπησεν ὁ θεὸς τὸν κόσμον (John 3:16)

- God loved **the world**

Sometimes a verb requires two objects in order to make sense. Often, not always, the word "of" is needed to translate the function into English.

3.5.2

Double Object

- ἐξέδυσαν αὐτὸν τὴν χλαμύδα (Matt 27:31)

- They stripped **him of** [his] **robe**

Like the other cases, the accusative can function in apposition.

3.5.3

Apposition

- πίστευσον ἐπὶ τὸν κύριον Ἰησοῦν (Acts 16:31)

- believe in the Lord **Jesus**

By now you might be feeling information overload. I don't blame you! Remember, once again, that you do not need to memorize all of this but you do need to understand when you see it in the Greek New Testament. Take the time before going on to the next section to go back and look at each small example sentence. Look at the words that are in bold and ask yourself, "What is it that I'm doing right now?" In many instances without looking at the description you would be able to say on your own already "this noun is the subject," or "this noun is indicating location," or "this noun is indicating relationship." The exercises for this chapter will further challenge you in identifying noun function.

3.6

NOUNS IN THE *DBL*

***GREEK* LEXICON**

The goal of the approach *Biblical Greek Made Simple* is to help you access the language using the best tools. One of the most important items in your toolkit when working with Greek is a good lexicon.[1] The *Dictionary of Biblical Languages with Semantic Domains* (*DBL Greek*) is a lexicon included in the Logos Bible Software base packages. The *DBL Greek* lexicon is a centralized resource that relies on *Greek-English Lexicon of the New Testament: Based on Semantic Domains* by Louw and Nida.[2]

You will come to see that all translation is interpretation.[3] Simply take a look at the entry of a few different words in your lexicon and you will see that there can sometimes be numerous translation options for a single word.[4] This is why it is important to not only learn the main gloss while learning vocabulary, but also to be able to access a lexicon when looking closer at New Testament passages. A proper translation of a word is only yielded when the meaning of the word in *that specific context* in understood.

3.6.1

A Word on Semantic

Domains

Because the *DBL Greek* lexicon relies on the Louw-Nida semantic domains lexicon, it is important to understand what semantic domains are. Semantic domains are classifications of meaning in a language—Louw-Nida has 93 domains in total. A word may have

---

1. Another lexicon that students may find helpful is the *Lexham Analytical Lexicon of the Greek New Testament*. It is similar to the *DBL Greek* lexicon in that it builds off of Louw-Nida, but because it is an analytical lexicon, it includes all instances of the word, displays all morphological forms, and lists cognates.

2. Johannes P. Louw and Eugene A. Nida, *Greek-English Lexicon Of The New Testament: Based On Semantic*

Domains, 2 vols. (New York: United Bible Societies, 1989); abbreviated Louw-Nida.

3. That's why not every English translation is the same and why it is important for you to be able to work with the primary language of the New Testament.

4. These options for translating a word are often called glosses.

only one meaning and so only be in a single domain, but usually words have multiple meanings, and so fit into several semantic domains.

Let's take κύριος as an example. Several words can be used to translate κύριος because it fits into several semantic domains. Two of the common translation options are (1) "Lord" and (2) "owner." κύριος is translated as "Lord" when referring to God; so it is in Louw-Nida's semantic domain 12, "Supernatural Beings and Powers" (there are 49 other Greek words that also fall into that domain). But when κύριος is best translated as "owner," κύριος falls into semantic domain 57, "Possess, Transfer, Exchange" (there are 248 other words that also fall into that domain). It is important to reiterate one more time that it is the context of a passage that determines the specific meaning of a word.

3.6.2
An Analysis of a DBL Greek Noun Entry

The following sections will detail the sections of a word entry. Through all *DBL Greek* entries, Greek words/phrases will include transliteration in italics and parentheses.

3.6.2.1
Lexical Form, Stem, Gender, and Part of Speech

Beyond giving you the various glosses for a noun, some of the first information a lexicon relates to a reader is the stem of a word and its gender. Remember, a noun's stem determines what declension endings a word uses. The biggest reason readers need a lexicon to help them with identifying a stem is because of third declension nouns (those that end in a consonant); remember that the lexical form (nominative singular) of a third declension noun does not show the stem the way first and second declension nominative singular nouns do (those pesky consonant interactions). A lexicon will help you identify the stem by showing you the genitive singular ending directly after the word is introduced (see examples below).

In chapter 6 you will learn more about the Greek article (the word "the") which was in the chapter 1 vocabulary. The masculine singular form of "the" is ὁ. The feminine singular form of "the" is ἡ. The neuter singular form of "the" is τό. In a lexicon, after a noun and its genitive ending, an article will occur to indicate the gender of the noun. *DBL Greek* will also then make it explicit by indicating the gender. As you work with other lexicons in the future, the article will often be the only gender indicator.

3.6.2.2
Links to Hebrew
Equivalents, Strong's,
and TDNT

When available, *DBL Greek* will link to Hebrew equivalents in the *DBL Hebrew* or *DBL Aramaic* lexicon. Following this is the Strong's number for the word.[1] The very beginning of every entry is also a number, the Goodrick-Kohlenberger number. These two numbering systems were created for the vocabulary of the Greek New Testament, particularly for the days of research using printed books.

A link to the *Theological Dictionary of the New Testament* (*TDNT*)[2] entry is also provided. Think of a theological dictionary as a commentary on the lexicon—it looks at the theological significance and usage of the word prior to and within the NT. *TDNT* is an important resource with invaluable information. As you begin to delve into Greek and do word studies, *TDNT* is a resource where you will find excellent information.

3.6.2.3
Louw-Nida Number

The entry in *DBL Greek* will list with numbers all of the relevant meanings of a word (the example below contains nine). Each of the numbered sections begins with the Louw-Nida (LN) number and link. This is the most valuable aspect of the *DBL Greek* lexicon—not only does it provide a tidy one paragraph overview of a word, it also provides direct links to the Louw-Nida lexicon. If you are not using *DBL Greek* to immediately access Louw-Nida, you are not using the lexicon correctly. The actual lexicon entries and discussion is in Louw-Nida, not *DBL Greek*.

3.6.2.4
Gloss

A gloss is the most often used English word to translate a Greek word in that particular semantic domain. A gloss will usually be in bold, unless the gloss is an idiom.

3.6.2.5
Brief Explanation,
Greek Example, and
Scripture Example

If any brief explanation on the gloss or notes is warranted, it will follow the gloss. This may be followed by a brief Greek example (with transliteration), and every numbered section will include at least one verse as an example. If the scripture example has a + sign, this

---

1. Although the Strong's number is linked, it will also take you to *TDNT* unless you own the Strong's lexicon in your Logos library.

2. *Theological Dictionary of the New Testament*, ed. Gerhard Kittel and Gerhard Friedrich, trans. Geoffrey W. Bromiley, 10 vols. (Grand Rapids: Eerdmans, 1964-1976).

indicates that the scripture example is the only verse in which the word is used in that manner.

Lexical form (nom.), genitive ending, gender	Links to Hebrew equivalents, Strong's, and TDNT	Louw-Nida number and link	**Gloss**	Brief explanation if necessary	**Greek example**	Scripture example (+ indicates only occurrence)

476 ἄνθρωπος (*anthrōpos*), ου (*ou*), ὁ (*ho*): n.masc.; ≡ DBL Hebr 132, 408, 632; Str 444; TDNT 1.364—**1.** LN 9.1 **human being** (Jn 10:33); **2.** LN 9.24 **man**, a male human (Mt 10:35); **3.** LN 10.53 **husband** (Mt 19:3, 10); **4.** LN 9.3 υἱὸς τοῦ ἀνθρώπου (*huios tou anthrōpou*), Son of Man (Mt 8:20); **5.** LN 9.2 υἱοὶ τῶν ἀνθρώπων (*huioi tōn anthrōpōn*), people, those of the class of humanity (Eph 3:5+); **6.** LN 41.43 παλαιὸς ἄνθρωπος (*palaios anthrōpos*), **former behavior** (Ro 6:6; Eph 4:22; Col 3:9+), note: others would see more than behavior in this idiom, but also ontological implications, see next entries; **7.** LN 8.3 ὁ ἔξω ἄνθρωπος (*ho exō anthrōpos*), **body, physical form** (2Co 4:16+); **8.** LN 26.1 ὁ ἔσω ἄνθρωπος (*ho esō anthrōpos*), **inner being** (Ro 7:22; Eph 3:16+); **9.** LN 26.1 ὁ ἐν τῷ κρυπτῷ ἄνθρωπος (*ho en tō kryptō anthrōpos*), **inner being** (1Pe 3:4+)

3.6.3
DBL Greek Noun Example

This noun example is typical of most *DBL Greek* entries. When necessary, future chapters will indicate any items of note for understanding different types of words in the lexicon.

As mentioned previously, it is absolutely necessary to move to Louw-Nida in order to gain a better understanding of the different semantic meanings of a word—*Louw-Nida is where the actual definition of the word occurs*. In the example of ἄνθρωπος above, clicking on entry 1 (LN 9.1) will open Louw-Nida to the word in that particular semantic domain. In this example, the user should note that ἄνθρωπος in this semantic domain has a synonym—ἀνήρ. Opening the table of

3.6.4
Reading a Louw-Nida Entry

contents panel on Louw-Nida will also reveal to you what semantic domain you are in—in this instance domain 9 is "People."

3.6.5
Determining The
Semantic Domain for
a Word Instance

The word entries in *DBL Greek* and Louw-Nida provide the definitions of a word based on its semantic domains. However, neither of these lexicons provides an exhaustive list for every time a word occurs, nor does it tell you which semantic domain is preferable.

Luckily, Logos has done the hard work for you by providing you with a direct link to the semantic domain for a word instance. For example, open your Greek NT to Matt 8:9, which has the word ἄνθρωπος. If you right-click the word in Logos, a Louw-Nida number is provided. This number is also provided in the reverse interlinear Bibles.

Keep in mind that lexicographers are not infallible—you may disagree with the choice made for the semantic domain. But in general we can trust the work of scholars who have made these determinations for users.

3.7
THE LEAST YOU
NEED TO KNOW

You should be able to clearly and accurately answer these questions. Use this link http://quizlet.com/_7tfw1 to memorize the answers:

- What does "predicate" mean?

- What is a predicate nominative?

- What is apposition? Which cases can indicate apposition?

- What is a genitive of relationship?

- What is an attributive genitive? Make up an English-sentence example.

- What is a genitive of comparison? Make up an English-sentence example.

- What is a subjective genitive? Make up an English-sentence example.

- What is an objective genitive? Make up an English-sentence example.

- What is a dative of interest? Make up an English-sentence example.

- What is a dative of reference? Make up an English-sentence example.

- What is a dative of association? Make up an English-sentence example.

- What is a dative of means? Make up an English-sentence example.

- What is a dative of cause? Make up an English-sentence example.

- How does a lexicon show you the root of the noun?

- What indicates the gender of a noun in a lexicon?

3.8 GREEK@LOGOS

Utilizing the Logos help file, Logos forums, Logos wiki, and videos provided, users should take the time to learn:

- How to build a filter to highlight nouns in the Greek New Testament

  - See the article on Visual Filters at https://support.logos.com

- How to access various ways you can learn more about a single word, particularly by using the context (right-click) menu

  - See the article on the Information Tool at https://support.logos.com

- How to do a Bible Word Study on a Greek noun

  - See the article on Bible Word Study at https://support.logos.com

3.9 VOCABULARY

In the above section on nouns in a lexicon (§3.6), you learned about how a lexicon shows you the stem of words, as well as what the gender is. These additional details are provided in your vocabulary lists from now on (these were gray font portions from chs. 1 and 2 vocabulary as well).

Word	Gloss	Type	Freq.	Derivatives
οὕτως	thus, so, in this manner	adv.	208	
ἐάν	if (ever), when (ever), although (+subj.)[1]	conj.	351	
τέ	and (so), so [consec: both . . . and]	conj.	215	
ἀνήρ, ἀνδρός, ὁ	man, husband	noun	216	android
γῆ, -ῆς, ἡ	land, earth	noun	250	geography
γυνή, -αικός, ἡ	woman, wife	noun	215	gynecology
μαθητής, -οῦ, ὁ	disciple, student	noun	261	math
νόμος, -ου, ὁ	law	noun	194	Deuteronomy
ὄνομα, -ματος, τό	name, reputation	noun	231	pseudonym
πίστις -εως, ἡ	faith, belief, trust	noun	243	
ἤ	or, than; (ἤ . . . ἤ either . . . or)	partic.	343	
κατά (κατ', καθ')	(+gen.) down from, against (+acc.) according to, throughout, during	prep.	473	cataclysm
μετά (μετ', μεθ')	(+gen.) with (+acc.) after	prep.	469	metaphor
περί	(+gen.) about, concerning (+acc.) around	prep.	333	perimeter
ὑπό (ὑπ', ὑφ')	(+gen.) by; (+acc.) under (prep.)	prep.	220	hypodermic

---

1. You will learn about the subjunctive mood in ch. 10.

Chapter 3 Exercises

LEARNING ACTIVITY 1: VOCABULARY (1 HOUR)
Be sure to review previous vocabulary as well as learn any new.

LEARNING ACTIVITY 2: TEXTBOOK READING (1 HOUR)
Read chapter 3 of the textbook.
Completed: _____ Yes _____ No

LEARNING ACTIVITY 3: READING PRACTICE (1 HOUR)
Take 30 minutes to practice your Greek reading using the Greek audio available in your Logos Greek package. Then take another 30 minutes and read 1 John 1:5–10 aloud several times. (If it helps you, write out a transliteration first)
Completed: _____ Yes _____ No

LEARNING ACTIVITY 4: DECLENSION ENDINGS
(30 MINUTES RECOMMENDED)
Review the declension endings again.

◢ Recommended for learning declension endings: ◣
The Singing Grammarian: (1) First Declension,
(2) Second Declension, and (3) Third Declension Songs.

Completed: _____ Yes _____ No

LEARNING ACTIVITY 5: 1 JOHN 1:5–10
(3–4 HOURS RECOMMENDED)
1. Open 1 John 1:5–10. Search for all nouns in this passage and list their form *as they occur* (and in proper order) in the passage <u>in the left column</u>. *Only do* column 1, then move on to step 2.

inflected form	parsing	meaning	declension
ἀγγελία	Nom., fem., sing., ἀγγελία	"message"	1st decl.
case usage: predicate nominative. *This is the object of an equative verb.*			
case usage:			
case usage:			
case usage:			
case usage:			
case usage:			
case usage:			
case usage:			
case usage:			
case usage:			
case usage:			
case usage:			
case usage:			
case usage:			
case usage:			

case usage:			
case usage:			
case usage:			
case usage:			
case usage:			

2. Now close your Bible software for 30 minutes. Using just your mind and your textbook try your hand at parsing the following words from above: ἀδικίας, αἷμα, ἁμαρτίαν, θεὸς, σκοτία, φωτί, ψεύστην (case, gender, number. Don't worry about the lexical form as you don't know all of the words). Parsing info goes in the second column.

3. Now that your brain is hurting, open your bible software again. Fill in the parsing for each word, check/correct your attempts, fill in a translation, and determine what declension endings the word uses in the final column. While you do this, check your own attempted answers, correcting along the way and filling in the lexical form in your parsing attempt.

4. Now the more difficult part. Working with chapter 3, determine what specifically each case is doing and record it in the "case usage" row. While making these decisions, work closely with an English translation, preferably a more literal one like LEB, NET, NASB, RSV, NRSV, or ESV. (Don't waste hours on this. If you are stuck on a noun for a long time, take an educated guess and move on.)

5. Bible Word Study: When studying passages, word studies are an excellent way to dig deeper into the passage. Use the Bible Word Study in Logos (launch from the context menu or open from the *Guides* menu). It is not always easy to identify keywords, but in the future take time to find recurring words or words for which more clarification is needed. For 1 John 1:5-10, I have chosen two nouns for a word study.

κοινωνία

1. Read the *Lexham Analytical Lexicon of the Greek New Testament* (*LALGNT*) or the *DBL Greek* lexicon entry and the linked Louw-Nida entries. In the section below, summarize the main ways this word can be translated, any nuances the word has in particular cases, and any idiomatic uses or constructions.

   _____

   _____

   _____

   _____

   _____

   _____

   _____

2. Read the entry for this word in a theological dictionary like the New International Dictionary of New Testament Theology and Exegesis (NIDNTTE), the Exegetical Dictionary of the New Testament (EDNT), or the single volume version of the Theological Dictionary of The New Testament ("Little Kittel").

   Summary of your findings: _____

   _____

   _____

   _____

   _____

   _____

   _____

3. Where else does this word appear in 1 John? Should it be translated the same there?_____

   _____

   _____

   _____

   _____

   _____

   _____

ἀδικία

1. Read the *LALGNT* or *DBL Greek* entry and the linked Louw-Nida entries. In the section below, summarize the main ways this word can be translated, any nuances the word has in particular cases, and any idiomatic uses or constructions.

   _____

   _____

   _____

   _____

   _____

2. Read the entry for this word in a theological dictionary like the *NIDNTTE*, the *EDNT*, or *Little Kittel*.

   Summary of your findings: _____

   _____

   _____

   _____

   _____

3. Where else does this word appear in 1 John? Should it be translated the same there?_____

   _____

   _____

   _____

   _____

LEARNING ACTIVITY 6: REVIEW (30 MINUTES RECOMMENDED)
You've just spent a good amount of time learning a lot of new things. Take 30 minutes to do one final read through of the chapter to solidify the knowledge, and make sure you can answer all of the questions in the *Least You Need to Know* section. Use the online flashcards link in the chapter to quiz yourself on the questions.
Completed: _____ Yes _____ No

3.10
THE SECOND
TIME AROUND

Please read the *Second Time Around* from the previous chapter, as these two chapters should be read and worked through together the second time around.

ADVANCED EXERCISES (CH. 3)

Learning Activity 1: Vocabulary (1 hour)

Learn your assigned vocabulary list from Appendix A. Be sure to review previous vocabulary as well as learn the new. Knowledge of this new vocabulary is assumed in the translation work.

Learning Activity 2: Reading (1 hour)

Read chapter 3 of the textbook again.

Completed: _____ Yes _____ No

Learning Activity 3: Memorize Declension Endings (30 minutes)

Memorize the first, second, and third declension endings. Use *The Singing Grammarian* as help, and practice filling in the paradigms from memory using the practice tables.

Completed: _____ Yes _____ No

Learning Activity 4: Parsing Practice (1.5 hours)

Drill yourself using either ParseGreek or Paradigms Master Pro

- For ParseGreek, choose any learned vocabulary range in conjunction with chapter 2 grammar concepts

- For Paradigms Master Pro, work on third declension nouns.

Completed: _____ Yes _____ No

Learning Activity 5: Parsing Work: Third Declension Focus (1.5 hours)

Parse the following nouns (case, gender, number, lexical form) and provide a translation.

1. πνεῦμα _____

2. γῆς _____

3. πατέρα _____

4. πίστεως _____

5. πνεύματος _____

6. πνεύματι _____

7. ὄνομα _____

8. γῆν _____

9. πατήρ _____

10. ὀνόματι _____

11. πόλιν _____

12. πατρός _____

13. ἄνδρες _____

14. γυνή _____

15. χάρις _____

16. σῶμα _____

17. πίστιν _____

18. πόδας _____

19. χεῖρας _____

Learning Activity 6: Translation (3.5 hours)

Translate the following sentences. Be ready to parse any nouns that appear in the sentences *and identify their functions*. The following sentences assume knowledge of all words occurring up to 79 times (chs. 1–11 and lists 1–2). For difficult forms, consult the morphological information in Logos Bible Software.

μεμέρισται (divided) ὁ Χριστός; μὴ Παῦλος ἐσταυρώθη (crucified) ὑπὲρ ὑμῶν (y'all), ἢ εἰς τὸ ὄνομα Παύλου ἐβαπτίσθητε (were you baptized); (1 Cor 1:13)

_____

_____

_____

_____

Τιμοθέῳ γνησίῳ (loyal) τέκνῳ ἐν πίστει, χάρις ἔλεος (mercy) εἰρήνη ἀπὸ θεοῦ πατρὸς καὶ Χριστοῦ Ἰησοῦ τοῦ κυρίου ἡμῶν (our). (1 Tim 1:2)

_____

_____

_____

_____

Τότε ὁ Ἰησοῦς ἐλάλησεν τοῖς ὄχλοις καὶ τοῖς μαθηταῖς αὐτοῦ (his) λέγων (saying)· ἐπὶ τῆς Μωϋσέως καθέδρας (seat) ἐκάθισαν (sit) οἱ γραμματεῖς καὶ οἱ Φαρισαῖοι. (Matt 23:1–2)

_____

_____

_____

_____

οὐ γάρ ἐστιν ἀνὴρ ἐκ γυναικὸς ἀλλὰ γυνὴ ἐξ ἀνδρός· καὶ γὰρ οὐκ ἐκτίσθη (created) ἀνὴρ διὰ τὴν γυναῖκα ἀλλὰ γυνὴ διὰ τὸν ἄνδρα. (1 Cor 11:8–9)

_____

_____

_____

_____

Καὶ ἔλαβον (I took) τὸ βιβλαρίδιον (little scroll) ἐκ τῆς χειρὸς τοῦ ἀγγέλου καὶ κατέφαγον αὐτό (ate it), καὶ ἦν ἐν τῷ στόματί (mouth) μου ὡς μέλι γλυκύ (sweet honey) (Rev 10:10)

_____

_____

_____

_____

CHAPTER 4

Greek Indicative Verbs Made Simple

What's the Point: 20 percent of the New Testament is verbs, 28,110 in total—half of these are in what is called the indicative mood (you'll understand what this means soon enough!). Verbs are a core component of any language, describing the action in sentences. Greek verbs are also very nuanced, robust, and flexible—and inflected like nouns. Having a thorough knowledge of Greek verbs is essential to understanding the Greek New Testament; they are quite literally where all of the action is!

G reek (and English) has three main types of verbs. It is not especially important that you always recognize what type every verb is, but one of them is more difficult to understand when working in a Greek sentence.

4.1

VERB BASICS

4.1.1

Types of Verbs

1. *Transitive*: A transitive verb is the standard way we think of verbs, transferring action from subject to object. "The dog *bites* the boy" is a transitive verb because action is being transferred from subject to object. Notice also that we can make the verb passive: "The boy *was bitten by* the dog."

2. *Intransitive*: An intransitive verb is not indicating transfer of action, it is only indicating the action of the subject. "The boy *went* to bed" is an intransitive verb because action is not being transferred to an object but is telling you about an action the subject is performing—the object is where the subject is going. Notice that we cannot neatly make the verb passive: "The bed *was being gone to by* the boy" is bad English! Intransitive verbs also do not need an object. Compare "the dog bites" and "I left." The

first statement expects an object—it is hard to discuss a dog biting without talking about what it is biting! With the second example, the statement does not need anything else.

3. *Equative:*[1] An equative verb does not indicate action at all. The verb is, rather, renaming or giving more information about the subject or is describing a state the subject is in—so the subject *equals* the object. "Danny *is* the author" is not transferring action nor is it telling you about an action the subject is performing. It is telling the reader something more about the subject. Notice how the subject and object can be flipped and it still means the same thing: "The author is Danny" works just as well. Because the subject and object are the same person and interchangeable, *both the subject and the object will be nominative in Greek.*[2] When in Greek (and English) an equative verb has a subject and an object, both will be nominative. The one acting as the "object" is properly called the *predicate nominative* (§3.2.2).

Because an equative verb has a nominative as subject *and* a nominative as object, there are rules for determining which one gets to be the subject and which one gets to be the object. Again, it is not essential that you memorize this, just that you recognize that there are rules that govern the decisions made by translators (some items in the image you will not understand until later in the book).

---

1. An equative verb is also often called a copulative verb.

2. There are numerous equative verbs used in the New Testament. These will be pointed out in your vocabulary lists and do need to be recognized in Greek, because the sentence will *not* have an accusative noun as the object. There will, rather, be two nominative nouns in the sentence. One is the subject and the other is the object. This special object of an equative verb is called a *predicate nominative*.

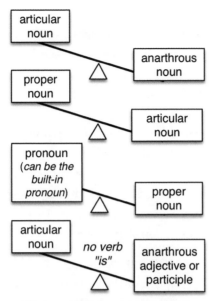

articular participle= usually object
anarthrous participle= object

Greek verbs pack quite a punch in that they contain a lot of information in a single word. Not only does a Greek verb tell you about
the actual action (*bite, run, know*, etc.), but a Greek verb can also have
the subject built in, as well as the type of action and sometimes even
when it happened. Consider the following English sentences:

4.1.2

The Efficiency of

Greek Verbs

- I will follow.

    □ "I" is the subject.
    □ "will" puts the action into the future.
    □ This sentence would translate a single Greek verb,
      ἀκολουθήσω. The verb means "follow" and is inflected to be
      future (the "will" part) and first-person (the "I" part).

- I have been found.

    □ "I" is the subject.
    □ "have" places the action into the past.
    □ "been" makes the subject passive, meaning the action is
      happening to the subject, rather than the subject doing the
      action.

▫ This sentence would translate a single Greek verb, εὑρέθην. The verb means "find" and is inflected to be in the past (the "have" part), first-person (the "I" part), and passive (the "been" part).

4.1.3 Greek Aspect

Greek tenses[1] are improperly named because the point of Greek's six[2] tenses is *not* primarily to tell you about when the action occurs (past, present, or future).[3] Just remember, when you hear the word tense when in reference to Greek, time is not the major issue. The aspect, or viewpoint, of the verb is the more important issue. Aspect relays how the author viewed the action of the verb.

- INTERNAL ASPECT: Internal aspect[4] views the action up close. It is more descriptive of the action of the verb. Think of it as a camera zooming in on the action showing you *unfolding action that is in process*. Using a popular parade analogy, internal aspect is like standing on the side of the street while a parade goes by. Your focus is not on the whole parade, but rather on one particular part of the parade unfolding before you. If someone were to ask you what you are looking at, you probably would not say you are looking at the parade, but that you are looking at the jugglers passing in front of you at that point.

- EXTERNAL ASPECT: External aspect[5] views the action like a snapshot, as *a whole and completed event* without regard for the details. Think of it as a camera zooming out on the action to show the whole thing. Using the parade analogy, you are lucky enough to be living on the 30th floor of an apartment that the parade is going by. As you sit on your balcony, you see the parade in its entirety from beginning to end, but you are so high up that the details are a little fuzzy.

1. Some grammarians prefer to use the term "tense-form" in attempts to avoid the issue of time that is so closely related to the word tense.

2. The New Testament actually has a seventh tense, but this final tense occurs just one time in Heb 8:11.

3. Scholars of New Testament Greek are divided on their understanding of Greek verbs. The issue basically boils down to whether verbs indicate time (past, present, future) or not. I have chosen to follow Wallace, *Greek Grammar Beyond the Basics*.

4. Other grammarians call this *imperfective aspect*.

5. Other grammarians call this *perfective aspect*.

- STATIVE ASPECT: Stative aspect views the action as *done and in a completed state*. This aspect combines both internal and external aspects in that the action is viewed as complete, but its result is viewed internally as having a continuing effect. Using the parade analogy, you are one of the unlucky crew members cleaning up after the parade (which had horses and elephants). You know the parade is complete but it had plenty of consequences affecting you now!

Greek (and English) verbs have six main components, one of which is the lexical form that contains the basic meaning. A verb's stem will take affixes[1] and endings (tags) to indicate tense, voice, person, and number.

In chapter 2 the components that made up noun parsing were introduced (case, gender, number, lexical form). For Greek verbs, the components are: tense, voice, mood, person, number, lexical form.[2] Each of these will be talked about in order.

4.2
COMPONENTS OF A
GREEK VERB

- *Aspect*: The present tense describes internal aspect.

- *Time*: Remember that time is not the primary part of Greek tenses, some grammarians would argue that time is not a factor in a Greek tense at all. The present tense will tend to be in the present time, but is not confined to it.

- *Translation*: The translation of Greek tenses is tricky business because Greek tenses can convey so many different things and are not confined to past, present, or future—though the present tense is usually in the present time. When the present tense is translated, translators will often use an "s" or "ing" on the verb to indicate the internal aspect (i.e., he kick*s* or he is kick*ing*). However, this is not always an exact science and the translation depends the most on the context in which it occurs.[3]

4.2.1
Tense
4.2.1.1
Present Tense

---

1. Affixes are parts added to the beginning or end of a word—prefixes and suffixes.

2. **TV M**akes **P**eople **N**auseous is a way I learned to remember the order of Greek parsing.

3. As you begin to work with Greek verbs and English translations, you will see how hard translation can be. It is often very difficult to convey Greek verbs into English without making a very unreadable translation. This is why learning the primary languages is so important.

4.2.1.2
Imperfect Tense

- *Aspect*: Like the present tense, the imperfect tense describes internal aspect.

  - *Time*: The difference from the present tense is that the imperfect tense is more often used in a past time context, and especially in narrative sequences to provide a "camera zoom in" on a particular detail.

  - *Translation*: Because the imperfect tense most often occurs in a narrative context, which is often past time, and also conveys the internal aspect, the imperfect will be translated as the present tense is, but with "was" before it (i.e., he *was* kick*ing*). Again, translation depends the most on the context in which the word occurs.

4.2.1.3
Future Tense

- *Aspect*: The future tense describes external aspect.

  - *Time*: As the name implies, the future tense describes a future action. The future tense in Greek is the truest tense by name in terms of time.

  - *Translation*: The future tense in Greek is translated the same as the future tense in English, using the word "will" (i.e., he *will* kick).

4.2.1.4
Aorist Tense

- *Aspect*: The aorist tense describes external aspect.

  - *Time*: Although time is not the main issue in Greek verbs, the aorist tends to be used mostly in past time, especially in narrative contexts.

  - *Translation*: The aorist is the most used tense in the indicative mood and is the default verb tense in narrative. Although aorist is most often used in a past time context, past time is not the main thing that is conveyed in the aorist tense form. The aorist tense is usually translated with a past time English form using "-ed," or using the simple form of the verb (i.e., "he kick*ed*" or "I kick").

- *Aspect*: The perfect tense portrays stative aspect.

- *Time*: Like the other tenses, the perfect tense is not very concerned about time but in general stays in the present tense.

- *Translation*: When used in a time-specific context, the perfect tense describes a completed action with ongoing results (i.e., he *has* kicked). When used to describe a state of affairs (stative) the perfect can be translated in different ways depending on context: I am (in a state of) hopefulness, I am hoping, I hope.

4.2.1.5
Perfect Tense

- *Aspect*: Like the perfect tense, the pluperfect tense portrays stative aspect.

- *Time*: The pluperfect tense works in much the same way as the perfect, but tends to be confined to narrative and most often in past time.

- *Translation*: When in a time-specific context the pluperfect refers to a completed action that had ongoing results in the past, but those results have also ceased (i.e., he *had* kicked). When used to describe a state of affairs (stative) the pluperfect can be translated much like the perfect.

4.2.1.6
Pluperfect Tense

In English, voice describes whether the subject is doing the action or having the action done to them. If the subject is doing the action, it is active voice. If the subject is having the action done to them, it is passive voice. Greek adds one more voice called middle. The middle voice is right in between active and passive—the subject does the action with self-interest. Middle voice is often hard to communicate and English translations of the middle voice often end up sounding active or reflexive.

4.2.2
Voice

1. ACTIVE: The subject performs the action.

   □ "The dog *bit* the child."

2. MIDDLE: The subject performs the action upon themselves or out of self-interest.

    □   "The student (himself) *took* the test." (the self-interest of the Greek voice is often left untranslated, or a reflexive pronoun may be used)

3. PASSIVE: The subject is having the action being done to them.

    □   "The child *was bitten by* the dog."

Every Greek tense can be combined with the active, middle, or passive voice. Of the six tenses, four of them (present, imperfect, perfect, pluperfect) have identical middle and passive forms. In these four tenses, context will decide whether to translate it as middle or passive.

4.2.3
Mood   The mood of a verb describes the action's relation to reality, or presentation of certainty. The action may be real or the action may just possibly happen depending on circumstances. English shares the first three moods with Greek, with one additional mood in Greek as well. Only the first mood, the indicative, will be covered in this chapter, with the final three moods being covered in chapter 10. The indicative mood is the presentation of certainty. Verbs in the indicative mood are being asserted as having happened, in the process of happening, or will happen.

4.2.4
Person   The person of a verb tells us about the subject.

1. FIRST-PERSON: "I" or "we" are first-person subjects. "I" is singular, "we" is plural.

2. SECOND-PERSON: "you" or "y'all"[1] are second-person subjects. "You" is singular; "y'all" is plural.

---

1. Only certain parts of the world use "y'all" as the second-person plural form of you. Most use "you" as singular and plural. I find it better to use "y'all" for learning Greek.

3. THIRD-PERSON: "he, she, it" or "they" are third-person subjects. "He, she, it" are singular, "they" is plural. Notice that "they" can be used for the plural of "he" to mean a bunch of men, or the plural of "she" to indicate a bunch of women, and so on.

The number of a verb is similar to a noun in that it makes it singular or plural. The difference is that a plural verb is telling you that the subject (the actor) is plural. "I kick" is singular, "we kick" is plural. "You kick" is singular, "y'all kick" is plural. "He/she/it kicks" is singular, "they kick" is plural.

4.2.5

Number

An easy(-ish) way to learn about the indicative mood is with the indicative slot machine. There are six slots that can be filled in the construction of a Greek verb (not every slot will be filled). Certain combinations in the slot machine will result in different tense and verb combination. This slot-type patterning is most recognizable with *strong verbs*. Strong verbs, in Greek and English, are verbs whose spelling stays consistent and/or follows recognizable patterns. For instance, "kick" is a strong verb because k-i-c-k always stays in the verb ("kick," "kicking," "was kicked," "will kick"). The verb "go" is a *weak verb*—its past tense is "went," which bears no resemblance to "go" whatsoever. English speakers have simply learned that "went" is the past tense of "go."

4.3

HOW GREEK INDICATIVE VERBS ARE FORMED

4.3.1

The Indicative Slot Machine

Table 16: Indicative Slot Machine

1 augment	2 reduplication	3 stem	4 suffix	5 connecting vowel	6 inflection

The first four attributes form the stem of each principal part[1]

Each slot of the slot machine will be discussed in turn. Before discussing these, though, examine closely the following table while

---

1. Principal parts will be discussed in §5.2.

reading about the different slots. You can see from the table that combinations of different slots create the different tense and voice combinations. Slot 6 (inflection tags) determines the person and number of a verb.

Table 17: Indicative Formation

principal part	tense and voice		augment	redupl.	stem	suffix	connecting vowel	inflection
First	present	active			λυ		ο/ε	primary active
		m/p			λυ		ο/ε	primary mid/pas
	imperfect	active	ε		λυ		ο/ε	secondary active
		m/p	ε		λυ		ο/ε	secondary mid/pas
Second	future	active			λυ	σ	ο/ε	primary active
		middle			λυ	σ	ο/ε	primary mid/pas
Third	aorist	active	ε		λυ	σα		secondary active
		middle	ε		λυ	σα		secondary mid/pas
Fourth	perfect	active		λε	λυ	κα		secondary active
	pluperfect	active	ε	λε	λυ	κει		secondary active
Fifth	perfect	m/p		λε	λυ			primary mid/pas
	pluperfect	m/p	ε	λε	λυ			secondary mid/pas
Sixth	aorist	passive	ε		λυ	θη		secondary active
	future	passive			λυ	θησ	ο/ε	primary mid/pas

composes the principal part

An augment is an *epsilon* added to the beginning of a verb. If the verb stem begins with a vowel, then the augment and the first vowel will contract together and result in a long vowel or diphthong. Aorist, imperfect, and pluperfect are the tenses that have an augment. Focus on the orange affixes below:

4.3.1.1

Slot 1: Augment

- Word with no augment: λύω[1]

- Word with augment: ἔλυον

- Word beginning with vowel (ἀκούω) with an augment: ἤκουον[2]

Reduplication takes the first consonant of a word and reduplicates it with an *epsilon*. If the verb stem begins with a (1) vowel, (2) a sibilant, or (3) two or three consonants in a row, it will use an augment instead of reduplicating, and the augment may or may not cause lengthening. If the word begins with a *rho* (ρ) it will still reduplicate it, but slightly differently. If the word begins with a stop consonant (see §1.3) the consonant will reduplicate with the smooth stop consonant. Perfect and pluperfect are the tenses that have reduplication. Focus on the purple affixes below:

4.3.1.2

Slot 2: Reduplication

- Word with no reduplication: λύω

- Word with reduplication: λέλυκας, πεφιλήκατε, ἐρρυήκατε

- Word beginning with a vowel, sibilant, or consonant group:[3] ἠγαπήκαμεν, ἐξήρανται, ἐσταύρωται

The stem of the verb is that which holds the core meaning of a verb. With the example of strong verbs, the stem does not change, or only changes in a very minor way. The strong verb that Greek students continually work with is λύω, "I loose." λύω is a strong verb because no matter what affixes are added to the word, the -λυ- part never

4.3.1.3

Slot 3: Verb Stems

---

1. In this example, the connecting vowel has been absorbed into the inflected ending.
2. Remember from §1.2.1 that vowels contract when next to one another.
3. Although these look like the augment and should be orange, it is reduplication.

changes. In reality, there are also so-called "weak pattern" verbs. There are in fact six potential ways a verb stem may be spelled, called *principal parts*. These will be discussed in chapter 5.

4.3.1.4
Slot 4: Tense Suffixes

Following the verb stem for some tenses is a tense suffix. The following are the different tense suffixes, along with some behaviors that may occur:

1. σ future active and future middle verbs take a *sigma* (σ) suffix.

   □ If you recall from chapter 1, the *sigma* is sinister;
   □ If the stem ends with a liquid verb, the *sigma* slips away entirely. These are called <u>liquid verbs</u>. (recall §1.3.1)
   □ If the stem ends with a stop consonant a change will occur (recall §1.3.2).

2. σα aorist active and aorist middle verbs take a *sigma-alpha* (σα) suffix.

   □ Like the σ future suffix, the same changes (*sigma* disappearing and *sigma*+stop interactions) will occur with the *sigma* in the σα suffix.
   □ In the third-person singular form, the σα suffix is σε.

3. κα perfect active verbs take a *kappa-alpha* (κα) suffix.

   □ The *kappa* at the beginning of the suffix may cause changes to the final letter of the stem (see table 4: Stop Interactions). This includes dentals on the end of the stem becoming a *sigma*.
   □ Some verbs like a buffer vowel between the stem and the κα-suffix and will first add an η or ω, particularly liquid consonants.
   □ In the third-person singular form, the κα suffix is κε.
   □ Some verb stems just don't like that *kappa* at all and will take just an *alpha* as the suffix.

4. κει pluperfect active verbs take *kappa-epsilon-iota* (κει) suffix.

   ◦ The same changes that occur because of the *kappa* (κ) in the above suffix also occur here.

5. θη aorist passive verbs take a *theta-eta* (θη) suffix.

   ◦ Like *sigma* (σ) and *kappa* (κ), *theta* causes changes when it follows a stop. (see table 4: Stop Interactions)
   ◦ Like the *kappa* in the above two suffixes, it may take a buffer vowel.

6. θησ future passive verbs take a *theta-eta-sigma* (θησ) suffix.

   ◦ All of the same θ interactions detailed in the previous suffix occur here.

4.3.1.5
Slot 5: Connecting Vowel

The connecting vowel (often called a thematic vowel) occurs in all present, imperfect, and future tense and voice combinations. These are the tense and voice combinations that are built off of the first and second principal parts. It is simply an *omicron* (ο) or *epsilon* (ε). The only real difficulty the connecting vowel can cause is in the present and imperfect tenses. Remember that when vowels are next to one another, they often contract into a long vowel or diphthong (§1.2.1). If a stem ends in a vowel, the connecting vowel will contract with the end of the stem. These verbs are called contract verbs, and will be discussed more below.

4.3.1.6
Slot 6: Primary and Secondary Endings

Different tense and voice combinations have either primary or secondary endings. There are both active voice endings and middle/passive voice endings. Therefore, the inflected endings in combination with a tense suffix will make it active or middle/passive. The inflected endings indicate the subject of the verb.

Table 18: Primary and Secondary Endings

							Primary	Primary	Secondary	Secondary
							Active	Middle/ Passive	Active	Middle/ Passive
		connecting vowel+inflection= ending[1]					*μι verbs*[2]			
1 sg	o	+	_[3]	=	ω		μι	μαι	ν, (-)	μην
2 sg	ε	+	ες[4]	=	εις		ς	σαι (η)	ς	ου, σο
3 sg	ε	+	ε[5]	=	ει		σι	ται	- (εν)[6]	το
1 pl	o	+	μεν	=	ομεν		μεν	μεθα	μεν	μεθα
2 pl	ε	+	τε	=	ετε		τε	σθε	τε	σθε
3 pl	o	+	οσι(ν)[7]	=	ουσι(ν)		ασι	νται	ν, σαν, σι(ν)	ντο

◢ Watch the video at ◣
http://youtu.be/6YSCYMLOZOk to solidify the previous section:

4.4 STRONG VERB EXAMPLE All of the information in §4.3 above is best understood by looking at an example. The following table displays the entire indicative paradigm of the strong verb λύω. *Stop and dwell on the following table for a long time.* Compare it to the information given to you above. Take the time to understand how every single form was built. You don't need to memorize and replicate this, just understand the formation of the verbs.

1. Because the connecting vowel and the primary active endings end up merging, these are broken down.

2. You will learn about verbs that use these endings in §5.3.5.

3. Because no ending is added, the connecting vowel is lengthened to an *omega* (ω).

4. Vowel contraction occurs here to create the ει

diphthong in the final form.

5. Vowel contraction occurs here to create the ει diphthong in the final form.

6. No ending is added here, so a *nu* (ν) is often added to the end. This is called an energic, or moveable, *nu*.

7. Vowel contraction occurs here to create the ου diphthong in the final form.

Table 19: λύω Indicative Paradigm

Parts	First λύω				Second λύσω	
tense and voice	present active	present m/p	imperfect active	imperfect m/p	future active	future middle
1 sg	λύω	λύομαι	ἔλυον	ἐλυόμην	λύσω	λύσομαι
2 sg	λύεις	λύῃ	ἔλυες	ἐλύου	λύσεις	λύσῃ
3 sg	λύει	λύεται	ἔλυε(ν)	ἐλύετο	λύσει	λύσεται
1 pl	λύομεν	λυόμεθα	ἐλύομεν	ἐλυόμεθα	λύσομεν	λυσόμεθα
2 pl	λύετε	λύεσθε	ἐλύετε	ἐλύεσθε	λύσετε	λύσεσθε
3 pl	λύουσι(ν)	λύονται	ἔλυον	ἐλύοντο	λύσουσι(ν)	λύσονται

Parts	Third ἔλυσα		Fourth λέλυκα	Fifth λέλυμαι	Sixth ἐλύθην	
tense and voice	aorist active	aorist middle	perfect active	perfect m/p	aorist passive	future passive
1 sg	ἔλυσα	ἐλυσάμην	λέλυκα	λέλυμαι	ἐλύθην	λυθήσομαι
2 sg	ἔλυσας	ἐλύσω	λέλυκας	λέλυσαι	ἐλύθης	λυθήσῃ
3 sg	ἔλυσε(ν)	ἐλύσατο	λέλυκε(ν)	λέλυται	ἐλύθη	λυθήσεται
1 pl	ἐλύσαμεν	ἐλυσάμεθα	λελύκαμεν	λελύμεθα	ἐλύθημεν	λυθησόμεθα
2 pl	ἐλύσατε	ἐλύσασθε	λελύκατε	λέλυσθε	ἐλύθητε	λυθήσεσθε
3 pl	ἔλυσαν	ἐλύσαντο	λελύκασι(ν)	λέλυνται	ἐλύθησαν	λυθήσονται

As you work with your Bible software of choice, take time to see how each verb is translated in your English translation. Use the following table as a guide in your understanding of the translation of verbs.

4.4.1

Verb Translation

Table 20: Indicative Verb Translation

		active		middle		passive
Present Tense						
		active		*middle*		*passive*
1 sg	λύω	*I am loosing* *I loose*	λύομαι	*I loose* *(for myself)*	λύομαι	*I am (being)* *loosed*
2 sg	λύεις	*you are loosing* *you loose*	λύῃ	*you loose* *(for yourself)*	λύῃ	*you are* *(being) loosed*
3 sg	λύει	*(s)he/it is loosing* *(s)he/it looses*	λύεται	*(s)he/it looses* *(for itself)*	λύεται	*(s)he/it is* *(being) loosed*
1 pl	λύομεν	*we are loosing* *we loose*	λυόμεθα	*we loose* *(for ourselves)*	λυόμεθα	*we are* *(being) loosed*
2 pl	λύετε	*y'all are loosing* *y'all loose*	λύεσθε	*y'all loose* *(for yourselves)*	λύεσθε	*y'all are* *(being) loosed*
3 pl	λύουσι(ν)	*they are loosing* *they loose*	λύονται	*they loose* *(for themselves)*	λύονται	*they are* *(being) loosed*
Imperfect Tense						
		active		*middle*		*passive*
1 sg	ἔλυον	*I was loosing* *I loose*	ἐλυόμην	*I was loosing* *(for myself)*	ἐλυόμην	*I was* *(being) loosed*
2 sg	ἔλυες	*you were loosing* *you loose*	ἐλύου	*you were loosing* *(for yourself)*	ἐλύου	*you were* *(being) loosed*
3 sg	ἔλυε(ν)	*(s)he/it was* *loosing* *(s)he/it looses*	ἐλύετο	*(s)he/it was* *loosing* *(for itself)*	ἐλύετο	*(s)he/it was* *(being) loosed*
1 pl	ἐλύομεν	*we were loosing* *we loose*	ἐλυόμεθα	*we were loosing* *(for ourselves)*	ἐλυόμεθα	*we were* *(being) loosed*
2 pl	ἐλύετε	*y'all were loosing* *y'all loose*	ἐλύεσθε	*y'all were loosing* *(for yourselves)*	ἐλύεσθε	*y'all were* *(being) loosed*
3 pl	ἔλυον	*they were loosing* *they loose*	ἐλύοντο	*they were* *loosing* *(for themselves)*	ἐλύοντο	*they were* *(being) loosed*
Future Tense						
		active		*middle*		*passive*
1 sg	λύσω	*I will loose*	λύσομαι	*I will loose (for* *myself)*	λυθήσομαι	*I will be* *loosed*
2 sg	λύσεις	*you will loose*	λύσῃ	*you will loose* *(for yourself)*	λυθήσῃ	*you will be* *loosed*

3 sg	λύσει	(s)he/it will loose	λύσεται	(s)he/it will loose (for himself)	λυθήσεται	(s)he/it will be loosed
1 pl	λύσομεν	we will loose	λυσόμεθα	we will loose (for ourselves)	λυθησόμεθα	we will be loosed
2 pl	λύσετε	y'all will loose	λύσεσθε	y'all will loose (for yourselves)	λυθήσεσθε	y'all will be loosed
3 pl	λύσουσι(ν)	they will loose	λύσονται	they will loose (for themselves)	λυθήσονται	they will be loosed

Aorist Tense

	active		middle		passive	
1 sg	ἔλυσα	I loose(d)	ἐλυσάμην	I loosed (for myself)	ἐλύθην	I was loosed
2 sg	ἔλυσας	you loose(d)	ἐλύσω	you loosed (for yourself)	ἐλύθης	you were loosed
3 sg	ἔλυσε(ν)	(s)he/it loose(d)	ἐλύσατο	(s)he/it loosed (for himself)	ἐλύθη	(s)he/it was loosed
1 pl	ἐλύσαμεν	we loose(d)	ἐλυσάμεθα	we loosed (for ourselves)	ἐλύθημεν	we were loosed
2 pl	ἐλύσατε	y'all loose(d)	ἐλύσασθε	y'all loosed (for yourselves)	ἐλύθητε	y'all were loosed
3 pl	ἔλυσαν	they loose(d)	ἐλύσαντο	they loosed (for themselves)	ἐλύθησαν	they were loosed

Perfect Tense
*note: for pluperfect translation "have/has" would be replaced with "had"

	active		middle		passive	
1 sg	λέλυκα	I have loosed	λέλυμαι	I have loosed (for myself)	λέλυμαι	I have (been) loosed
2 sg	λέλυκας	you have loosed	λέλυσαι	you have loosed (for yourself)	λέλυσαι	you have (been) loosed
3 sg	λέλυκε(ν)	(s)he/it has loosed	λέλυται	(s)he/it has loosed (for himself)	λέλυται	(s)he/it has (been) loosed
1 pl	λελύκαμεν	we have loosed	λελύμεθα	we have loosed (for ourselves)	λελύμεθα	we have (been) loosed
2 pl	λελύκατε	y'all have loosed	λέλυσθε	y'all have loosed (for yourselves)	λέλυσθε	y'all have (been) loosed
3 pl	λελύκασι(ν)	they have loosed	λέλυνται	they have loosed (for themselves)	λέλυνται	they have (been) loosed

4.5
VERB PARSING

The main difference in the approach of *Biblical Greek Made Simple* as compared to other grammars is that other grammars take many chapters to teach you how to parse a verb from memory. In this approach, the assumption is that you are not (at least initially) aiming on parsing on your own. Bible software is there to do the parsing for you. What you need to know, rather, is what the information provided to you by Bible software means. Verb parsing will be provided to you in the following way (as per §4.2):

tense	voice	mood	person	number	lexical form
present	active	indicative	3	singular	λύω

T.V. Makes **P**eople **N**auseous is a simple way to remember the order in which the information is usually given to you. Most importantly, though, you need to understand what these things mean. What does the present tense convey? What does it mean to have active voice? What is the indicative mood? And related questions. These are the types of questions you need to ask and be able to answer from memory.

4.6
THE LAST WORD

You are likely dazed and confused right now—I don't blame you. This is a whirlwind of information. As you work through the exercises things will become clearer. Remember, this approach aims to help you understand how Greek verbs are formed and what verb parsing means. Familiarity with all of the items is important, but not memorization.

4.7
THE LEAST YOU
NEED TO KNOW

You should be able to clearly and accurately answer these questions. Use the flashcards at http://quizlet.com/_7tfwd to memorize the answers:

- What are the three types of verbs?

- What is internal aspect?

- What is external aspect?

- What is stative aspect?

- What does the Greek present tense convey? In what time is it most often used?

- What does the Greek imperfect tense convey? In what time is it most often used?

- What does the Greek future tense convey? In what time is it most often used?

- What does the Greek aorist tense convey? In what time is it most often used?

- What does the Greek perfect tense convey? In what time is it most often used?

- What does the Greek pluperfect tense convey? In what time is it most often used?

- What three voices occur in Greek? What does each one convey?

- What is the indicative mood?

- What are the six slots of the indicative slot machine?

- What tenses receive the augment?

- What tenses receive reduplication?

- Which tenses take which suffixes (slot 4)?

- Which tense and voice combinations take primary endings?

- Which tense and voice combinations take secondary endings?

Utilizing the Logos help file, Logos forums, Logos wiki, and videos provided, users should take the time in this chapter to learn:

4.8 GREEK@LOGOS

- How to make a filter to highlight indicative verbs

  - See the article on Visual Filters at https://support.logos.com

- How to search for a lexical form of a verb and how to search for an inflected form of a verb

- See the article on Morph Search at https://support.logos.com

• How to access the parsing of any Greek verb using the information window and its translation

- See the article on the Information Tool at https://support.logos.com

4.9 VOCABULARY

One of the things this chapter has in the verb stem section (§4.3.1.4) is that verbs are built upon six principal parts. In other words, there are six possible variations on how a verb can look (yikes!). Lexicons (and the vocabulary tables in this textbook) list the lexical form as the one to learn. The reality, though, is that the other principal parts are just as, and sometimes more, important to recognize as well. In the vocabulary below, and in the remaining chapters, principal parts will be listed with verbs as they occur. The lexical form (the one you memorize) is the first principal part. When a dash appears in the principal parts, it is because that form of the word does not occur in the NT.

You don't fully understand principal parts yet, so don't worry; I am not expecting you to. You will learn about them in the next chapter, and the gray words added below the verbs here will start to make more sense to you over time.

Word	Gloss	Type	Freq.	Derivatives
ἄγγελος, -ου, ὁ	messenger, angel	noun	175	*angel*
κόσμος, -ου, ὁ	world, universe	noun	186	*cosmos*
χείρ, χειρός, ἡ	hand; arm; finger	noun	177	*chiropractor*
παρά (παρ')	(+gen.) from (+dat.) beside, in the presence of, with (+acc.) alongside of, other than	prep.	194	*parallel*
ἀκούω	I hear	verb	428	*acoustics*
ἀκούω, ἀκούσω, ἤκουσα, ἀκήκοα, ἤκουσμαι, ἠκούσθην				
ἀποκρίνομαι	I answer	verb	231	
ἀποκρίνομαι, — —, ἀπεκρινάμην, — —, — —, ἀπεκρίθην				

Word	Gloss	Type	Freq.	Derivatives
γράφω	I write	verb	191	*graphics*
γράφω, γράψω, ἔγραψα, γέγραφα, γέγραμμαι, ἐγράφην				
δύναμαι	I am able, I am powerful, I can	verb	210	*dynamic*
δύναμαι, δυνήσομαι, — —, — —, — —, ἠδυνήθην				
ἔχω	I have	verb	708	
ἔχω (imperfect εἶχον), ἕξω, ἔσχον, ἔσχηκα, ἔσχημαι, — —				
θέλω	I want, wish, will, desire	verb	208	
θέλω (imperfect ἤθελον), θελήσω, ἠθέλησα, ἠθέληκα, — —, ἠθελήθην				
καλέω	I call, name, invite	verb	148	
καλέω, καλέσω, ἐκάλεσα, κέκληκα, κέκλημαι, ἐκλήθην				
λαλέω	I sound, talk, speak	verb	296	*glossalalia*
λαλῶ, λαλήσω, ἐλάλησα, λελάληκα, λελάλημαι, ἐλαλήθην				
λύω	I loosen, release	verb	42	
λύω, λύσω, ἔλυσα, λέλυκα, λέλυμαι, ἐλύθην				
πιστεύω	I believe (in), have faith, trust	verb	241	
πιστεύω, πιστεύσω, ἐπίστευσα, πεπίστευκα, πεπίστευμαι, ἐπιστεύθην				
ποιέω	I do, make	verb	568	
ποιέω, ποιήσω, ἐποίησα, πεποίηκα, πεποίημαι, ἐποιήθην				
πορεύομαι	I go, proceed, live	verb	153	
πορεύομαι, πορεύσομαι, ἐπορευσάμην, πεπόρευκα, πεπόρευμαι, ἐπορεύθην				

Chapter 4 Exercises

LEARNING ACTIVITY 1: VOCABULARY (1 HOUR)
Be sure to review previous vocabulary as well as learn the new.

LEARNING ACTIVITY 2: READING (30 MINUTES)
Read chapter 4 of the textbook.
Completed: _____ Yes _____ No

LEARNING ACTIVITY 3: VERB TENSES (1.5–2 HOURS RECOMMENDED)
Take some time to become as familiar as possible with all of the indicative paradigms and endings. Sing along with the songs below over and over until you have memorized them.

◢ Recommended for learning about the indicative mood: ◣
The Singing Grammarian: (1) Present Active Indicative Song, (2) Present Middle/Passive Song, (3) Future Active and Middle Song, (4) Secondary Endings-Imperfect Tense Song, (5) Aorist Active and Middle Song, (6) The Passives Song, and (7) The (Plu)Perfect Song.

Completed: _____ Yes _____ No

LEARNING ACTIVITY 4: VERB FORMATION (3–4 HOURS RECOMMENDED)
The following two tables should be photocopied as necessary. Work on filling them from memory.

	Primary			*Secondary*	
	Active		**Middle/Passive**	**Active**	**Middle/Passive**
	final ending	*μι verbs*			
1 sg					
2 sg					
3 sg					
1 pl					
2 pl					
3 pl					

principal part	tense & voice							composes the principal part
1st								
2nd								
3rd								
4th								
5th								
6th								

LEARNING ACTIVITY 5: FORMATION OF INDICATIVE VERBS (1.5–2 HOURS RECOMMENDED)

Using only the verb λυω, and only your textbook (the tables above should suffice), create the verbs listed. (Don't worry about accents or breathing marks.)

1. present, active, indicative, 3, plural = _____

2. present, active, indicative, 2, singular = _____

3. present, middle/passive, indicative, 1, plural = _____

4. present, middle/passive, indicative, 2, singular = _____

5. imperfect, active, indicative, 2, singular = _____

6. imperfect, active, indicative, 3, plural = _____

7. imperfect, middle/passive, indicative, 1, singular = _____

8. imperfect, middle/passive, indicative, 2, plural = _____

9. future, active, indicative, 3, singular = _____

10. future, active, indicative, 1, plural = _____

11. future, middle, indicative, 2, singular = _____

12. future, middle, indicative, 3, plural = _____

13. future, passive, indicative, 3, singular = _____

14. future, passive, indicative, 2, plural = _____

15. aorist, active, indicative, 2, singular = _____

16. aorist, active, indicative, 1, plural = _____

17. aorist, middle, indicative, 2, singular = _____

18. aorist, middle, indicative, 3, plural = _____

19. aorist, passive, indicative, 3, singular = _____

20. aorist, passive, indicative, 1, plural = _____

21. perfect, active, indicative, 2, singular = _____

22. perfect, active, indicative, 3, plural = _____

23. perfect, middle/passive, indicative, 2, singular = _____

24. perfect, middle/passive, indicative, 3, plural = _____

25. pluperfect, active, indicative, 1, singular = _____

26. pluperfect, active, indicative, 2, plural = _____

27. pluperfect, middle/passive, indicative, 2, singular = _____

28. pluperfect, middle/passive, indicative, 3, plural = _____

LEARNING ACTIVITY 6: REVIEW (30 MINUTES RECOMMENDED)
You've just spent a good amount of time learning a lot of new things. Take 30 minutes to do one final read through of the chapter to solidify the knowledge, and make sure you can answer all of the questions in the *Least You Need to Know* section. Use the online flashcards link in the chapter to quiz yourself on the questions.
Completed: _____Yes _____No

4.10 THE SECOND TIME AROUND

The second time around in this chapter is all about memorization and paradigms. You should not only thoroughly memorize the endings and indicative slot machine, but be able to create the paradigms from memory.

The following is the pluperfect paradigm of λύω, which wasn't presented during the chapter.

Table 21: Pluperfect Indicative Paradigm

Parts	Fourth λέλυκα	Fifth λέλυμαι
tense and voice	*pluperfect active*	*pluperfect middle/passive*
1 sg	ἐλελύκειν	ἐλελύμην
2 sg	ἐλελύκεις	ἐλέλυσο
3 sg	ἐλελύκει	ἐλέλυτο
1 pl	ἐλελύκειμεν	ἐλελύμεθα
2 pl	ἐλελύκειτε	ἐλέλυσθε
3 pl	ἐλελύκεισαν	ἐλέλυντο

ADVANCED EXERCISES (CH. 4)

Learning Activity 1: Vocabulary (1 hour)

Learn your assigned vocabulary list from Appendix A. Be sure to review previous vocabulary as well as learn the new. Knowledge of this new vocabulary is assumed in the translation work.

Learning Activity 2: Reading (1 hour)

Read chapter 4 of the textbook again.

Completed: _____ Yes _____ No

Learning Activity 3: Memorize Declension Endings (1.5 hour)

Take a good amount of time to review the Greek strong verb paradigms with *The Singing Grammarian*. (Present Active, Present Middle/Passive, Future, Imperfect/Secondary Endings, Aorist, Perfect, Passives, and Liquid Verbs Songs)

Completed: _____ Yes _____ No

Learning Activity 4: Parsing Practice (1.5 hours)

Drill yourself using either ParseGreek or Paradigms Master Pro

- For ParseGreek, choose By Frequency; λύω; narrow your verb mood to indicative.

- For Paradigms Master choose Verbs by moods: Forms of λύω; Indicative forms of λύω until you can get them all right every single time.

Completed: _____ Yes _____ No

Learning Activity 5: Parsing Work (1.5 hours)

Parse the following verbs (**TV M**akes **P**eople **N**auseous + Lexical form) and provide a translation.

1. λέγει _____

2. λέγω _____

3. ἔχει _____

4. ἔρχεται _____

5. ἔλεγον _____

6. δύναται _____

7. ἔλεγεν _____

8. λέγουσιν _____

9. ἔχετε _____

10. ἔχομεν _____

11. ἤρξατο _____

12. ἤκουσα _____

13. ἔχουσιν _____

14. ἐλάλησεν _____

15. δύνασθε _____

16. ἐποίησεν _____

17. ἐγέννησεν _____

Learning Activity 6: Translation (3.5 hours)

Translate the following sentences. Be ready to parse any verbs that appear in the sentences. The following sentences assume knowledge of all words occurring up to 70 times (chs. 1–11 and lists 1–3). For some difficult forms, the lexical form is provided. For any remaining difficult forms, consult the morphological information in Logos Bible Software or the notes in *The UBS Greek New Testament: A Reader's Edition*.

ὅτι αἴρεται ἀπὸ τῆς γῆς ἡ ζωὴ αὐτοῦ (Acts 8:33)

_____

_____

_____

ὅτε ἤμην *νήπιος* (child), *ἐλάλουν* (lex = λαλέω) ὡς νήπιος, *ἐφρόνουν* (I thought) ὡς νήπιος, *ἐλογιζόμην* (lex = λογίζομαι) ὡς νήπιος (1 Cor 13:11)

_____

_____

_____

_____

ἐν αὐτῷ ζωὴ ἦν, καὶ ἡ ζωὴ ἦν τὸ φῶς τῶν ἀνθρώπων (John 1:4)

_____

_____

_____

_____

Αἱ μὲν οὖν ἐκκλησίαι *ἐστερεοῦντο* (were strengthened) τῇ πίστει καὶ *ἐπερίσσευον* (increased) τῷ *ἀριθμῷ* (number) καθ᾽ ἡμέραν. (Acts 16:5)

_____

_____

_____

_____

ἔκραζεν (he called out) ἐν τῷ *συνεδρίῳ* (Sanhedrin)· ἄνδρες ἀδελφοί, ἐγὼ Φαρισαῖός εἰμι, υἱὸς Φαρισαίων, περὶ *ἐλπίδος* (hope) καὶ *ἀναστάσεως* (resurrection) νεκρῶν ἐγὼ κρίνομαι. (Acts 23:6)

_____

_____

_____

_____

ἀλλὰ λέγω, Ἰσραὴλ οὐκ *ἔγνω* (understand); πρῶτος Μωϋσῆς λέγει· ἐγὼ *παραζηλώσω* (will make jealous) ὑμᾶς ἐπ᾽ οὐκ ἔθνει (Rom 10:19)

_____

_____

_____

_____

CHAPTER 5

Principal Parts and Alternative-Pattern Indicative Verbs Made Simple

What's the Point: In the same way that the English verb "go" can be written in three alternative ways ("go," "went," and "going"), Greek verbs have six spelling pattern variations. While some are very similar (like those introduced in the previous chapter), many differ greatly (like comparing "go" to "went"). This chapter introduces you to the spelling pattern variations of Greek verbs.

5.1 INTRODUCTION

While you may feel like you just barely understand the Greek indicative verb system from the last chapter, the truth is that Greek verbs get even more complicated. (Don't blame me!) The last chapter focused on the strong verb, using the example of λύω, as well as vowel contractions and consonant interactions that can happen. With λύω, the -λυ- part was consistent. Because it was consistent, we could clearly see the affixes attached to make the different tense and voice combinations. The reality, though, is that most verbs aren't neat and tidy like this. Furthermore, there is another group of verbs, called μι verbs, that are very different. This chapter will begin by discussing principal parts and then introduce you to various alternative patterns. The chapter will conclude with discussing how to read about verbs in a Greek lexicon.

5.2 GREEK PRINCIPAL PARTS

In the previous chapter you learned about the indicative slot machine and how the slot patterns is best seen with a strong verb like λύω. It is important to understand that the slot machine *is a recognition of patterns in a verb*. The slot patterns are easily recognizable with strong verbs. For some verbs, the pattern can change a little bit:

- If a verb stem begins with a vowel there will be contraction when slot 1 (the augment) is attached. The vowel that begins the stem also cannot be reduplicated (slot 2) and so will lengthen instead.

- If a verb stem ends with a vowel and a connecting vowel (slot 5) is added, there will be vowel contraction.

- If a verb stem ends in a liquid letter, the *sigma* that is part of the future and aorist suffix will disappear (they will slip on the liquid).

- If a verb stem ends with any of the stop consonants, there will be consonant interaction with all of the suffixes, because the suffixes begin with *sigma*, *kappa*, or *theta* (see §1.3.2).

All of these changes are manageable because the slot machine pattern is there, though altered slightly. BUT, this is not the only problem we can run into. Another problem is *the stem itself*. There are many verbs whose stem (slot 3) will change depending on the tense and voice combination. This is where Greek principal parts comes in.

Unlike nouns, a Greek verb stem is not always consistent in its spelling. In the approach of *Biblical Greek Made Simple* you do not need to worry about learning all the various ways a verb may look, just know that *it is not always consistent*—there are more weak verbs than strong verbs in Greek. Using our English example, the past tense of "go" is "went." Children will often say "goed" because they have not yet learned that for this particular verb you don't simply stick "-ed" on the end of the verb to make it past tense. The same thing occurs in Greek. Sometimes a verb stem is consistent and stays the same no matter what tense; this is a strong verb like λύω (e.g., kill, kills, killed). Other times a Greek verb will be somewhat consistent—it will change a little bit because of the affixes but the stem will still be recognizable (e.g., fight, fights, fought). Finally, some Greek verbs will be very different depending on the tense; this a weak verb (e.g., go, goes, *went*).

For English speakers, there are three primary ways every verb is spelled, that is, there are three *principal parts*. A principal part is one of three possible spelling variations for a verb (*go, going, went; fight, fighting, fought*). As native speakers, we learn these as related words even when they are spelled very differently. Greek has *six* principal parts for each verb, in other words there are six possible spelling variations.

Look at the following λύω table again, but this time note how the stem of the principal part in the top row (the bold and underlined portion) flows down to all of the forms that are built off of it (also underlined):

Table 22: λύω Indicative Paradigm

Parts	First λύω				Second λύσω	
tense and voice	*present active*	*present m/p*[1]	*imperfect active*	*imperfect m/p*	*future active*	*future middle*
1 sg	λύω	λύομαι	ἔλυον	ἐλυόμην	λύσω	λύσομαι
2 sg	λύεις	λύῃ	ἔλυες	ἐλύου	λύσεις	λύσῃ
3 sg	λύει	λύεται	ἔλυε(ν)	ἐλύετο	λύσει	λύσεται
1 pl	λύομεν	λυόμεθα	ἐλύομεν	ἐλυόμεθα	λύσομεν	λυσόμεθα
2 pl	λύετε	λύεσθε	ἐλύετε	ἐλύεσθε	λύσετε	λύσεσθε
3 pl	λύουσι(ν)	λύονται	ἔλυον	ἐλύοντο	λύσουσι(ν)	λύσονται

Parts	Third ἔλυσα		Fourth λέλυκα	Fifth λέλυμαι	Sixth ἐλύθην	
tense and voice	*aorist active*	*aorist middle*	*perfect active*[2]	*perfect m/p*	*aorist passive*	*future passive*
1 sg	ἔλυσα	ἐλυσάμην	λέλυκα	λέλυμαι	ἐλύθην	λυθήσομαι
2 sg	ἔλυσας	ἐλύσω	λέλυκας	λέλυσαι	ἐλύθης	λυθήσῃ
3 sg	ἔλυσε(ν)	ἐλύσατο	λέλυκε(ν)	λέλυται	ἐλύθη	λυθήσεται
1 pl	ἐλύσαμεν	ἐλυσάμεθα	λελύκαμεν	λελύμεθα	ἐλύθημεν	λυθησόμεθα
2 pl	ἐλύσατε	ἐλύσασθε	λελύκατε	λέλυσθε	ἐλύθητε	λυθήσεσθε
3 pl	ἔλυσαν	ἐλύσαντο	λελύκασι(ν)	λέλυνται	ἐλύθησαν	λυθήσονται

1. See §4.2.2.
2. Pluperfect active and middle is also built off of this part. It is rare so is not added here.

Notice how, for the most part, the inflected endings (the red font along with the connecting vowel), is the main change that occurs as one goes down the columns (with a few exceptions). Because λύω is a strong verb, the patterns work out nicely. The following table takes ἀκούω, which is not as "strong" as λύω. First, it begins with a vowel, so there will be some vowel contraction. But as we get to the fourth-sixth principal parts, it starts to look quite different and the slot machine pattern (§4.3.1) is not as easy to recognize. Notice, again, how the principal part stem flows down through the forms that are built off of it, and the endings (the red font) is the main change.

Table 23: ἀκούω Indicative Paradigm

Parts	First ἀκούω				Second ἀκούσω	
tense and voice	present active	present m/p[1]	imperfect active	imperfect m/p	future active	future middle
1 sg	ἀκούω	ἀκούομαι	ἤκουον	ἠκουόμην	ἀκούσω	ἀκούσομαι
2 sg	ἀκούεις	ἀκούῃ	ἤκουες	ἠκούου	ἀκούσεις	ἀκούσῃ
3 sg	ἀκούει	ἀκούεται	ἤκουε(ν)	ἠκούετο	ἀκούσει	ἀκούσεται
1 pl	ἀκούομεν	ἀκουόμεθα	ἠκούομεν	ἠκουόμεθα	ἀκούσομεν	ἀκουσόμεθα
2 pl	ἀκούετε	ἀκούεσθε	ἠκούετε	ἠκούεσθε	ἀκούσετε	ἀκούσεσθε
3 pl	ἀκούουσι(ν)	ἀκούονται	ἤκουον	ἠκούοντο	ἀκούσουσι(ν)	ἀκούσονται

Parts	Third ἤκουσα		Fourth ἀκήκοα	Fifth ἤκουσμαι	Sixth ἠκούσθην	
tense and voice	aorist active	aorist middle	perfect active[2]	perfect m/p	aorist passive	future passive
1 sg	ἤκουσα	ἠκουσάμην	ἀκήκοα	ἤκουσμαι	ἠκούσθην	ἠκουσθήσομαι
2 sg	ἤκουσας	ἠκούσου	ἀκήκοας	ἤκουσαι	ἠκούσθης	ἀκουσθήσῃ
3 sg	ἤκουσε(ν)	ἠκούσετο	ἀκήκοε(ν)	ἤκουσται	ἠκούσθη	ἀκουσθήσεται
1 pl	ἠκούσαμεν	ἠκουσάμεθα	ἀκηκόαμεν	ἠκούσμεθα	ἠκούσθημεν	ἠκουσθησόμεθα
2 pl	ἠκούσατε	ἠκούσεσθε	ἀκηκόατε	ἤκουσθε	ἠκούσθητε	ἠκουσθήσεσθε
3 pl	ἤκουσαν	ἠκούσοντο	ἀκηκόασιν	ἤκουσνται	ἠκούσθησαν	ἠκουσθήσονται

1. See §4.2.2.
2. Pluperfect active and middle is also built off of this part. It is rare so is not added here.

So to recap, Greek verbs have six potential ways they can be spelled to which the inflection tags (the primary or secondary endings) are attached. It is these endings that change. The six principal parts of each Greek verb is the representation of the variances in spelling for that Greek verb. For some verbs, like λύω, the slot machine pattern is easy to recognize because the -λυ- part stays the same. For a verb like ἀκούω, the pattern is somewhat consistent in that much of the slot machine pattern is recognizable. But some verbs will be *very* different from part to part. This final example is λέγω, one of the highest frequency verbs in the New Testament. Notice how different the principal parts are from each other. *But* you should also notice how the stem of the principal part flows down to all of the forms that are built off of it.

Table 24: λέγω Indicative Paradigm

Parts	First λέγω				Second ἐρῶ	
tense and voice	present active	present m/p[1]	imperfect active	imperfect m/p	future active	future middle
1 sg	λέγω	λέγομαι	ἔλεγον	ἐλεγόμην	ἐρῶ	-[2]
2 sg	λέγεις	λέγῃ	ἔλεγες	ἐλέγου	ἐρεῖς	-
3 sg	λέγει	λέγεται	ἔλεγε(ν)	ἐλέγετο	ἐρεῖ	-
1 pl	λέγομεν	λεγόμεθα	ἐλέγομεν	ἐλεγόμεθα	ἐροῦμεν	-
2 pl	λέγετε	λέγεσθε	ἐλέγετε	ἐλέγεσθε	ἐρεῖτε	-
3 pl	λέγουσι(ν)	λέγονται	ἔλεγον	ἐλέγοντο	ἐροῦσιν	-

1. See §4.2.2.
2. No NT forms.

Table 24: λέγω Indicative Paradigm *(continued)*

Parts	Third εἶπον		Fourth εἴρηκα	Fifth εἴρημαι	Sixth ἐρρέθην	
tense and voice	aorist active	aorist middle	perfect active[1]	perfect m/p	aorist passive	future passive
1 sg	εἶπον	εἰπόμην	εἴρηκα	εἴρημαι	ἐρρέθην	-
2 sg	εἶπες	εἶπου	εἴρηκας	εἴρησαι	ἐρρέθης	-
3 sg	εἶπε(ν)	εἶπετο	εἴρηκε(ν)	εἴρηται	ἐρρέθη	-
1 pl	εἴπομεν	εἰπόμεθα	εἰρήκαμεν	εἰρήμεθα	ἐρρέθημεν	-
2 pl	εἴπετε	εἴπεσθε	εἰρήκατε	εἴρησθε	ἐρρέθητε	-
3 pl	εἶπον	εἴποντο	εἰρήκασι(ν)	εἴρηνται	ἐρρέθησαν	-

A final word about principal parts that I hope you recognize by now—if you had a photographic memory and memorized all Greek principal parts and the primary and secondary endings, you would be able to recognize any verb form! You do not need to memorize all of that, but you do need to understand the formation of indicative verbs. The table below is a sampling of Greek verb principal parts. Some are strong, some are manageable, some are annoying, and some are downright ugly. I have color-coded these principal parts as best as can be done—with some verbs, the slot machine pattern is not easily recognizable. Appendix B has a fuller list of Greek principal parts.

As you go through the remainder of this chapter, keep your head in "principal-part mode." As tables of different types of verbs are introduced, see how the stem of the principal part flows down to all of the forms that are built off of it.

---

1. Pluperfect active and middle is also built off of this part. It is rare so is not added here.

Table 25: Principal Parts

First	Second	Third	Fourth	Fifth	Sixth
λύω[1]	λύσω	ἔλυσα	λέλυκα	λέλυμαι	ἐλύθην
ἀκούω	ἀκούσω	ἤκουσα	ἀκήκοα	ἤκουσμαι	ἠκούσθην
γινώσκω[2]	γνώσομαι	ἔγνων	ἔγνωκα	ἔγνωσμαι	ἐγνώσθην
γίνομαι[3]	γενήσομαι	ἐγενόμην	γέγονα	γεγένημαι	ἐγενήθην
λαλῶ[4]	λαλήσω	ἐλάλησα	λελάληκα	λελάλημαι	ἐλαλήθην
πληρῶ	πληρώσω	ἐπλήρωσα	πεπλήρωκα	πεπλήρωμαι	ἐπληρώθην
γεννῶ	γεννήσω	ἐγέννησα	γεγέννηκα	γεγέννημαι	ἐγεννήθην
ἀποστέλλω[5]	ἀποστελῶ	ἀπέστειλα	ἀπέσταλκα	ἀπέσταλμαι	ἀπεστάλην
λέγω	ἐρῶ	εἶπον	εἴρηκα	εἴρημαι	ἐρρέθην
ὁράω	ὄψομαι	εἶδον	ἑώρακα	ἑώραμαι	ὤφθην
δίδωμι[6]	δώσω	ἔδωκα	δέδωκα	δέδομαι	ἐδόθην
tense and voice combinations that build off of these principal parts					
present (all), imperfect (all)	future active and middle	aorist active and middle	(plu)perfect active	(plu)perfect middle/ passive	aorist and future passive

In the nouns chapter you learned that the nominative singular form of every noun is the lexical form. With verbs, the first principal part is the lexical form of every verb (usually the present, active, indicative, first-person, singular). This is why it is important to understand that the Greek verb system is built upon principal parts—sometimes the form of a verb is *very* different from its lexical form.

5.3 DIFFERENT TYPES OF VERBS

5.3.1 Lexical Middle Verbs

Certain Greek verbs do not have active voice forms. They look like a middle/passive verb because they only take the middle/passive endings. It is fairly easy to recognize a lexical middle verb because their lexical form ends with -μαι, not -ω. So for example, the word γίνομαι has μαι as the ending (the middle/passive ending). This verb,

1. In both the first and second principal parts, certain inflected endings will absorb the connecting vowel.

2. This is a future middle verb. You will read about these in §5.3.1.

3. This is a lexical middle verb. You will read about these in §5.3.1.

4. The following three verbs are called contract verbs. You will read more about them in §5.3.2.

5. This is a compound verb. You will read more about them in §5.3.3.

6. This is a μι verb. You will read more about them in §5.3.5.

γίνομαι, will not take active voice endings (γίνω never occurs). In the table below, all of the verbs are middle or passive, with the exception of perfect which has an active form. Remember that middle voice indicates that the action is being done with self-interest, and is often translated into English as an active.[1]

Table 26: Lexical Middle Indicative Forms

Parts	First γίνομαι				Second γενήσομαι	
tense and voice	present active	present m/p	imperfect active	imperfect m/p	future active	future middle
1 sg	-	γίνομαι	-	ἐγινόμην	-	γενήσομαι
2 sg	-	γίνῃ	-	ἐγίνου	-	γενήσῃ
3 sg	-	γίνεται	-	ἐγίνετο	-	γενήσεται
1 pl	-	γινόμεθα	-	ἐγινόμεθα	-	γενησόμεθα
2 pl	-	γίνεσθε	-	ἐγίνεσθε	-	γενήσεσθε
3 pl	-	γίνονται	-	ἐγίνοντο	-	γενήσονται
Parts	**Third** ἐγενόμην		**Fourth** γέγονα	**Fifth** γεγένημαι	**Sixth** ἐγενήθην	
tense and voice	aorist active	aorist middle	perfect active	perfect m/p	aorist passive	future passive
1 sg	-	ἐγενόμην	γέγονα	γεγένημαι	ἐγενήθην	γενήθησομαι
2 sg	-	ἐγένου	γέγονας	γεγένησαι	ἐγενήθης	γενηθήσῃ
3 sg	-	ἐγένετο	γέγονε(ν)	γεγένηται	ἐγενήθη	γενηθήσεται
1 pl	-	ἐγενόμεθα	γέγοναμεν	γεγενήμεθα	ἐγενήθημεν	γενηθησόμεθα
2 pl	-	ἐγένεσθε	γεγόνατε	γεγένησθε	ἐγενήθητε	γενηθήσεσθε
3 pl	-	ἐγενοντο	γεγόνασι(ν)	γεγένηνται	ἐγενήθησαν	γενηθήσονται

5.3.2

Contract Verbs

You have already learned from chapter 1 that vowels frequently contract when placed side by side. Verb stems that end in an *alpha* (α), *epsilon* (ε), or *omicron* (ο) are called contract verbs because the vowel at

---

1. Many past and current grammars have called these forms "deponent verbs." A deponent verb is a Latin concept, where verbs look like middle, but are translated as active. Research in the past few decades, however, has shown that deponency is foreign to Greek. These lexical middle forms do indeed get translated as active in English, but the idea of self-interest is still core to its meaning in Greek.

the end of the stem contracts with the connecting vowel *for all present and imperfect forms* (i.e., the first principal part). When a contract verb occurs in the rest of the tenses the vowel at the end of the stem will automatically lengthen: α/ε = η and ο = ω. In the following paradigms I've underlined the vowel contraction or lengthening.

Table 27: φιλέω Indicative Paradigm

Parts	First φιλέω				Second -	
tense and voice	*present active*	*present m/p*	*imperfect active*	*imperfect m/p*	*future active*	*future middle*
1 sg	φιλ<u>ῶ</u>	φιλ<u>οῦ</u>μαι	ἐφίλ<u>ου</u>ν	ἐφιλ<u>ού</u>μην	-	-
2 sg	φιλ<u>εῖ</u>ς	φιλ<u>ῇ</u>	ἐφίλ<u>ει</u>ς	ἐφιλ<u>οῦ</u>	-	-
3 sg	φιλ<u>εῖ</u>	φιλ<u>εῖ</u>ται	ἐφίλ<u>ει</u>	ἐφιλ<u>εῖ</u>το	-	-
1 pl	φιλ<u>οῦ</u>μεν	φιλ<u>ού</u>μεθα	ἐφιλ<u>οῦ</u>μεν	ἐφιλ<u>ού</u>μεθα	-	-
2 pl	φιλ<u>εῖ</u>τε	φιλ<u>εῖ</u>σθε	ἐφιλ<u>εῖ</u>τε	ἐφιλ<u>εῖ</u>σθε	-	-
3 pl	φιλ<u>οῦ</u>σι(ν)	φιλ<u>οῦ</u>νται	ἐφίλ<u>ου</u>ν	ἐφιλ<u>οῦ</u>ντο	-	-
Parts	**Third** ἐφίλησα		**Fourth** πεφίληκα	**Fifth** -	**Sixth** -	
tense and voice	*aorist active*	*aorist middle*	*perfect active*	*perfect m/p*	*aorist passive*	*future passive*
1 sg	ἐφίλ<u>η</u>σα	ἐφίλ<u>η</u>σάμην	πεφίλ<u>η</u>κα	-	-	-
2 sg	ἐφίλ<u>η</u>σας	ἐφίλ<u>η</u>σω	πεφίλ<u>η</u>κας	-	-	-
3 sg	ἐφίλ<u>η</u>σε(ν)	ἐφίλ<u>η</u>σάτο	πεφίλ<u>η</u>κε(ν)	-	-	-
1 pl	ἐφίλ<u>η</u>σαμεν	ἐφιλ<u>ή</u>σάμεθα	πεφιλ<u>ή</u>καμεν	-	-	-
2 pl	ἐφίλ<u>η</u>σατε	ἐφιλ<u>ή</u>σασθε	πεφιλ<u>ή</u>κατε	-	-	-
3 pl	ἐφίλ<u>η</u>σαν	ἐφιλ<u>ή</u>σαντο	πεφιλ<u>ή</u>κασι(ν)	-	-	-

Table 28: ἀγαπάω Indicative Paradigm

Parts	First ἀγαπάω				Second ἀγαπήσω	
tense and voice	present active	present m/p	imperfect active	imperfect m/p	future active	future middle
1 sg	ἀγαπῶ	ἀγαπῶμαι	ἠγάπων	ἠγαπώμην	ἀγαπήσω	ἀγαπήσομαι
2 sg	ἀγαπᾷς	ἀγαπᾷ	ἠγάπας	ἠγαπῶ	ἀγαπήσεις	ἀγαπήσῃ
3 sg	ἀγαπᾷ	ἀγαπᾶται	ἠγάπα	ἠγαπᾶτο	ἀγαπήσει	ἀγαπήσεται
1 pl	ἀγαπῶμεν	ἀγαπώμεθα	ἠγαπῶμεν	ἠγαπώμεθα	ἀγαπήσομεν	ἀγαπησόμεθα
2 pl	ἀγαπᾶτε	ἀγαπᾶσθε	ἠγαπᾶτε	ἠγαπᾶσθε	ἀγαπήσετε	ἀγαπήσεσθε
3 pl	ἀγαπῶσι	ἀγαπῶνται	ἠγάπων	ἠγαπῶντο	ἀγαπήσουσιν	ἀγαπήσονται

Parts	Third ἠγάπησα		Fourth ἠγάπηκα	Fifth ἠγάπημαι	Sixth ἠγαπήθην	
tense and voice	aorist active	aorist middle	perfect active	perfect m/p	aorist passive	future passive
1 sg	ἠγάπησα	ἠγαπησάμην	ἠγάπηκα	ἠγάπημαι	ἠγαπήθην	ἀγαπηθήσομαι
2 sg	ἠγάπησας	ἠγαπήσω	ἠγάπηκας	ἠγάπησαι	ἠγαπήθης	ἀγαπηθήσῃ
3 sg	ἠγάπησε(ν)	ἠγαπήσατο	ἠγάπηκεν	ἠγάπηται	ἠγαπήθη	ἀγαπηθήσεται
1 pl	ἠγάπησαμεν	ἠγαπήσαμεθα	ἠγαπήκαμεν	ἠγάπημεθα	ἠγαπήθημεν	ἀγαπηθησόμεθα
2 pl	ἠγάπησατε	ἠγαπήσασθε	ἠγαπήκατε	ἠγάπησθε	ἠγαπήθητε	ἀγαπηθήσεσθε
3 pl	ἠγάπησαν	ἠγαπήσαντο	ἠγαπήκασι(ν)	ἠγάπησαν	ἠγαπήθησαν	ἀγαπηθήσονται

5.3.3
Compound Verbs

Compound verbs are made up of a normal verb with the addition of a preposition to the front of it.[1] This will make an entirely new verb with a meaning somewhat similar to the original form. For instance:

- γινώσκω = I know

- ἀναγινώσκω = I read (the preposition ἀνά, which means "up," has been added to the front of the verb to make a new word)

---

1. You've already learned numerous prepositions in vocabulary and you will learn more about them in §7.2.

The addition changes the meaning, but still retains some similarity in meaning. It is like the knowledge of the written word floats "up" so you can "know" it.

The most important thing to know about compound verbs is that the *epsilon* augment (slot 1) will come *after the preposition* that has been added to make the new word. So ἀνά + [ε] + γινώσκω. In the table below the example used is ἀπαγγέλλω, ἀπ᾽[1] + [ε] + αγγέλλω. The underlined letters represent the contraction that has occurred because of the augment. The behavior shows up in the imperfect, aorist, and perfect.

Table 29: ἀπαγγέλλω Indicative Paradigm

Parts	First ἀπαγγέλλω				Second ἀπαγγελῶ	
tense and voice	present active	present m/p[2]	imperfect active	imperfect m/p	future active	future middle
1 sg	ἀπαγγέλλω	ἀπαγγέλλομαι	ἀπήγγελλον	ἀπηγγελλόμην	ἀπαγγελῶ	ἀπαγγελοῦμαι
2 sg	ἀπαγγέλλεις	ἀπαγγέλλη	ἀπήγγελλες	ἀπηγγέλλου	ἀπαγγελεῖς	ἀπαγγελῇ
3 sg	ἀπαγγέλλει	ἀπαγγέλλεται	ἀπήγγελλεν	ἀπηγγέλλετο	ἀπαγγελεῖ	ἀπαγγελεῖται
1 pl	ἀπαγγέλλομεν	ἀπαγγελλόμεθα	ἀπήγγελλομεν	ἀπηγγελλόμεθα	ἀπαγγελοῦμεν	ἀπαγγελούμεθα
2 pl	ἀπαγγέλλετε	ἀπαγγέλλεσθε	ἀπήγγελλετε	ἀπηγγέλλεσθε	ἀπαγγελεῖτε	ἀπαγγελεῖσθε
3 pl	ἀπαγγέλλουσι	ἀπαγγέλλονται	ἀπήγγελλον	ἀπηγγέλλοντο	ἀπαγγελοῦσι	ἀπαγγελοῦνται

Parts	Third ἀπήγγειλα		Fourth -	Fifth ἀπήγγελμαι	Sixth ἀπηγγέλην	
tense and voice	aorist active	aorist middle	perfect active	perfect m/p	aorist passive	future passive
1 sg	ἀπήγγειλα	ἀπηγγειλάμην	-	ἀπήγγελμαι	ἀπηγγέλην	ἀπαγγελήσομαι
2 sg	ἀπήγγειλας	ἀπηγγείλω	-	ἀπήγγελσαι	ἀπηγγέλης	ἀπαγγελήσῃ
3 sg	ἀπήγγειλε	ἀπηγγείλατο	-	ἀπήγγελται	ἀπηγγέλη	ἀπαγγελήσεται
1 pl	ἀπηγγείλαμεν	ἀπηγγειλάμεθα	-	ἀπήγγελμεθα	ἀπηγγέλημεν	ἀπαγγελησόμεθα
2 pl	ἀπηγγείλατε	ἀπηγγείλασθε	-	ἀπήγγελσθε	ἀπηγγέλητε	ἀπαγγελήσετε
3 pl	ἀπήγγειλαν	ἀπηγγείλαντο	-	ἀπήγγελνται	ἀπηγγέλησαν	ἀπαγγελήσονται

1. This is the shortened form for ἀπό.   2. See §4.2.2.

5.3.4
Second Aorist Verbs

Some aorist stems are so different in their principal part that their is no trace of the σα suffix. These aorists are often called second aorist. Because no σα suffix remains, these second aorist forms end up looking just like an imperfect tense in that they only take an augment (slot 1) and secondary endings. The key, again, is that the principal part is different.

Table 30: Second Aorist Indicative Paradigm

Parts	First ἄγω				Second ἄξω	
tense and voice	present active	present m/p¹	imperfect active	imperfect m/p	future active	future middle
1 sg	ἄγω	ἄγομαι	ἦγον	ἠγόμην	ἄξω	ἄξομαι
2 sg	ἄγεις	ἄγῃ	ἦγες	ἤγου	ἄξεις	ἄξῃ
3 sg	ἄγει	ἄγεται	ἦγε(ν)	ἤγετο	ἄξει	ἄξεται
1 pl	ἄγομεν	ἀγόμεθα	ἤγομεν	ἠγόμεθα	ἄξομεν	ἀξόμεθα
2 pl	ἄγετε	ἄγεσθε	ἤγετε	ἤγεσθε	ἄξετε	ἄξεσθε
3 pl	ἄγουσι(ν)	ἄγονται	ἦγον	ἤγοντο	ἄξουσι(ν)	ἄξονται

Parts	Third ἤγαγον		Fourth ἀγείοχα	Fifth ἦγμαι	Sixth ἤχθην	
tense and voice	aorist active	aorist middle	perfect active²	perfect m/p	aorist passive	future passive
1 sg	ἤγαγον	ἠγαγόμην	ἀγείοχα	ἦγμαι	ἤχθην	ἀχθήσομαι
2 sg	ἤγαγες	ἠγάγου	ἀγείοχας	ἦγσαι	ἤχθης	ἀχθήσῃ
3 sg	ἤγαγε(ν)	ἠγάγετο	ἀγείοχεν	ἦγται	ἤχθη	ἀχθήσεται
1 pl	ἠγάγομεν	ἠγαγόμεθα	ἀγειόχαμεν	ἦγμεθα	ἤχθημεν	ἀχθησόμεθα
2 pl	ἠγάγετε	ἠγάγεσθε	ἀγειόχατε	ἦγσθε	ἤχθητε	ἀχθήσεσθε
3 pl	ἤγαγον	ἠγάγοντο	ἀγειόχασι(ν)	ἦγνται	ἤχθησαν	ἀχθήσονται

5.3.5
μι Verbs

The μι verbs are a special class of Greek verbs that occur pretty regularly in the New Testament. Their stems are often short and end in a vowel, which causes them to act much like contract verbs in that the vowel may lengthen to a long vowel or diphthong. The other oddity

---

1. See §4.2.2.
2. Pluperfect active and middle is also built off of this part. It is rare so is not added here.

of a μι verb occurs mainly in the present and imperfect tenses (those built off of the first principal part). In the first principal part, μι verbs have a special type of *iota* (ι) reduplication. It is like perfect reduplication, but using an *iota* (ι) instead. The present active forms of μι verbs also have their own set of endings (see Table 18: Primary and Secondary Endings). Finally, aorist active μι verbs have a -κα suffix instead of -σα. In the middle forms it has no suffix. The following table shows the full indicative paradigm of δίδωμι, with the unique *iota* reduplication in the first principal part underlined.

Table 31: δίδωμι Indicative Paradigm

Parts	First δίδωμι				Second δώσω	
tense and voice	present active	present m/p	imperfect active	imperfect m/p	future active	future middle
1 sg	δ<u>ί</u>δωμι	δ<u>ί</u>δομαι	ἐδ<u>ί</u>δουν	ἐδ<u>ι</u>δόμην	δώσω	δώσομαι
2 sg	δ<u>ί</u>δως	δ<u>ί</u>δοσαι	ἐδ<u>ί</u>δους	ἐδ<u>ί</u>δοσο	δώσεις	δώσῃ
3 sg	δ<u>ί</u>δωσι(ν)	δ<u>ί</u>δοται	ἐδ<u>ί</u>δου	ἐδ<u>ί</u>δοτο	δώσει	δώσεται
1 pl	δ<u>ί</u>δομεν	δ<u>ι</u>δόμεθα	ἐδ<u>ί</u>δομεν	ἐδ<u>ι</u>δόμεθα	δώσομεν	δωσόμεθα
2 pl	δ<u>ί</u>δοτε	δ<u>ί</u>δοσθε	ἐδ<u>ί</u>δοτε	ἐδ<u>ί</u>δοσθε	δώσετε	δώσεσθε
3 pl	δ<u>ι</u>δόασι(ν)	δ<u>ί</u>δονται	ἐδ<u>ί</u>δοσαν	ἐδ<u>ί</u>δοντο	δώσουσι(ν)	δώσονται
Parts	Third ἔδωκα		Fourth δέδωκα	Fifth δέδομαι	Sixth ἐδόθην	
tense and voice	aorist active	aorist middle	perfect active[1]	perfect middle	aorist passive	future passive
1 sg	ἔδωκα	ἐδόμην	δέδωκα	δέδομαι	ἐδόθην	δοθήσομαι
2 sg	ἔδωκας	ἔδου	δέδωκας	δέδοσαι	ἐδόθης	δοθήσῃ
3 sg	ἔδωκε(ν)	ἔδοτο	δέδωκε(ν)	δέδοται	ἐδόθη	δοθήσεται
1 pl	ἐδώκαμεν	ἐδόμεθα	δεδώκαμεν	δεδόμεθα	ἐδόθημεν	δοθησόμεθα
2 pl	ἐδώκατε	ἔδοσθε	δεδώκατε	δέδοσθε	ἐδόθητε	δοθήσεσθε
3 pl	ἔδωκαν	ἔδοντο	δεδώκαν	δέδονται	ἐδόθησαν	δοθήσονται

◢ Watch the video at ◣
http://youtu.be/lj1Nq53zpEU to solidify the previous section.

---

1. Pluperfect active and middle is also built off of this part. It is rare so is not added here.

5.3.5.1   The Greek verb εἰμί is an equative verb (see §4.1). It is also a μι verb, but
εἰμί   is treated separately because it is so frequent in the New Testament.
εἰμί only occurs in the present, imperfect, and future in the indicative
mood. It is also unique from other verbs in that it does not have voice.
So a form of εἰμί would be parsed as tense, mood, person, number,
lexical form (e.g., present, indicative, second-person, singular, εἰμί).

Table 32: εἰμί Indicative

	Present		**Imperfect**		**Future**	
1 sg	εἰμί	*I am*	ἤμην	*I was*	ἔσομαι	*I will be*
2 sg	εἶ	*you are*	ἦς (ἦσθα)	*you were*	ἔσῃ	*you will be*
3 sg	ἐστί(ν)	*(s)he/it is*	ἦν	*(s)he/it was*	ἔσται	*(s)he/it will be*
1 pl	ἐσμέν	*we are*	ἦμεν (ἤμεθα)	*we were*	ἐσόμεθα	*we will be*
2 pl	ἐστέ	*y'all are*	ἦτε	*y'all were*	ἔσεσθε	*y'all will be*
3 pl	εἰσί(ν)	*they are*	ἦσαν	*they were*	ἔσονται	*they will be*

5.4   You should be able to clearly and accurately answer these questions.
THE LEAST YOU   Use the flashcards at http://quizlet.com/_7tfwx to memorize the
NEED TO KNOW   answers:

- What are principal parts?

- Which tense and voice combinations build off of the first
  principal part?

- Which tense and voice combinations build off of the second
  principal part?

- Which tense and voice combinations build off of the third
  principal part?

- Which tense and voice combinations build off of the fourth
  principal part?

- Which tense and voice combinations build off of the fifth
  principal part?

- Which tense and voice combinations build off of the sixth principal part?

- What are deponent verbs?

- What are future deponent verbs?

- What are contract verbs? Describe their behavior.

- What are compound verbs? Describe their behavior, particularly with the augment.

- What are second aorists?

- What are μι verbs? What makes μι verbs different from other verb forms?

- What is the first bit of information a lexicon gives about verbs?

Utilizing the Logos help file, Logos forums, Logos wiki, and videos provided, users should take the time in this chapter to learn:

**5.5
GREEK@LOGOS**

- Get started on managing your Logos library to empower your searching

  - See the article on Using Your Library at https://support.logos.com

- How to highlight and take notes in Logos

  - See the articles on Highlighting and Notes at https://support.logos.com

5.6 VOCABULARY

Word	Meaning	Type	Freq.	Derivatives
μέν	on the one hand, indeed [or left untranslated]	partic.	179	
γίνομαι	I become, am, exist, happen, take place, am born, am created	verb	669	
γίνομαι, γενήσομαι, ἐγενόμην, γέγονα, γεγένημαι, ἐγενήθην				
γινώσκω	I know, come to know, realize, learn	verb	222	diagnostic
γινώσκω, γνώσομαι, ἔγνων, ἔγνωκα, ἔγνωσμαι, ἐγνώσθην				
δίδωμι	I give (out), entrust, give back, put, grant, allow	verb	415	
δίδωμι, δώσω, ἔδωκα, δέδωκα, δέδομαι, ἐδόθην				
εἰμί	I am	verb	2462	
εἰμί, ἔσομαι, ἤμην, — —, — —, — —				
εἰσέρχομαι	I enter, come in(to), go in(to)	verb	194	
εἰσέρχομαι, εἰσελεύσομαι, εἰσῆλθον, εἰσελήλυθα, — —, — —				
ἐξέρχομαι	I go out	verb	218	
ἐξέρχομαι, ἐξελεύσομαι, ἐξῆλθον, ἐξελήλυθα, — —, — —				
ἔρχομαι	I come, go	verb	634	
ἔρχομαι, ἐλεύσομαι, ἦλθον, ἐλήλυθα, — —, — —				
ἐσθίω	I eat	verb	158	
ἐσθίω, φάγομαι, ἔφαγον, ἐδήδοκα, ἐδήδεσμαι, ἠδέσθην				
εὑρίσκω	I find	verb	176	heuristic
εὑρίσκω, εὑρήσω, εὗρησα (εὗρον), εὕρηκα, — —, εὑρέθην				
ἵστημι	I stand, set, place; I cause to stand	verb	155	
ἵστημι, στήσω, ἔστησα (ἔστην), ἔστηκα, — —, ἐστάθην				
λαμβάνω	I take, receive	verb	258	
λαμβάνω, λήμψομαι, ἔλαβον, εἴληφα, — —, ἐλήμφθην				
λέγω	I say, speak	verb	2354	legend
λέγω, ἐρῶ, εἶπον, εἴρηκα, εἴρημαι, ἐρρέθην				
οἶδα	I know, understand	verb	318	
οἶδα, εἰδήσω, ᾔδειν, — —, — —, — —				
ὁράω	I see, notice, experience	verb	454	panorama
ὁράω, ὄψομαι, εἶδον, ἑώρακα (ἑόρακα), ἑώραμαι, ὤφθην				

Chapter 5 Exercises

LEARNING ACTIVITY 1: VOCABULARY (1 HOUR)

Be sure to review previous vocabulary as well as learn the new.

LEARNING ACTIVITY 2: READING (1 HOUR)

Read chapter 5 of the textbook.

Completed: _____ Yes _____ No

LEARNING ACTIVITY 3: VERB TENSES (30–45 MINUTES RECOMMENDED)

Take some more time to become as familiar as possible with all of the indicative paradigms and endings. Sing along with the songs below over and over. The two new songs to add this week are in bold below.

◣ Recommended for learning about the indicative mood: ◥
The Singing Grammarian: (1) Present Active Indicative Song,
(2) Present Middle/Passive Song, (3) Future Active and Middle Song, (4) Secondary Endings–Imperfect Tense Song,
(5) Aorist Active and Middle Song, (6) The Passives Song,
(7) The (Plu)Perfect Song, **(8) The Liquid Verbs Song, and (9) The μι Verbs Song**.

Completed: _____ Yes _____ No

LEARNING ACTIVITY 4: PARSING (2.5–3.5 HOURS RECOMMENDED)

The following list of verbs are some of the most frequently occurring indicative forms.

1. Open a Logos search window and search for each inflected word to fill in the parsing of the following verbs. (Confirm the lexical form by double-clicking the word to open it in your prioritized lexicon.)

2. In the second row, indicate which principal part the verb is built off of (appendix B)

3. In the second row, indicate the unique characteristics of the verb from section §5.2 of your textbook. For example: contract, compound, μι verb, lexical middle, liquid, second aorist. (It can be more than one of these!)

   Appendix B will help with this, particularly looking at the first three principal parts of a verb.

4. In the second row, indicate the unique characteristics of the verb from section §5.2 of the textbook (i.e., contract, compound, μι verb, lexical middle, liquid, 2 Aorist — a verb can be more than one of these).

inflected form	tense	voice	mood	person	number	lexical form
εἶπεν example	aorist	active	indicative	3	singular	εἶπον / λέγω [hover details indicate εἶπον as lemma, but looking it up in a lexicon reveals that εἶπον is the 2 Aorist of λέγω]
principal part: third			characteristic(s): second aorist			
ἐστιν						
principal part:			characteristic(s):			
λέγει						
principal part:			characteristic(s):			
ἦν						
principal part:			characteristic(s):			
γέγονεν						
principal part:			characteristic(s):			
ἐγένετο						
principal part:			characteristic(s):			
ἔσται						
principal part:			characteristic(s):			
ἔχει						
principal part:			characteristic(s):			
ἀπέστειλεν						
principal part:			characteristic(s):			
εἶπαν						
principal part:			characteristic(s):			
ἤκουσα						
principal part:			characteristic(s):			

(continued)

inflected form	tense	voice	mood	person	number	lexical form
ἔρχεται						
principal part:			characteristic(s):			
ἦλθεν						
principal part:			characteristic(s):			
ἀπεκρίθη						
principal part:			characteristic(s):			
ἔλεγον						
principal part:			characteristic(s):			
ἐποίησεν						
principal part:			characteristic(s):			
ἐξῆλθεν						
principal part:			characteristic(s):			
ἔδωκεν						
principal part:			characteristic(s):			
ἦλθον						
principal part:			characteristic(s):			
γέγραπται						
principal part:			characteristic(s):			
ἔλεγεν						
principal part:			characteristic(s):			
λέγουσιν						
principal part:			characteristic(s):			
εἶπον						
principal part:			characteristic(s):			
ἐστάθη						
principal part:			characteristic(s):			
ἔχετε						
principal part:			characteristic(s):			
ἐγέννησεν						
principal part:			characteristic(s):			

(continued)

inflected form	tense	voice	mood	person	number	lexical form
ἔφη						
principal part:			characteristic(s):			
εἰσῆλθεν						
principal part:			characteristic(s):			
γέγονεν						
principal part:			characteristic(s):			
ἐδόθη						
principal part:			characteristic(s):			
ἐλάλησεν						
principal part:			characteristic(s):			

LEARNING ACTIVITY 5: REVIEW (30 MINUTES RECOMMENDED)

You've just spent a good amount of time learning a lot of new things. Take 30 minutes to do one final read through of the chapter to solidify the knowledge, and make sure you can answer all of the questions in the *Least You Need to Know* section. Use the online flashcards link in the chapter to quiz yourself on the questions.

Completed: _____ Yes _____ No

**5.7
THE SECOND
TIME AROUND**

This chapter very much builds off of the foundation laid in the previous chapter. Learning the differences in these alternative patterns, in addition to the paradigms and endings learned in the previous chapter, will help you to recognize them when parsing. Take the time also to memorize the εἰμί indicative paradigm, as it is the most frequent verb in the NT.

ADVANCED EXERCISES (CH. 5 PART 1)

Learning Activity 1: Vocabulary (1 hour)

Learn your assigned vocabulary list from Appendix A. Be sure to review previous vocabulary as well as learn the new. Knowledge of this new vocabulary is assumed in the translation work.

Learning Activity 2: Reading (1 hour)
Read chapter 5 of the textbook again.
Completed: _____ Yes _____ No

Learning Activity 3: Memorize Indicative Verb Endings (1 hour)
Memorize the indicative verb endings. Use *The Singing Grammarian* as help, and practice filling in the paradigms from memory using the practice tables.
Completed: _____ Yes _____ No

Learning Activity 4: Parsing Practice (1.5 hours)
Drill yourself using either ParseGreek or Paradigms Master Pro

- For ParseGreek, choose any learned vocabulary range in conjunction with chapters 4 and 5 grammar concepts

- For Paradigms Master Pro, choose
  Verbs by moods: All verbs: Indicatives.

Completed: _____ Yes _____ No

Learning Activity 4: Parsing Work (1.5 hours)

1. εἶπεν _____

2. ἐστιν _____

3. ἦν _____

4. ἔσται _____

5. εἶ _____

6. εἰσιν _____

7. ἦσαν _____

8. γέγραπται _____

9. ἐσμεν _____

10. ἔσονται _____

11. ἐγένετο _____

12. εἶπαν _____

13. ἦλθεν _____

14. ἦσαν _____

15. ἀπεκρίθη _____

Learning Activity 6: Translation (3.5 hours)

Translate the following sentences. Be ready to parse any indicative verbs that appear in the sentences. The following sentences assume knowledge of all words occurring up to 62 occurrences (chs. 1–11 and lists 1–4). For some difficult forms, the lexical form is provided. For any remaining difficult forms, consult the morphological information in Logos Bible Software.

αὕτη δέ ἐστιν ἡ κρίσις (judgment) ὅτι τὸ φῶς ἐλήλυθεν (has come) εἰς τὸν κόσμον καὶ ἠγάπησαν οἱ ἄνθρωποι μᾶλλον τὸ σκότος (darkness) ἢ τὸ φῶς (John 3:19)

_____

_____

_____

εἴτε προφάσει εἴτε (whether false motives or) ἀληθείᾳ, Χριστὸς καταγγέλλεται (is proclaimed), καὶ ἐν τούτῳ χαίρω. Ἀλλὰ καὶ χαρήσομαι (lex = χαίρω) (Phil 1:18)

_____

_____

_____

νόμον οὖν καταργοῦμεν (we overthrow) διὰ τῆς πίστεως; μὴ γένοιτο (by no means)· ἀλλὰ νόμον ἱστάνομεν (lex = ἵστημι). (Rom 3:31)

_____

_____

_____

ἔλαβεν τοὺς ἑπτὰ ἄρτους καὶ τοὺς ἰχθύας (fish) καὶ εὐχαριστήσας (after giving thanks) ἔκλασεν (he broke) καὶ ἐδίδου τοῖς μαθηταῖς, οἱ δὲ μαθηταὶ τοῖς ὄχλοις. (Matt 15:36)

_____

_____

_____

_____

Ἐγώ εἰμι ὁ ποιμὴν (shepherd) ὁ καλός. ὁ ποιμὴν ὁ καλὸς τὴν ψυχὴν αὐτοῦ τίθησιν ὑπὲρ τῶν προβάτων (sheep)· (John 10:11)

_____

_____

_____

_____

Εἰρήνην ἀφίημι ὑμῖν, εἰρήνην τὴν ἐμὴν δίδωμι ὑμῖν· οὐ καθὼς ὁ κόσμος δίδωσιν ἐγὼ δίδωμι ὑμῖν. (John 14:27)

_____

_____

_____

_____

ADVANCED EXERCISES (CH. 5 PART 2)

Learning Activity 1: Vocabulary (1 hour)
Learn your assigned vocabulary list from Appendix A. Be sure to review previous vocabulary as well as learn the new. Knowledge of this new vocabulary is assumed in the translation work.

Learning Activity 2: Reading (30 minutes)
Review chapter 5 of the textbook again.
Completed: _____ Yes _____ No

Learning Activity 3: Memorize the Indicative Verb Endings (1 hour)

Memorize the indicative verb endings. Use *The Singing Grammarian* as help, and practice filling in the paradigms from memory using the practice tables.

Completed: _____ Yes _____ No

Learning Activity 4: Parsing Practice (1.5 hours)

Drill yourself using either ParseGreek or Paradigms Master Pro

- For ParseGreek, choose any learned vocabulary range in conjunction with chapter 5 grammar concepts

- For Paradigms Master Pro, work on first, second, and third declension nouns until you can get them all right every single time.

note The program gives you the lexical form in the parsing. Take time to practice recognizing the lexical form on your own, as you will be responsible for providing the lexical form in testing.

Completed: _____ Yes _____ No

Learning Activity 4: Parsing Work (1.5 hours)

1. εἶδον _____

2. γέγραπται _____

3. ἐξῆλθεν _____

4. ἔδωκεν _____

5. ἦλθον _____

6. οἴδατε _____

7. εἶπον _____

8. εἶδεν _____

9. ἔφη _____

10. εἰσῆλθεν _____

11. ἀπῆλθεν _____

12. ἀπέστειλεν _____

13. ἀπέθανεν _____

14. γέγονεν _____

15. εὗρον _____

16. δώσω _____

Learning Activity 6: Translation (3.5 hours)

Translate the following sentences. Be ready to parse any indicative verbs that appear in the sentences. The following sentences assume knowledge of all words occurring up to 56 times (chs. 1–11 and lists 1–5). For difficult forms, consult the morphological information in Logos Bible Software.

λέγει αὐτῇ ὁ Ἰησοῦς· ἀναστήσεται (lex = ἀνίστημι) ὁ ἀδελφός σου. (John 11:23)

_____

_____

_____

μέλλει γὰρ ὁ υἱὸς τοῦ ἀνθρώπου ἔρχεσθαι (to come) ἐν τῇ δόξῃ τοῦ πατρὸς αὐτοῦ μετὰ τῶν ἀγγέλων αὐτοῦ, καὶ τότε ἀποδώσει (he will repay) ἑκάστῳ κατὰ τὴν πρᾶξιν (deeds) αὐτοῦ. (Matt 16:27)

_____

_____

_____

ἵνα παραστήσωμεν (we may present) πάντα ἄνθρωπον τέλειον (complete) ἐν Χριστῷ· (Col 1:28)

_____

_____

_____

_____

τότε <u>ἐπετίθεσαν</u> (they laid) τὰς χεῖρας ἐπ᾽ αὐτοὺς καὶ ἐλάμβανον πνεῦμα ἅγιον. (Acts 8:17)

_____

_____

_____

<u>ὃν</u> (he whom) γὰρ <u>ἀπέστειλεν</u> (lex = <u>ἀποστέλλω</u>) ὁ θεὸς τὰ ῥήματα τοῦ θεοῦ λαλεῖ, οὐ γὰρ ἐκ <u>μέτρου</u> (measure) δίδωσιν τὸ πνεῦμα. (John 3:34)

_____

_____

_____

καὶ εἶδον (lex = ὁράω) τοὺς νεκρούς, τοὺς μεγάλους καὶ τοὺς <u>μικρούς</u> (small) (Rev 20:12)

_____

_____

_____

μετὰ δὲ <u>πολὺν χρόνον</u> (long time) ἔρχεται ὁ κύριος τῶν δούλων ἐκείνων καὶ <u>συναίρει</u> (settled) λόγον μετ᾽ αὐτῶν. (Matt 25:19)

_____

_____

_____

CHAPTER 6

The Article, Adjectives, Pronouns, and Numbers Made Simple

What's the Point: 32 percent of the New Testament is composed of words that fill in detail and give life to the text. Pronouns stand in place of nouns; the word "the" in Greek does a lot more than "the" in English; and adjectives have a robust life in the Greek language. Learning and appreciating these types of words will bring out the life and color of the Greek New Testament as you read and study it.

6.1

TWENTY-FOUR WAYS TO SAY "THE"

Greek has no word like "a" or "an," but the definite article "the" comes in abundance in Greek. In English, "the" always come right before the word it is paired with.[1] The article can be paired with any Greek noun, no matter how it is inflected. When words are paired together in Greek, they have to be inflected in the exact same way (same case, gender, and number). So, unlike Greek nouns which are only one gender (masculine, feminine, or neuter) the article can be any gender.

6.1.1

How the Article is Formed

Because the article has to be inflected the same way as the noun it is paired with, it has 24 forms.

---

1. Recall in §2.1 that the article was color-coded along with the noun it is paired with.

Table 33: The Article

| | masculine | | feminine | | neuter | |
	singular	plural	singular	plural	singular	plural
nominative	ὁ(ς)	οἱ	ἡ	αἱ	τό(ν)	τά
genitive	τοῦ	τῶν	τῆς	τῶν	τοῦ	τῶν
dative	τῷ	τοῖς	τῇ	ταῖς	τῷ	τοῖς
accusative	τόν	τούς	τήν	τάς	τό(ν)	τά

Notice that apart from the masculine and feminine nominative forms, all of the articles start with a *tau* (τ). Those four that do not have a *tau* (τ) have rough breathing instead. Finally, take note that the masculine and neuter articles use second declension endings and feminine articles use first declension endings. I have added in gray font the letters that complete the declension endings. It is only the gray font portions that are not used in article formation.

6.1.2
What the
Article Can Do
6.1.2.1
Make Something
Definite

The article will simply say "the" to make something definite when it is directly before a noun that it is paired with. Remember, when the article is paired with a noun they are inflected exactly the same in case, gender, and number. The case of the article and noun pair will be translated accordingly. For example: ὁ λογός = the word, τοῖς λόγοις = to the words. Even though the article makes something definite, it is not always translated into English. For example, God and proper names like Jesus often occur with an article. Translations usually do not say "the God" or "the Jesus."

This exact pairing is why grammarians often tell students that the article is one of your best friends. It never lies to the reader. Whereas some nouns are more difficult to figure out (especially those pesky third declension nouns) the article is always crystal clear.

6.1.2.2
The Article As
a Pronoun

The article can stand all by itself in Greek. When this happens it is functioning in a unique way that is unparalleled in English. The first thing the article can do when it is by itself is act like a pronoun. Consider this example:

- ὁ δὲ εἶπεν αὐτοῖς (Matt 12:3)

  □ ὁ (article="the") δὲ ("but" or untranslated) εἶπεν (verb = "said") αὐτοῖς (pronoun="to them")

  □ Translation: He said to them (Matt 12:3, NRSV)

Notice how the translation is NOT "the said to them." Notice also that the article is *all by itself*. Whenever the article is all by itself, it is not saying "the." In this example, the article is working like a pronoun, and just like a pronoun it has an antecedent (the "he" is Jesus). In this example, the article is nominative, masculine, singular. Therefore it is translated as "he." The English pronoun used to translate the article will correspond to the inflection of the noun:

- ἡ δὲ εἶπεν αὐτοῖς

  She said to them

- τό δὲ εἶπεν αὐτοῖς

  It said to them

- οἱ δὲ εἶπαν αὐτοῖς

  they said to them

The second thing a Greek article can do when it is *sitting all by itself* is rope in a prepositional phrase. Consider the following Greek sentence (and its breakdown):

6.1.2.3
Rope in a Prepositional Phrase

word	ὁ	ναὸς	τοῦ	θεοῦ	ὁ	ἐν	τῷ	οὐρανῷ
meaning	the	temple	the	God	the	in	the	heaven
type	article	noun	article	noun	article	preposition	article	noun
parsing	nom., masc., sg.		gen., masc., sg.		nom., masc., sg.	-		dat., masc., sg.
translation:	"the temple of God which is in heaven (Rev 11:19) *or* "the temple of God that is in heaven (Rev 11:19)							

Looking at the English translation ask yourself, what is "in heaven," the temple or God? In English it is unclear, in Greek it is crystal clear. In the example, there are four articles. The article all by

itself is not paired with anything and comes right before the prepositional phrase. You will learn more about prepositions and phrases in
chapter 7. For now what you need to know is that a preposition works
with a few other words to further describe something in the sentence.

Now take note that the lone article is identical to the very first article. That is what the lone article is doing, it is telling you that the following prepositional phrase is *telling you more about the matching word*.

Table 34: Lone Article Function

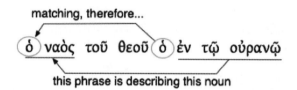

Because the lone article matches "the temple" (ὁ ναός) the thing "in
heaven" is the temple. If we were to change the lone article to match
God, then it would be saying that God is in heaven:

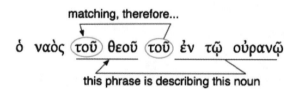

In both cases the English translation would be the same. They are
both ambiguous as to what is in heaven, but the Greek is clear. Finally,
notice that this type of article is translated with "which" or "that."

6.2
ADJECTIVES
Adjectives in Greek function in much the same way they do in English.
They can attribute value to a noun (*good* person, *bad* dog, *ugly* house) or
they can sit all by themselves and act like a noun (the *good*, the *bad*, and
the *ugly*). This last function is called acting as a substantive (i.e., it has
substance all on its own and can stand alone). Therefore, as you work
with Greek and come across an adjective, the main question to ask is: Is
it attributing value to a noun? If so, what noun is it paired with?

The great thing about adjectives (*and* the article) is that they use the declension endings just like nouns do, so there are no new endings to become familiar with. Just like nouns, the last letter on the stem determines which declension endings are chosen. Like the article, adjectives are also multigendered. In the following examples the case inflection is colored red—the red inflection is what will change the pronoun depending on its case and number. Finally, remember that the case ending affects the translation of adjectives just like it does nouns: nominative adjectives are the subject, genitive adjectives indicate possession, and so on.

6.2.1

How Adjectives Are Formed

Table 35: Adjective following First and Second Declension

	Masculine		Feminine		Neuter	
	sg.	pl.	sg.	pl.	sg.	pl.
nominative	ἀγαθός	ἀγαθοί	ἀγαθή	ἀγαθαί	ἀγαθόν	ἀγαθά
genitive	ἀγαθοῦ	ἀγαθῶν	ἀγαθῆς	ἀγαθῶν	ἀγαθοῦ	ἀγαθῶν
dative	ἀγαθῷ	ἀγαθοῖς	ἀγαθῇ	ἀγαθαῖς	ἀγαθῷ	ἀγαθοῖς
accusative	ἀγαθόν	ἀγαθούς	ἀγαθήν	ἀγαθάς	ἀγαθόν	ἀγαθά

Table 36: Adjective following Third Declension (for Masculine and Neuter)

stem is παντ for masc/neut	Masculine		Feminine		Neuter	
	sg.	pl.	sg.	pl.	sg.	pl.
nominative	πᾶς	πάντες	πᾶσα	πᾶσαι	πᾶν	πάντα
genitive	παντός	πάντων	πάσης	πασῶν	παντός	πάντων
dative	παντί	πᾶσι(ν)	πάση	πασαις	παντί	πᾶσι(ν)
accusative	πάντα	πάντας	πᾶσαν	πάσας	πᾶν	πάντα

Just like English, Greek has comparatives and superlatives.

- "Good" is an adjective.
- "Better" is the comparative of good.
- "Best" is the superlative of good.

6.2.1.1

Comparatives and Superlatives

Greek comparatives and superlatives are built off of Greek adjectives. Like English, some comparatives and superlatives are just like their adjectives (small, smaller, smallest). Greek adjectives that are more regular will add to the word -τερ- (comparative) or ταῖ (superlative), then the declension endings. Other adjectives, though, will be totally different (good, better, best). Higher frequency comparatives and superlatives will appear in vocabulary as their own words. All comparatives and superlatives will take declension endings just like any other adjective.

	normal	**comparative**	**superlative**
regular	νεός	νεώτερος	νεώτατος
irregular	ἀγαθός	κρείσσων	ἄριστός

6.2.2
What Adjectives Can Do

Adjectives in Greek do the same things English adjectives do, but Greek grammar determining the function is different from English.

6.2.2.1
Attribute Value to a Noun

Take a look at these three English examples and the three different ways Greek can say the same thing. Each noun used is a different gender and all are nominative singular:

- the good man (*masculine noun*)

   ◦ ἀγαθὸς ἄνθρωπος
   ◦ ὁ ἀγαθὸς ἄνθρωπος
   ◦ ὁ ἀγαθὸς ὁ ἄνθρωπος
   ◦ ὁ ἄνθρωπος ὁ ἀγαθὸς

- the good woman (*feminine noun*)

   ◦ ἀγαθὴ γυνή
   ◦ ἡ ἀγαθὴ γυνή
   ◦ ἡ ἀγαθὴ ἡ γυνή
   ◦ ἡ γυνὴ ἡ ἀγαθή

- the good tree (*neuter noun*)

   ◦ ἀγαθὸν δένδρον
   ◦ τόν ἀγαθὸν δένδρον

- τόν ἀγαθὸν τόν δένδρον
- τόν δένδρον τόν ἀγαθὸν

Take the time to look carefully at each set above to recognize the similarities in every group. The first thing to notice is that the adjective and the noun it is paired with are *identical in case, gender, and number* (the articles are identical too). The second thing to notice is that in examples 2–4 *the adjective always has an article*. Think of this as the **AAA rule** = an **A**djective preceded by an **A**rticle is **A**ttributive. Even when the noun does not have the article, the adjective still does. This demonstrates a simple maxim about Greek adjectives: *the article is key to understanding adjective function*. Here are the rules governing an attributive adjective:

1. The adjective *must* be in concord (i.e., same case, gender, number) as the noun it is paired with.

2. If the noun has an article, the adjective *must* have it too.

Like English, an adjective can act alone. In this case, the gender of the adjective *may* become part of the translation. When an adjective stands alone, words are sometimes added to make it more substantive. Examples:

6.2.2.2
Act Like a Noun (Act Substantivally)

- ὁ ἀγαθός
  - This is nominative, masculine, singular.
  - It can be translated as "the good," "the good *one*," or "the good *man*."
  - This same adjective without an article, and with no nearby noun in concord, would also be translated substantivally, that is, "a good (man)"

- ἡ ἀγαθή
  - This is nominative, feminine, singular.
  - It can be translated as "the good," "the good *one*," or "the good *woman*."
  - This same adjective without an article, and with no nearby noun in concord, would also be translated substantivally, that is, "a good (woman)"

- *τόν ἀγαθόν*
    - This is nominative, neuter, singular.
    - It can be translated as "the good," "the good *one*," or "the good *thing*."
    - This same adjective without an article, and with no nearby noun in concord, would also be translated substantivally, that is, "a good (thing)."

In all of the above cases, the adjective has the article but **it is not in concord with a nearby noun** (remember the rules from above). Think of it as the **A(A) noN rule** = an **A**djective (that can also have an **A**rticle) but **no N**oun in concord is <u>substantival</u>.

6.2.2.3
Act as a Predicate Nominative

This is a bit of a hybrid function of the previous two. Here is an example:

- *ἀγαθὸς ὁ ἄνθρωπος*
    - Both the noun and the adjective are nominative, masculine, singular.
    - Notice that the noun has the article but the adjective **does not.**
    - It is translated as "the man *is* good."

You may be wondering where "is" came from? It is a good question because it is foreign to English. In English, we always need a verb for a proper sentence—not so in Greek. In Greek (and other languages) a sentence can be verbless. This does not mean that you can insert any verb you want there, only one verb in particular. When a Greek sentence has no verb, the verb assumed to be invisibly present is a form of εἰμί. In this type of Greek sentence, "is," "was," "am," "were," or "are" is added in translation. In this type of verbless sentence, the adjective *with no article* will be *the object* (properly called the predicate nominative) of the invisible equative verb (review the equative verb in §4.1). We can call this the **noA noV rule** = an adjective with **no** Article and in a clause with **no V**erb is a *predicate nominative*.

Greek has a somewhat complicated set of pronouns that have different functions beyond a traditional English pronoun. The base meaning of a pronoun from Greek to English remains the same: it is a smaller word that stands in the place of a noun. For example, "John ate pizza. *He* liked it," uses the pronoun "he." Readers know from context that the "he" is John—this is called the antecedent. In the same way, most Greek pronouns have an antecedent. It is not necessary to cover every pronoun in detail, as some are infrequent and others essentially act like adjectives. The pronouns will be discussed in order of importance and frequency, and some pronouns that do not occur regularly will only be discussed in the *Second Time Around* section. In the future, if you come across pronouns you are unfamiliar with, you can also take the time to read about them in Wallace's *Greek Grammar Beyond the Basics*.

6.3

PRONOUNS

The great thing about pronouns (*and* the article *and* adjectives) is that they use the declension endings just like nouns do, so there are no new endings to become familiar with. Just like nouns and adjectives, the last letter on the stem determines which declension endings are chosen. Like adjectives and the article, pronouns are also multigendered. In the following examples the case inflection is colored red—the red inflection is what will change on the pronoun depending on its case and number. Finally, remember that the case ending affects the translation of pronouns just like it does nouns: nominative pronouns are the subject; genitive pronouns indicate possession; and so on.

6.3.1

How Pronouns are Formed

Personal pronouns are the most frequently occurring. The previous chapter on verbs taught how verbs have the subject built into them—person and number indicate the subject. When a verb is translated on its own, a personal pronoun is used in the translation. For example: *I* loose, *you* loose, *they* loose. These pronouns are built into Greek verbs, but they also have a life of their own. As you come across personal pronouns in the Greek New Testament, you will find that they are not always necessary. This is one case where Greek seems inefficient—a personal pronoun will occur with a verb that already has the subject built in. For example:

6.3.2

Personal Pronouns

- ἐγὼ βαπτίζω ἐν ὕδατι = I baptize in water (verb is pres., act., ind., first-person, sg.)

- βαπτίζω ἐν ὕδατι = I baptize in water (verb is pres., act., ind., first-person, sg.)

In the above examples the sentence is translated the same, as the verb has the subject built in, so the presence of the pronoun "I" (ἐγὼ) does not seem necessary.[1]

6.3.2.1
First- and Second-Person Personal Pronoun

There is no gender in the first- and second-person personal pronoun. In the singular forms of the first-person, the *epsilon* is in parentheses as it does not always occur. Although these personal pronouns are inflected for case and number, they do not take a very recognizable pattern of inflection—the genitive and dative forms are similar to the noun declensions, but not the nominative and accusative.

Table 37: First-Person Personal Pronoun

	singular		*plural*	
nominative	ἐγώ	*I*	ἡμεῖς	*we*
genitive	(ἐ)μοῦ	*my or of/from me*	ἡμῶν	*our or of/from us*
dative	(ἐ)μοί	*to/in me*	ἡμῖν	*to/in us*
accusative	(ἐ)μέ	*me*	ἡμᾶς	*us*

Table 38: Second-Person Personal Pronoun

	singular		*plural*	
nominative	σύ	*you*	ὑμεῖς	*y'all*
genitive	σοῦ	*your or of/from you*	ὑμῶν	*your or of/from y'all*
dative	σοί	*to you*	ὑμῖν	*to y'all*
accusative	σέ	*you*	ὑμᾶς	*y'all*

---

1. At times the Greek authors may be emphasizing the subject when they use the pronoun.

The third-person personal pronoun is fully inflected and multigendered like adjectives.

Table 39: Third-Person Personal Pronoun

	Masculine			Feminine			Neuter		
	sg.		pl.		sg.		pl.		sg.		pl.	
nom	αὐτός	he	αὐτοί	they	αὐτή	she	αὐταί	they	αὐτό	it	αὐτά	they
gen	αὐτοῦ	his	αὐτῶν	their	αὐτῆς	her	αὐτῶν	their	αὐτοῦ	its	αὐτῶν	their
dat	αὐτῷ	to him	αὐτοῖς	to them	αὐτῇ	to her	αὐταῖς	to them	αὐτῷ	to it	αὐτοῖς	to them
acc	αὐτόν	him	αὐτούς	them	αὐτήν	her	αὐτάς	them	αὐτό	it	αὐτά	them

The third-person personal pronoun can function like a regular pronoun (as per the translations given in Table 39 above) but can also function in an adjectival way. The word will look exactly the same as above, but an article may be involved in the construction. There are two different ways this can work:

6.3.3
Pronouns That Act
Like Adjectives
6.3.3.1
Special Functions
of the Third-Person
Personal Pronoun

- Intensive Attributive

  τὸν αὐτὸν λόγον, "the same word" (Mark 14:39) or
  αὐτῇ τῇ ὥρᾳ, "the same hour" (Luke 10:21)
  □ The pronoun is in full concord with the noun it is paired with.
  □ The noun and pronoun may or may not have an article.

- Intensive Predicative

  αὐτὴ ἡ κτίσις, "the creation itself" (Rom 8:21)
  □ The pronoun is in full concord with the noun it is paired with but never has the article.
  □ The pronoun is translated like a reflexive pronoun (himself, herself, itself, etc.).

6.3.3.2
Demonstrative
Pronouns

Demonstrative pronouns function just like adjectives (refer to §6.2.2) and so will be in *full concord* with the nouns they are paired with. The one exception is that demonstrative pronouns *never take an article*. Like adjectives, the demonstrative will pair with a nearby noun in full concord. Far more frequent, however, is the demonstrative by itself acting substantivally (see §6.2.2.2). "This/these" are often referred to as the close or proximate demonstrative. "That/those" are often referred to as the far or remote demonstrative. Demonstrative pronouns use second declension for masculine and neuter, and first declension for feminine. The following are some examples:

1. Demonstrative Paired with a Noun

   □ Ἔχομεν δὲ τὸν θησαυρὸν <u>τοῦτον</u> ἐν ὀστρακίνοις σκεύεσιν
     But we have *this treasure* in clay jars (2 Cor 4:7)

   □ Ἐν δὲ ταῖς ἡμέραις <u>ἐκείναις</u> παραγίνεται Ἰωάννης ὁ βαπτιστὴς
     But in *those days* John the baptizer appeared (Matt 3:1)

2. Demonstrative by Itself

   □ <u>οὗτός</u> ἐστιν ὁ υἱός μου
     this is my son (Matt 3:17)

   □ <u>ταῦτα</u> δὲ αὐτοῦ ἐνθυμηθέντος
     But just when he had resolved to do *these things* (Matt 1:20)

Table 40: Demonstrative Pronouns

Near	Masculine		Feminine		Neuter	
	sg.	*pl.*	*sg.*	*pl.*	*sg.*	*pl.*
nominative "this/these"	οὗτος	οὗτοι	αὕτη	αὗται	τοῦτο	ταῦτα
genitive "of this/these"	τούτου	τούτων	ταύτης	τούτων	τούτου	τούτων
dative "to this/these"	τούτῳ	τούτοις	ταύτῃ	ταύταις	τούτῳ	τούτοις
accusative "this/these"	τοῦτον	τούτους	ταύτην	ταύτας	τοῦτο	ταῦτα

(continued)

Far	Masculine		Feminine		Neuter	
	sg.	*pl.*	*sg.*	*pl.*	*sg.*	*pl.*
nominative "that/those"	ἐκεῖνος	ἐκεῖνοι	ἐκείνη	ἐκεῖναι	ἐκεῖνο	ἐκεῖνα
genitive "of that/those"	ἐκείνου	ἐκείνων	ἐκείνης	ἐκείνων	ἐκείνου	ἐκείνων
dative "to that/those"	ἐκείνῳ	ἐκείνοις	ἐκείνῃ	ἐκείναις	ἐκείνῳ	ἐκείνοις
accusative "that/those"	ἐκεῖνον	ἐκείνους	ἐκείνην	ἐκείνας	ἐκεῖνο	ἐκεῖνα

Notice that the near demonstrative is like the article, with the masculine and feminine nominative singular having rough breathing and no *tau*, but the rest do.

Correlative pronouns and possessive pronouns also act just like adjectives, but occur infrequently. As you come across them, you can take time to read about them in the *Second Time Around* section. You can also read Wallace's *Greek Grammar Beyond the Basics*.

6.3.3.3
Correlative and Possessive Pronouns

Clauses will be introduced in the next chapter but for now the important thing to know is that clauses are units of words centered around a verb. In English we separate clauses by periods, commas, semicolons, colons, and so on. If you take a minute to look at your Greek New Testament in Bible software or paperback, you will notice that there is punctuation. This punctuation is not original to the text, but modern editors know where to put the punctuation because of the way Greek grammar works. The following two types of pronouns are examples: they introduce clauses and thus the editors knew to place punctuation immediately prior to these pronouns. These pronouns are unique, then, in that they are both a pronoun *and* they work like a conjunction between clauses.

6.3.4
Pronouns That Introduce a Dependent Clause

A relative pronoun will be translated as "who," "whom," "which," or "that" depending on context. They are a pronoun with an antecedent (they will match the antecedent in gender and number), and they also

6.3.4.1
Relative Pronouns

introduce a new clause. The relative pronoun will be the subject or the object of the new clause it introduces. Relative pronouns are fairly easy to recognize because they look just like the declension endings with rough breathing. Relative pronouns use second declension for masculine and neuter, and first declension for feminine. The following are some examples:

1. αὕτη ἐστὶν ἡ ἀγγελία <u>ἣν ἠκούσατε ἀπ' ἀρχῆς</u> (1 John 3:11)
   this is the message <u>which you heard from the beginning</u>.

2. ἐπίστευσαν τῇ γραφῇ καὶ τῷ λόγῳ <u>ὃν εἶπεν ὁ Ἰησοῦς</u>
   (John 2:22)
   they believed in the scripture and in the word <u>that Jesus spoke</u>.

Table 41: Relative Pronouns

who, whom, which, that	Masculine		Feminine		Neuter	
	sg.	pl.	sg.	pl.	sg.	pl.
nominative	ὅς	οἵ	ἥ	αἵ	ὅ	ἅ
genitive	οὗ	ὧν	ἧς	ὧν	οὗ	ὧν
dative	ᾧ	οἷς	ᾗ	αἷς	ᾧ	οἷς
accusative	ὅν	οὕς	ἥν	ἅς	ὅ	ἅ

Another frequent way readers will see a relative pronoun is with ἄν following it. ἄν is often an untranslated word, but when it follows a relative pronoun it will add "-ever" to the pronoun. So ὅς ἄν would be translated as "whoever" or "whatever."

6.3.4.2
Indefinite Relative
Pronouns

Indefinite relative pronouns occur infrequently. They are translated like the relative pronoun followed by ἄν and function in the same way that relative pronouns do. As you come across them, you can take time to read about them in the *Second Time Around* section. You can also read Wallace's *Greek Grammar Beyond the Basics*.

Like the relative pronouns above, three types of pronouns sit at the front of a clause that is asking a question and so the editors know where to put question marks.

Interrogative pronouns ask "who?" "which?" "what?" or "why?" The context determines the best English translation. An accusative interrogative often ends up being translated like the subject. These pronouns use third declension endings, and are interesting because they are identical to the indefinite pronoun (§6.3.6.1) except that the indefinite does *not* have an accent. The stem of the interrogative pronoun is τιν-, which classifies it as third declension (review the changes to the final consonant of a third declension word in §2.7.3).

1. Τίς [δέ] ἐστιν ὁ νικῶν τὸν κόσμον εἰ μὴ ὁ πιστεύων ὅτι Ἰησοῦς ἐστιν ὁ υἱὸς τοῦ θεοῦ; (1 John 5:5)

   Who is it that conquers the world but the one who believes that Jesus is the Son of God?

   □ Notice how the sentence ends with a Greek question mark (;).

Table 42: Interrogative Pronouns

"who? which? what? why?"	Masculine		Feminine		Neuter	
	sg.	*pl.*	*sg.*	*pl.*	*sg.*	*pl.*
nominative	τίς	τίνες	τίς	τίνες	τί	τίνα
genitive	τίνος	τίνων	τίνος	τίνων	τίνος	τίνων
dative	τίνι	τίσι(ν)	τίνι	τίσι(ν)	τίνι	τίσι(ν)
accusative	τίνα	τίνας	τίνα	τίνας	τί	τίνα

The qualitative (which? what?) and quantitative (how much? how many?) interrogative pronouns also ask questions but occur infrequently. As you come across them, you can take time to read about them in the *Second Time Around* section. You can also read Wallace's *Greek Grammar Beyond the Basics.*

6.3.6
More Pronouns
Acting Like Pronouns

The remaining pronoun types stand on their own (i.e., not paired with a noun) and are translated in the same way as personal pronouns.

6.3.6.1
Indefinite Pronouns

The indefinite pronoun makes inexact reference and is a pronoun that does not have an antecedent. They are usually translated as "any-(one)," "some(one)," "a certain one," etc. The stem of the interrogative pronoun is τιν-, which classifies it as third declension (review the changes to the final consonant of a third declension word in §2.7.3). Indefinite pronouns are identical to interrogative pronouns with the exception of the accent position.

1.   ἐάν τις εἴπη ὅτι ἀγαπῶ τὸν θεὸν . . . (1 John 4:20)

If anyone says "I love God" . . .

Table 43: Indefinite Pronouns

someone, something, a certain one/person	**Masculine**		**Feminine**		**Neuter**	
	sg.	*pl.*	*sg.*	*pl.*	*sg.*	*pl.*
nominative	τις	τινές	τις	τινές	τι	τινά
genitive	τινός	τινῶν	τινός	τινῶν	τινός	τινῶν
dative	τινί	τισί(ν)	τινί	τισί(ν)	τινί	τισί(ν)
accusative	τινά	τινάς	τινά	τινάς	τι	τινά

6.3.6.2
Reflexive, Reciprocal,
and Negative
Pronouns

Reflexive pronouns ("myself," "yourself," "himself," etc.), reciprocal pronouns ("one another"), and negative pronouns ("no one" or "nothing") occur infrequently. As you come across them, you can take time to read about them in the *Second Time Around* section. You can also read Wallace's *Greek Grammar Beyond the Basics*.

6.4
NUMBERS

As in English, Greek numbers do not occur with great frequency in prose, but happen often enough that a reader needs to be familiar with some high frequency numbers.

Cardinal numbers are normal counting numbers (1, 2, 3, or one, two, three). Only the numbers 1, 2, 3, 7, and 12 occur in high frequency. Only numbers one through four are declined, and occur in all genders just like adjectives. All remaining cardinals are not declined. As far as numbers one through four, the number one is always and only singular, two through four are always and only plural. All of them follow third declension, except for three which follows first declension for feminine, though like other third-declension words, they do not always follow a neat and tidy pattern.

6.4.1

Cardinals

Table 44: Declined Cardinal Numbers

	Masculine				Feminine				Neuter			
	sing	*plural*			*sing*	*plural*			*sing*	*plural*		
	one	*two*	*three*	*four*	*one*	*two*	*three*	*four*	*one*	*two*	*three*	*four*
nom	εἷς	δύο	τρεῖς	τέσσαρες	μία	δύο	τρεῖς	τέσσαρες	ἕν	δύο	τρία	τέσσαρα
gen	ἑνός	δύο	τριῶν	τεσσάρων	μιᾶς	δύο	τριῶν	τεσσάρων	ἑνός	δύο	τριῶν	τεσσάρων
dat	ἑνί	δυσί	τρισί	τέσσαρσι	μιᾷ	δυσί	τρισί	τέσσαρσι	ἑνί	δυσί	τρισί	τέσσαρσι
acc	ἕνα	δύο	τρεῖς	τέσσαρας	μίαν	δύο	τρεῖς	τέσσαρας	ἕν	δύο	τρία	τέσσαρα

The higher cardinal numbers do not occur in high frequency, but it is good to understand how Greek formulates numbers.

- ten is its own word, δέκα. To make a teen number, the number ten is added to the numbers one through nine. So for example δεκατέσσαρες is 14 (δέκα = ten and τέσσαρες = four).

- 20 is its own word (εἴκοσι).

  □ A suffix which means "times ten" is -κοντα. So for example τεσσεράκοντα is 40 (τέσσαρες = four and –κοντα = times ten).

- 100 is its own word (ἑκατόν).

  □ A suffix which means "times 100" is -κοσιοι. So for example πεντακόσιοι is 500 (πέντε = five and –κοσιοι = times 100).

- 1,000 is its own word (χίλιοι).

  ▫ A suffix which means "times 1,000" is -χιλιοι. So for example πεντακισχίλιοι is 5,000 (πέντε = 5 and –χιλιοι = times 1,000).

- There is also a word for 10,000 (μύριοι) and for an innumerable number (μυριάδες).

All of the numbers in between these are strung together. Here is an example from the end of the Gospel of John: "Simon Peter went aboard and hauled the net ashore, full of large fish, ἑκατὸν πεντήκοντα τριῶν of them" (John 21:11). From the information above you should be able to determine that the number is 153.

6.4.2
Ordinals

Ordinal numbers are the ordering numbers (first, second, third). Only the word "first" occurs in high frequency. Ordinals function and are declined just like adjectives.

Table 45: Ordinal Number "First"

	Masculine		Feminine		Neuter	
	sg.	*pl.*	*sg.*	*pl.*	*sg.*	*pl.*
nominative	πρῶτος	πρῶτοι	πρώτη	πρῶται	πρῶτον	πρῶτα
genitive	πρώτου	πρώτων	πρώτης	πρώτων	πρώτου	πρώτων
dative	πρώτῳ	πρώτοις	πρώτῃ	πρώταις	πρώτῳ	πρώτοις
accusative	πρῶτον	πρώτους	πρώτην	πρώτας	πρῶτον	πρῶτα

In translation, "first" may not always be the best choice. An ordinal may also be used to mean "prominent," "former," "earlier," or even "above all else."

6.5
THE LEAST YOU NEED TO KNOW

You should be able to clearly and accurately answer these questions. Use the flashcards at http://quizlet.com/_7tfxi to memorize the answers:

- What endings does the article take?

- What two things can the article do when it is all by itself?

- What does it mean for an adjective to be in concord with a noun?

- What is an attributive adjective?

- What is a substantival adjective?

- What is a predicate adjective?

- What is the **AAA rule**?

- What is the **A(A)noN rule**?

- What is the **noA noV rule**?

- What are the special functions of third-person personal pronouns? How do you know when the special functions have kicked in?

- What are demonstrative pronouns? How do they function?

- What do relative pronouns do?

- What do interrogative pronouns do?

- What do interrogative pronouns look just like? How do you tell them apart?

- What are cardinal numbers?

- Which cardinal numbers are declined?

- How are teen numbers formed?

- How are multiples of ten formed?

- How are multiples of 100 formed?

- How are multiples of 1,000 formed?

- What are ordinals? How do they work?

6.6

GREEK@LOGOS

Utilizing the Logos help file, Logos forums, Logos wiki, and videos provided, users should take the time this chapter to learn:

- Basic Searches

    □ See the article on Bible Search at https://support.logos.com

- Clause Search

    □ See the article on Clause Search at https://support.logos.com

6.7

VOCABULARY

Word	Meaning	Type	Freq.	Derivatives
ἅγιος, -α, -ον	holy; pl. saints	adj.	233	*hagiography*
εἷς, μία, ἕν	one	adj.	345	
μέγας, -η, -α	large, great	adj.	243	*megaphone*
οὐδείς, οὐδεμία, οὐδέν	no one; nothing	adj.	234	
πᾶς, πᾶσα, πᾶν	every, each; [pl.] all	adj.	1243	*panoramic*
πολύς, πολλή, πολύ	much, [pl.] many; (adv.) often	adj.	416	*poly*theism
αὐτός, αὐτή, τουτό	he, she, it (-self, same); pl. they	pron.	5597	*automatic*
ἑαυτοῦ, -ῆς, -οῦ	himself/herself/itself; our/your/themselves	pron.	319	
ἐγώ (pl. ἡμεῖς)	I; we	pron.	2666	*ego*
ἐκεῖνος, -η, -ο	that, [pl.] those	pron.	265	
ὅς, ἥ, ὅ	who, which, what	pron.	1398	
οὗτος, αὕτη, τοῦτο	this (one); pl. these	pron.	1387	*tautology*
σύ (pl. ὑμεῖς)	you (sg.); y'all (pl.)	pron.	2907	
τίς, τί	who? which? what? why?	pron.	556	
τις, τι	someone, anyone; something, certain one	pron.	525	

Chapter 6 Exercises

LEARNING ACTIVITY 1: VOCABULARY (1 HOUR)

Be sure to review previous vocabulary as well as learn the new.

LEARNING ACTIVITY 2: READING PRACTICE (30 MINUTES)

Take 30 minutes to practice your Greek reading using the Greek audio Bible resource in Logos.

Completed: _____ Yes _____ No

LEARNING ACTIVITY 3: TEXTBOOK READING (1 HOUR)

Read chapter 6 of the textbook.

Completed: _____ Yes _____ No

LEARNING ACTIVITY 4: DECLENSION ENDINGS
(15 MINUTES RECOMMENDED)

You've just learned that the article, adjectives, and pronouns use declension endings just like nouns. Take some time to review the declension songs once again. Sing along until you've memorized them.

> ◢ Recommended for learning declension endings: ◤
> The Singing Grammarian: (1) First Declension, (2) Second
> Declension, and (3) Third Declension Songs.

Completed: _____ Yes _____ No

LEARNING ACTIVITY 5: THE GREEK DEFINITE ARTICLE
(15-30 MINUTES RECOMMENDED)

Take some time to become as familiar as possible with the Greek definite article.

> ◢ Recommended for learning the Greek article: ◤
> *The Singing Grammarian: The Article Song.*

Completed: _____ Yes _____ No

LEARNING ACTIVITY 6: ARTICLE, ADJECTIVE, AND PRONOUN FUNCTIONS (2–3 HOURS RECOMMENDED)

The following examples use the adjective "good," the noun "person/man," an article, the third-person personal pronoun, a demonstrative pronoun, and the verb λυέι ("he/she/it looses"). They will *always* be nominative, masculine, singular. Using just your textbook, translate each example and determine how they are functioning. Take notice of how similar some of the constructions are.

1. ὁ ἄνθρωπος

    a. translation: _____

    b. function of article: _____

2. ὁ ἀγαθὸς ἄνθρωπος

    a. translation: _____

    b. function of article: _____

    c. function of adjective: _____

3. ὁ αὐτός ἄνθρωπος

    a. translation: _____

    b. function of article: _____

    c. function[1] of pronoun: _____

4. ὁ ἀγαθὸς ὁ ἄνθρωπος

    a. translation: _____

    b. function of article: _____

    c. function of adjective: _____

---

1. I am NOT asking what type of pronoun this is, but how it is functioning.

5. οὗτος ὁ ἄνθρωπος

    a. translation: _____

    b. function of article: _____

    c. function of pronoun: _____

6. ὁ αὐτός ὁ ἄνθρωπος

    a. translation: _____

    b. function of article: _____

    c. function of pronoun: _____

7. ἀγαθὸς ὁ ἄνθρωπος

    a. translation: _____

    b. function of article: _____

    c. function of adjective: _____

8. αὐτός ὁ ἄνθρωπος

    a. translation: _____

    b. function of article: _____

    c. function of pronoun: _____

9. ὁ ἀγαθὸς ἄνθρωπος λυέι

    a. translation: _____

    b. function of article: _____

    c. function of adjective: _____

    d. What is the subject? _____

10. αὐτός λυέι

    a. translation: _____

    b. function of pronoun: _____

11. ὁ λύει

    a. translation: _____

    b. function of article: _____

12. ὁ ἀγαθὸς λύει

    a. translation: _____

    b. function of adjective: _____

13. οὗτος λύει

    a. translation: _____

    b. function of pronoun: _____

14. ὁ ἄνθρωπος λύει ὁ ἐν τῳ οἰκῳ [in the house]

    a. function of first article: _____

    b. function of second article: _____

ὁ ἀγαθὸς ἄνθρωπος ἐκ τοῦ ἀγαθοῦ θησαυροῦ τῆς καρδίας προφέρει τὸ ἀγαθόν, καὶ ὁ πονηρὸς ἐκ τοῦ πονηροῦ προφέρει τὸ πονηρόν· (Luke 6:45)

1. First, take a few minutes to observe how your preferred English translation translates this verse.

2. Now close your Bible software. Using just your mind and the textbook, try to parse the articles, nouns and adjectives in the table below (take no more than 30 minutes).

3. Confirm/complete the parsing with your Bible software.

4. This chapter has taught you the different ways the article and adjectives can function. Fill out the "article function" and "adjective function" boxes.

5. word	case	gender	number	lexical form
ὁ				
article function:				
ἀγαθὸς				
adjective function:				
ἄνθρωπος				
τοῦ				
article function:				
ἀγαθοῦ				
adjective function:				
τῆς				
article function:				
καρδίας				
τὸ				
article function:				
ἀγαθόν				
adjective function:				

5. Use your Bible software now. What is the verb in this section?

_____

    a. How is it parsed? _____

_____

    b. What does the tense indicate (aspect and time)? _____

_____

_____

    c. What does the voice indicate? _____

_____

    d. What does the mood indicate? _____

           _____

    e. What kind of endings does this verb take? _____

           _____

LEARNING ACTIVITY 7: BIBLE SOFTWARE ACTIVITIES (2–3 HOURS RECOMMENDED)

Up to this point you have searched for single words. The following activities ask you to do a "search string"—meaning you will now search for more than one word under certain conditions. Restrict the first 7 questions to the Gospel of John. Open the LEB or ESV and place your Greek NT in parallel. In the inline search, choose "morph" for the following questions.

1. Search for: [any article] + δὲ + [any indicative verb].

    (hint: put this into your Logos morph search – *lemma:δέ AFTER 1 WORDs @D BEFORE 1 WORD @V??I*)

    a. How often does this occur? _____

           _____

    b. In all of these examples, how is the article functioning?

           _____

           _____

    c. How do you know the article is functioning this way (what are the grammatical clues)? _____

           _____

2. Now search for all demonstrative pronouns with the inline search (hit @ and choose "pronoun" and "demonstrative"). This will highlight the Greek demonstrative and the English word that translates it.

    a. Look at the first 5 hits. How is the demonstrative functioning here? _____.

    How should these be translated?

           _____

b. Now look at John 1:39. How is the demonstrative functioning here? _____.

c. How do you know? _____
_____
_____

3. Now search for all adjectives with the inline search (hit @ and choose "adjective"). This will highlight the Greek adjective and the English word that translates it.

a. There are 2 adjectives in John 1:3. How are these functioning? How do you know? _____
_____

b. Scroll down to John 3:16. There are 2 adjectives here. How are these functioning? How do you know? _____
_____

4. In the inline search, hit the @ sign. Notice that you can hover over each word in the morph menu to get a brief description.

a. Search for all first-person personal pronouns. How many occur in John? _____

b. Scroll down to John 1:33. The first word κἀγώ is called a crasis word form, a smashing together of καί and ἐγώ. Now go to the tools menu and click on "Information" to open the very helpful Information window. Click on κἀγώ to fill the information window. The *translation* section of Information shows you how different English translations translate this word utilizing Logos' *Text Comparison* feature. Which versions use the word "myself" in their translation? _____

c. Search for all second-person personal pronouns. How many occur in John? _____

5. As you recall, the third-person personal pronoun can have special functions. These special functions are tagged in Logos as "Intensive Attributive" and "Intensive Predicative" in the Morph

menu. Search for the third-person personal pronouns with intensive predicative function. The first hit is John 2:24. How is the intensive predicative translated in various translations? (use the Information pane) _____

6. Now search for the third-person personal pronoun with intensive attributive (but search the entire NT, not just John). The first two hits are where?_____
   What is the difference between the constructions in these hits?

   _____

7. Find an example of a comparative adjective. What is the first result from John? _____
   What is this word's lexical form? _____

8. Find the number of the beast in Revelation and write it out in Greek: _____

9. _____ κύριος, _____ πίστις (faith), _____ βάπτισμα (baptism) (Eph 4:5).

   a. Why are these 3 words different? _____

   _____

10. ὁ _____ ἄνθρωπος ἐκ γῆς χοϊκός, ὁ _____ ἄνθρωπος ἐξ οὐρανοῦ (1 Cor 15:47)

    a. What kind of words are these? _____

    _____

    b. Translation: _____

    _____

LEARNING ACTIVITY 8: REVIEW (30 MINUTES RECOMMENDED)
You've just spent a good amount of time learning a lot of new things. Take 30 minutes to do one final read through of the chapter to solidify your knowledge, and make sure you can answer all of the questions in the *Least You Need to Know* section. Use the online flashcards link in the chapter to quiz yourself on the questions.

Completed: _____Yes _____No

As you recognized, adjectives and pronouns use case endings, so if you have those down you do not need to focus heavily on memorization in this chapter. Instead, focus heavily on what adjectives can do (§6.2.2) and the special functions of the third-person personal pronoun (§6.3.3.1).

6.8 THE SECOND TIME AROUND

Greek has numerous types of pronouns, and not all of them are particularly frequent. Through the chapter, several pronoun types were mentioned but not shown. The following tables cover the pronouns that were not shown through the chapter.

Table 46: Correlative Pronouns

	"such"	"so much/great"	Masculine		Feminine		Neuter	
			sg.	pl.	sg.	pl.	sg.	pl.
nom.	τοι-	τοσ-	-οὗτος	-οὗτοι	-αὐτη	-αὖται	-τοῦτο	-ταῦτα
gen.	τοι-	τοσ-	-τούτου	-τούτων	-ταύτης	-τούτων	-τούτου	-τούτων
dat.	τοι-	τοσ-	-τούτῳ	-τούτοις	-ταύτῃ	-ταύταις	-τούτῳ	-τούτοις
acc.	τοι-	τοσ-	-τοῦτον	-τούτους	-ταύτην	-ταύτας	-τοῦτο	-ταῦτα

"such as"	Masculine		Feminine		Neuter	
	sg.	pl.	sg.	pl.	sg.	pl.
nominative	οἷος	οἷοι	οἵα	οἷαι	οἷον	οἷα
genitive	οἵου	οἵων	οἵας	οἵων	οἵου	οἵων
dative	οἵῳ	οἵοις	οἵᾳ	οἵαις	οἵῳ	οἵοις
accusative	οἷον	οἵους	οἵαν	οἵας	οἷον	οἷα

"as many as"	Masculine		Feminine		Neuter	
	sg.	pl.	sg.	pl.	sg.	pl.
nominative	ὅσος	ὅσοι	ὅση	ὅσαι	ὅσον	ὅσα
genitive	ὅσου	ὅσων	ὅσης	ὅσων	ὅσου	ὅσων
dative	ὅσῳ	ὅσοις	ὅσῃ	ὅσαις	ὅσῳ	ὅσοις
accusative	ὅσον	ὅσους	ὅσην	ὅσας	ὅσον	ὅσα

Table 47: Possessive Pronouns

		Masculine		**Feminine**		**Neuter**	
		Singular	*Plural*	*Singular*	*Plural*	*Singular*	*Plural*
1 sg "my"	nom.	ἐμός	ἐμοί	ἐμή	ἐμαί	ἐμόν	ἐμά
	gen.	ἐμοῦ	ἐμῶν	ἐμῆς	ἐμῶν	ἐμοῦ	ἐμῶν
	dat.	ἐμῷ	ἐμοῖς	ἐμῇ	ἐμαῖς	ἐμῷ	ἐμοῖς
	acc.	ἐμόν	ἐμούς	ἐμήν	ἐμάς	ἐμόν	ἐμά
1 pl "our"	nom.	ἡμέτερος	ἡμέτεροι	ἡμέτερα	ἡμέτεραι	ἡμέτερον	ἡμέτερα
	gen.	ἡμετέρου	ἡμετέρων	ἡμέτερας	ἡμέτερων	ἡμέτερου	ἡμέτερων
	dat.	ἡμετέρῳ	ἡμέτεροις	ἡμέτερα	ἡμέτεραις	ἡμέτερῳ	ἡμέτεροις
	acc.	ἡμέτερον	ἡμέτερους	ἡμέτεραν	ἡμέτερας	ἡμέτερον	ἡμέτερα
		Masculine		**Feminine**		**Neuter**	
		Singular	*Plural*	*Singular*	*Plural*	*Singular*	*Plural*
2 sg "your"	nom.	σός	σοί	σή	σαί	σόν	σά
	gen.	σοῦ	σῶν	σῆς	σῶν	σοῦ	σῶν
	dat.	σῷ	σοῖς	σῇ	σαῖς	σῷ	σοῖς
	acc.	σόν	σούς	σήν	σάς	σόν	σά
2 pl "your"	nom.	ὑμέτερος	ὑμέτεροι	ὑμέτερα	ὑμέτεραι	ὑμέτερον	ὑμέτερα
	gen.	ὑμετέρου	ὑμέτερων	ὑμέτερας	ὑμέτερων	ὑμέτερον	ὑμέτερων
	dat.	ὑμετέρῳ	ὑμέτεροις	ὑμέτερα	ὑμέτεραις	ὑμέτερῳ	ὑμέτεροις
	acc.	ὑμέτερον	ὑμέτερους	ὑμέτεραν	ὑμέτερας	ὑμέτερον	ὑμέτερα
		Masculine		**Feminine**		**Neuter**	
		Singular	*Plural*	*Singular*	*Plural*	*Singular*	*Plural*
3 "his/her/ its/their"	nom.	ἴδιος	ἴδιοι	ἴδια	ἴδιαι	ἴδιον	ἴδια
	gen.	ἰδίου	ἰδίων	ἰδίας	ἰδίων	ἰδίου	ἰδίων
	dat.	ἰδίῳ	ἰδίοις	ἰδίᾳ	ἰδίαις	ἰδίῳ	ἰδίοις
	acc.	ἴδιον	ἰδίους	ἰδίαν	ἰδίας	ἴδιον	ἴδια

The indefinite relative is exactly as it sounds—the indefinite pronoun and the relative pronoun are put together. So a dative singular feminine form takes the dative singular feminine form of the indefinite and the relative and puts them together. The following table shows just the nominatives.

Table 48: Indefinite Relative Pronouns

Masculine		Neuter		Feminine	
singular	*plural*	*singular*	*plural*	*singular*	*plural*
ὅστις	οἵτινες	ὅτι	ἅτινα	ἥτις	αἵτινες

Table 49: Qualitative and Quantitative Pronouns

QUALITATIVE *"what type?"*	Masculine		Feminine		Neuter	
	sg.	*pl.*	*sg.*	*pl.*	*sg.*	*pl.*
nominative	ποῖος	ποῖοι	ποῖα	ποῖαι	ποῖον	ποῖα
genitive	ποῖου	ποῖων	ποῖας	ποῖων	ποῖου	ποῖων
dative	ποῖῳ	ποῖοις	ποῖᾳ	ποῖαις	ποῖῳ	ποῖοις
accusative	ποῖον	ποῖους	ποῖαν	ποῖας	ποῖον	ποῖα
QUANTITATIVE *"how much?"*	Masculine		Feminine		Neuter	
	sg.	*pl.*	*sg.*	*pl.*	*sg.*	*pl.*
nominative	πόσος	πόσοι	πόση	πόσαι	πόσον	πόσα
genitive	πόσου	πόσων	πόσης	πόσων	πόσου	πόσων
dative	πόσῳ	πόσοις	πόση	πόσαις	πόσῳ	πόσοις
accusative	πόσον	πόσους	πόσην	πόσας	πόσον	πόσα

Table 50: Reflexive Pronouns

MASCULINE	Singular			Plural		
	1 *"myself"*	2 *"yourself"*	3 *"himself"*	1 *"ourselves"*	2 *"yourselves"*	3 *"themselves"*
genitive	ἐμαυτοῦ	σεαυτοῦ	ἑαυτοῦ	ἑαυτῶν	ἑαυτῶν	ἑαυτῶν
dative	ἐμαυτῷ	σεαυτῷ	ἑαυτῷ	ἑαυτοῖς	ἑαυτοῖς	ἑαυτοῖς
accusative	ἐμαυτόν	σεαυτόν	ἑαυτόν	ἑαυτούς	ἑαυτούς	ἑαυτούς
NEUTER	Singular			Plural		
	1	2	3	1	2	3
genitive	-	-	ἑαυτοῦ	ἑαυτῶν	ἑαυτῶν	ἑαυτῶν
dative	-	-	ἑαυτῷ	ἑαυτοῖς	ἑαυτοῖς	ἑαυτοῖς
accusative	-	-	ἑαυτόν	ἑαυτούς	ἑαυτούς	ἑαυτούς
FEMININE	Singular			Plural		
	1	2	3	1	2	3
genitive	ἐμαυτῆς	σεαυτῆς	ἑαυτῆς	ἑαυτῶν	ἑαυτῶν	ἑαυτῶν
dative	ἐμαυτῇ	σεαυτῇ	ἑαυτῇ	ἑαυταῖς	ἑαυταῖς	ἑαυταῖς
accusative	ἐμαυτήν	σεαυτήν	ἑαυτήν	ἑαυτάς	ἑαυτάς	ἑαυτάς

Table 51: Reciprocal Pronouns

Only three forms of the reciprocal pronoun exist in the NT.

- ἀλλήλων = of one another (genitive)

- ἀλλήλοις = to one another (dative)

- ἀλλήλους = one another (accusative)

Table 52: Negative Pronouns

singular only	MASCULINE "no one"	FEMININE "no one"	NEUTER "nothing"
nom.	οὐδείς	οὐδεμία	οὐδέν
gen.	οὐδενός	οὐδεμιᾶς	οὐδενός
dat.	οὐδενί	οὐδεμιᾷ	οὐδενί
acc.	οὐδένα	οὐδεμίαν	οὐδέν

ADVANCED EXERCISES (CH. 6)

Learning Activity 1: Vocabulary (1 hour)
Learn your assigned vocabulary list from Appendix A. Be sure to review previous vocabulary as well as learn the new. Knowledge of this new vocabulary is assumed in the translation work.
Completed: _____Yes _____No

Learning Activity 2: Reading (1 hour)
Read chapter 6 of the textbook again.
Completed: _____Yes _____No

Learning Activity 3: Memorize Declension Endings (30–60 minutes)
Review and make sure you have memorized the first, second, and third declension endings. Use *The Singing Grammarian* as help, and practice filling in paradigms from memory using the practice tables.
Completed: _____Yes _____No

Learning Activity 4: Parsing Practice (1.5 hours)
Drill yourself using either ParseGreek or Paradigms Master Pro

- For ParseGreek, choose any learned vocabulary range in conjunction with chapter 6 grammar concepts.

- For Paradigms Master Pro, choose
  Adjectives: Cardinals, Pronouns (all 4), and The article.
Completed: _____Yes _____No

Learning Activity 5: Parsing Work (1.5 hours)

1. αὐτοῦ _____

2. αὐτῷ _____

3. αὐτόν _____

4. ὑμῖν _____

5. αὐτῶν _____

6. ὑμῶν _____

7. αὐτοῖς _____

8. μου _____

9. ὑμᾶς _____

10. σου _____

11. ἡμῶν _____

12. τί _____

13. τοῦτο _____

14. με _____

15. τις _____

16. ταῦτα _____

17. ὅ _____

18. ὅς _____

19. αὐτῆς _____

20. ᾧ _____

21. ἀλλήλους _____

22. ἐμοί _____

23. ἑαυτόν _____

24. οἵτινες _____

25. ὅσα _____

26. ἐκεῖνος _____

Learning Activity 6: Translation (3.5 hours)

Translate the following sentences. Be ready to parse any articles/ adjectives/pronouns/numbers that appear in the sentences. The following sentences assume knowledge of all words occurring up to 50 times (chs. 1–11 and lists 1–6). For difficult forms, consult the morphological information in Logos Bible Software.

καὶ ἐξεπορεύετο (going) πρὸς αὐτὸν πᾶσα ἡ Ἰουδαία χώρα (countryside) καὶ οἱ Ἱεροσολυμῖται (Jerusalemites) πάντες, καὶ ἐβαπτίζοντο ὑπ' αὐτοῦ ἐν τῷ Ἰορδάνῃ (Jordan) ποταμῷ (river) ἐξομολογούμενοι (confessing) τὰς ἁμαρτίας αὐτῶν. (Mark 1:5)

_____

_____

_____

_____

καὶ λέγει αὐτῷ· πᾶς ἄνθρωπος πρῶτον τὸν καλὸν οἶνον (lex = οἶνος) τίθησιν καὶ ὅταν μεθυσθῶσιν (drunk) τὸν ἐλάσσω (inferior)· σὺ τετήρηκας τὸν καλὸν οἶνον (wine) ἕως ἄρτι (now). (John 2:10)

_____

_____

_____

_____

ὁ ἀγαθὸς ἄνθρωπος ἐκ τοῦ ἀγαθοῦ θησαυροῦ (treasure) τῆς καρδίας προφέρει (produces) τὸ ἀγαθόν, καὶ ὁ πονηρὸς ἐκ τοῦ πονηροῦ προφέρει τὸ πονηρόν· ἐκ γὰρ περισσεύματος (abundance) καρδίας λαλεῖ τὸ στόμα αὐτοῦ. (Luke 6:45)

_____

_____

_____

καὶ ὁ Κορνήλιος (Cornelius) ἔφη· ἀπὸ τετάρτης ἡμέρας (days) μέχρι (until) ταύτης τῆς ὥρας ἤμην τὴν ἐνάτην (nine) προσευχόμενος (I was praying) ἐν τῷ οἴκῳ μου, καὶ ἰδοὺ ἀνὴρ ἔστη (lex = ἵστημι) ἐνώπιόν μου ἐν ἐσθῆτι λαμπρᾷ (dazzling clothes) (Acts 10:30)

τὰ πρόβατα (sheep) τὰ ἐμὰ τῆς φωνῆς μου ἀκούουσιν, κἀγὼ γινώσκω αὐτὰ καὶ ἀκολουθοῦσίν μοι, κἀγὼ δίδωμι αὐτοῖς ζωὴν αἰώνιον καὶ οὐ μὴ ἀπόλωνται (perish) εἰς τὸν αἰῶνα καὶ οὐχ ἁρπάσει (will snatch) τις αὐτὰ ἐκ τῆς χειρός μου. (John 10:27–28)

Καὶ ἀπεσταλμένοι ἦσαν (they had been sent) ἐκ τῶν Φαρισαίων. καὶ ἠρώτησαν αὐτὸν καὶ εἶπαν αὐτῷ· τί οὖν βαπτίζεις εἰ σὺ οὐκ εἶ ὁ χριστὸς οὐδὲ Ἠλίας (Elijah) οὐδὲ ὁ προφήτης; ἀπεκρίθη (lex = ἀποκρίνομαι) αὐτοῖς ὁ Ἰωάννης λέγων (saying)· ἐγὼ βαπτίζω ἐν ὕδατι· μέσος ὑμῶν ἔστηκεν (lex = ἵστημι) ὃν ὑμεῖς οὐκ οἴδατε (John 1:24–26)

Adverbs, Prepositions, Phrases, and Clauses Made Simple

What's the Point: Phrases and clauses are groups of words that work together to say something. Every word in the Greek New Testament is in a phrase or clause. While we can trust for the most part the editors of our modern Greek New Testament who added commas, colons, and periods, it is because of the the knowledge of Greek clauses that they knew where to place those marks in the first place. Understanding how these units are introduced and what they do in larger paragraphs will help you better understand Greek structure.

7.1

ADVERBS

Adverbs are the last of the primary parts of speech to cover in Greek (the others being nouns, verbs, and adjectives). Recall from grade school days that adverbs give more information about the verb, answering the questions *when?*, *where?*, *why?*, and so on. Adverbs are simple to master in Greek because there are only a dozen or so that occur in high frequency and *adverbs are not declined* (yippee!).

About the only thing that adverbs do differently in Greek is that they can, on occasion, take an article. When this occurs, the adverb is changed into a substantive. So, for example, the adverb κακῶς means "badly." But when κακῶς has the article it comes to mean "the one(s) feeling badly," or more neatly translated as "the sick." Here is a NT example: "his fame spread throughout all Syria, and they brought to him all τοὺς κακῶς" (Matt 4:24).

7.2

PREPOSITIONS

Prepositions are little words that *never* work alone, in English or Greek. You have already been briefly introduced to prepositions that attach themselves to verbs to create compound verbs (§5.3.3). When prepositions occur they will *always* work with at least one noun (or substantive), but often even more than that. For instance, the noun may have an article, or the noun may also have a genitive following it. This group of words, introduced by a preposition, is called a *prepositional phrase*.[1] Remember too that the prepositional phrase may be introduced with an article to help the reader to know what the phrase is talking about (see §6.1.2.3 to review this). Although prepositions are small words, they can be slippery like eels. A preposition can be translated with numerous English words depending on their context. You do not need to worry about deciding how best to translate a preposition, just know that there are numerous options, based on context, that you will come across as you work with the Greek New Testament and your preferred English translation.[2]

The most immediate factor in determining a preposition's translation and function is the case of the noun it is attached to (remember that a preposition is always followed by a noun/substantive). Some prepositions are snobs—they will only work with one case. Others are a little more friendly—they will work with two cases. Finally there are three prepositions that are extroverts—they work with genitive, dative, or accusative (prepositions never work with nominatives). See the following examples, which use the same preposition, where the nouns following it are in different cases, resulting in different translations of the preposition:

- ἐξεπλήσσοντο ἐπὶ τῇ διδαχῇ αὐτοῦ
  They were astounded by his teaching (Mark 1:22)

- ὁ Παῦλος ἑστὼς ἐπὶ τῶν ἀναβαθμῶν
  Paul stood on the steps (Acts 21:40)

- Ἰδοὺ ἕστηκα ἐπὶ τὴν θύραν
  Behold I stand at the door (Rev 3:20)

As you can see, ἐπί is followed by a dative in the first instance, a genitive in the second, and an accusative in the third. The case of the noun that follows determines how the preposition is translated.

---

1. You will learn more about what a phrase is in §7.4.1.
2. The spatial translations of the prepositions are
often the easiest to learn (see table 55).

Remember also from the nouns chapter that dative and genitive have a "built-in" preposition that is used when translating them—so for a dative often the word "in" is used before it. If a dative or a genitive noun has a preposition before it, then the "built-in" preposition is no longer used—the visible is more powerful than the invisible.

Prepositions are not declined so they are easy to spot. However, prepositions may change slightly depending on whether the following word starts with a vowel or if the next word begins with rough breathing. A coronis will replace the vowel on the end of the preposition and before rough breathing prepositions that have a stop consonant, it will change to a rough stop (§1.3.2).

7.2.1

Preposition Forms

Table 53: Preposition Forms

prep.	when followed by a word beginning with a vowel	when followed by a word beginning with rough breathing
ἀνά	ἀν'	ἀν'
ἀντί	ἀντ'	ἀνθ'
ἀπό	ἀπ'	ἀφ'
διά	δι'	δι'
ἐκ	ἐξ	ἐξ
ἐπί	ἐπ'	ἐφ'
κατά	κατ'	καθ'
μετά	μετ'	μεθ'
παρά	παρ'	παρ'
ὑπό	ὑπ'	ὑφ'

As you work with NT Greek and use grammars, lexicons, and commentaries, you will often come across descriptions of how prepositions work (words like ablative, locative, instrumental, means, agency, etc., will often come up). Look at the following English examples of the preposition "by":

7.2.2

Preposition Functions

- I stayed in a cabin by the lake.

- I made the dog happy by feeding it.

- The door was opened by my daughter.

The preposition is the same, yet it is giving you different types of information in every sentence. The first example of "by" is giving you location information (called *locative* function), the second is telling you the means by which something happened (called *instrumental* function), and the third one is giving us information on who did the action (called *agency* function). It is not important to memorize these functions right now, but do not discount or dismiss these little words as you interpret the NT, as they can have such a range of translation and function. See, for example, Wallace's presentation of the basic uses of ἐπί:[1]

1. With Genitive

    a. Spatial: on, upon, at, near

    b. Temporal: in the time of, during

    c. Cause: on the basis of

2. With Dative

    a. Spatial: on, upon, against, at, near

    b. Temporal: at, at the time of, during

    c. Cause: on the basis of

3. With Accusative

    a. Spatial: on, upon, to, up to, against

    b. Temporal: for, over a period of

As you can see from this list, a preposition has numerous translation options, and can function in numerous ways. As you come across prepositions in your work with the NT, you may at times need to dig deeper into them and use a lexicon and grammar to better understand

---

1. Wallace, *Greek Grammar Beyond the Basics*, 375.

the function of a preposition. (And lest you want to curse the person who created Greek prepositions, English prepositions are just as complex!)

In previous chapters you have learned some of the different functions of the noun case endings. It is important to know that when a noun is in a prepositional phrase, you no longer ask the question, "What is the case of the noun doing?" The question instead becomes, "What is the prepositional phrase doing?" Reading about the preposition in a lexicon or grammar will help you answer this and other questions.

7.3 MORE LITTLE WORDS

This last set of word types almost completes your introduction to the types of words in Greek (participles and infinitives each receive their own chapter). These little words are simple in that they are not inflected, and they do not pair themselves with other words as do adjectives or prepositions.

7.3.1 Conjunctions

Conjunctions *connect things* together, in both Greek and English. You will be introduced to the highest frequency conjunctions in the vocabulary sections. The following is a list of some of the main functions of conjunctions:

1. INTRODUCE A SENTENCE: Some conjunctions may introduce a sentence (they will come after a period or colon in your Greek NT). Conjunctions like οὖν ("therefore") and γάρ ("for") frequently, but not always, introduce a new sentence. These two conjunctions, as well as δέ, always occur as the second word in their clause.[1]

2. INTRODUCE A DEPENDENT CLAUSE: Many conjunctions introduce a dependent clause (which you will learn about in §7.4.2.2): ἵνα, ἐάν, ὅταν, ὅτε, and a few others fall into this function. These conjunctions are good to know as you come to work with and recognize Greek clauses.

---

1. These are called postpositive conjunctions and frequently come between an article and its noun.

3. CONNECT INDEPENDENT CLAUSES TOGETHER: Several high frequency conjunctions can at times connect two independent clauses (which you will learn about in §7.4.2.1). Καί, δέ, and ἀλλά are the ones that can function this way.

4. CONNECT EQUALS: Καί is one of the most frequent words in Greek and can do several things. Καί is often a "teeter-totter" conjunction, in that it will immediately connect things of equal grammatical weight. It may connect verbs together,[1] nouns together, or clauses together. If you recall from when you first learned καί as vocabulary, it can mean "also" as well. When translated as "also," καί is an adverb, not a conjunction.

7.3.2
Interjections

Interjections *inject emotion* into a sentence. They are small words unconnected and not paired with any other words in the sentence. English too has interjections like "wow" or "hey." The most frequent interjection in Greek is ἰδού, which means "look!" or "pay attention!" Oftentimes interjections are left untranslated into English, but they add an element of emotion in the Greek NT.

7.3.3
Particles

A particle is a tricky word that is used in different ways, but for the sake of being thorough, it is introduced here. Often a particle simply means "little word," and so conjunctions and interjections are often considered particles. In other cases, particles are simply words that do not fall into any other category. Some Greek particles function as word-group markers and are often left untranslated as well.

7.4
WORD GROUPS

You have now been introduced to all but two types of words in Greek (participles and infinitives both will receive their own chapters). Now that we've talked about individual words, let's discuss how groups of words work together. The following discussion applies to both English and Greek.

---

1. As you will learn in §7.4.2, a clause has only one verb. An exception is when a καί directly connects two verbs together. In these cases, the two verbs are acting as one in the clause.

In English and Greek, the primary parts of speech are (1) nouns, (2) verbs, (3) adjectives, and (4) adverbs. The primary parts (excluding verbs) are generally thought of as one word, but a *group of words* can also function like a noun, adjective, or adverb. Other types of words can also function in these positions—for instance recall from chapter 6 that an article, adjective, and pronoun can all act like a noun (substantive). Word groups can also work together to act like a noun, an adjective, or an adverb.

The prepositions section introduced the concept of "prepositional phrase." Notice how the following examples of prepositional phrases (word groups) function in the sentence:

1. AS A NOUN: "In the house was very hot." The phrase is acting as the subject in the sentence.

2. AS AN ADJECTIVE: "I saw the child with his mother." The phrase is acting like an adjective, telling us more about the child.

3. AS AN ADVERB: "I hit the ball with a wooden bat." The phrase is acting like an adverb, telling us the "how" of the verb.

The following table breaks down how word groups work. The remainder of this chapter will be a commentary on this table.

Table 54: Greek Word Groups

Phrase *no verb*	Clause *verb or verbal*
prepositional phrase	Dependent clause indicative, subjunctive, imperative, optative
or substantive phrase nouns, participles, adjectives, or infinitives	Participle clause
or vocative phrase	Infinitive clause

acts like

acts like

noun adverb adjective

in a clause

for an

Independent clause

Sentence
Composed of at least one independent clause

7.4.1
Phrases

Phrases, then, are groups of words that act like a noun, an adjective, or an adverb in a sentence. A phrase does not contain a regular verb,[1] so a phrase cannot be a sentence all on its own. A phrase may be a single word (like adverbs, participles, and infinitives) or a group of words. You have been shown above how a phrase can function as a

---

1. Participles and infinitives, as you will learn, are verbal forms, but not true verbs.

noun, adjective, or adverb, which means that this group of words work together to function as a unit. Phrases are groups of words (or just one word) that have a function *within a clause* (follow the solid arrow in the table above).

Clauses are groups of words that have a subject and verb. A clause can be as simple as just a subject and verb ("I yelled") which can be one word in Greek, or a more complex group of words with a subject, verb, object, and indirect object ("Joe yelled commands to the soldiers"). *A clause has ONE verb,*[1] *the main verb, around which the entire clause is centered.* Think of a clause like a wheel, with the verb at its center and spokes (subject, object, etc.) coming off of it.

7.4.2
Clauses

There are two types of clauses. The first is an independent clause. An independent clause stands independently—it needs no help from anyone. *A sentence has at least one independent clause*; if you do not have an independent clause; you don't have a sentence either. A sentence can have more than one independent clause, but if too many independent clauses are connected together, run-on sentences appear!

7.4.2.1
Independent Clauses

Dependent clauses (built upon an indicative, imperative, subjunctive, or optative verb) as well as participle and infinitive clauses are a bit harder to understand, as they possesses the qualities of a clause, but function like a phrase. As a clause they have their own subject and verb(al), but they *are not* the main thought of a sentence—they are **dependent** on another clause for their existence. These clauses cannot exist on their own, they are always connected to an independent clause. Oftentimes a complex sentence will have one independent clause and several dependent clauses, all of them tied to the central independent clause.

7.4.2.2
Dependent,
Participle, and
Infinitive Clauses

Dependent clauses are like phrases, though, in that they are a word group that together function like a noun, adjective, or adverb to the independent clause (follow the dotted arrows in the table above). Like a phrase, they cannot live on their own, but depend on an

---

1. See p. 158, n. 1 for the exception to this rule.

independent clause for their existence. In the following examples, the main verbs are colored blue, the independent clauses are highlighted yellow, the dependent clauses are highlighted green, and phrases are underlined.

- We declare to you what was from the beginning, what we have heard, what we have seen with our eyes, what we have looked at and touched with our hands (1 John 1:1).

  ◦ Notice how each clause has one verb.
  ◦ Notice how each dependent clause is telling you what is being "declared" in the independent clause. Each dependent clause is functioning as a noun—they are the objects of the main verb.
  ◦ Each of the phrases in their respective clauses are functioning like a noun—the object of the verb they are with.
  ◦ Although the independent clause comes first in the sentence this is not always the case.

- And this is the message which we have heard from him and announce to you (1 John 1:5).

  ◦ Notice how each clause has one verb.
  ◦ Notice how the dependent clauses provide the substance of what "the message" is in the independent clause.
  ◦ This means that the dependent clauses are functioning adjectivally, as they modify the noun "message."

7.4.2.3
Dependent Clause
Introducers

You have already been introduced to relative pronouns (§6.3.4.1), which are one of the main dependent clause introducers. When you see a relative pronoun it is always the first word in a dependent clause. There are various other Greek words that often (not always) introduce dependent clauses—the equivalent English words do the same thing as well.

- ὅς, ἥ, ὅ: who, which, that

- ἵνα: that, in order that

- ὅπως: how, that

- ὅταν: when(ever)

- ἕως: until, while

- ἄχρι: until, as far as

- ἐάν: if

Infinitive and participle clauses will be discussed further in separate chapters. For now it is sufficient to know that most participles and infinitives, when they occur, are working within a clause.

By now you know that Bible software can quickly provide you with the parsing information of Greek words, and you also know how to search for specific forms of words.

7.5 SYNTAX AND BIBLE SOFTWARE

Some Bible software programs go a step further by also providing syntactical information. So, for instance, you can search for a noun acting like an object (rather than just an accusative noun). The syntax information helps you to see the flow of the scriptural text. Logos Bible Software also provides a number of syntax resources, one in particular is called the OpenText syntax resource. This resource is also advantageous in that it is available for free online at www.opentext.org. The other main Logos resource is called the *Lexham Syntactic Greek New Testament*. When and if the time comes that you want to work more with the syntax of the NT, be sure to read about the resource of your choosing, as they often use their own nomenclature.

You should be able to clearly and accurately answer these questions. Use the flashcards at http://quizlet.com/_7tfxu to memorize the answers:

7.6 THE LEAST YOU NEED TO KNOW

- What is an adverb?
- How are Greek adverbs declined?

- What is a preposition?
- What changes may occur to a preposition and why?
- How do Greek prepositions work?
- What noun cases are prepositions coupled with?
- What is a conjunction?
- What type of conjunctions are there?
- What are interjections?
- What is a phrase and what does a phrase do?
- What types of phrases are there?
- What is an independent clause?
- What is a dependent clause and what does it do?
- What composes a sentence?
- What words can introduce dependent clauses?

7.7
GREEK@LOGOS
Utilizing the Logos help file, Logos forums, Logos wiki, and videos provided, users should take the time this chapter to learn:

- Lexham clausal outlines
  - Open it alongside your Greek New Testament in a link group and explore how it displays verses.

- Lexham Syntactic Greek New Testament
  - Open it alongside your Greek New Testament in a link group and explore how it displays verses.

7.8
VOCABULARY

Word	Meaning	Type	Freq.	Derivatives
Ἰουδαῖος, -α, -ον	Jewish, Judean	adj.	195	

νῦν	now (adv.); the present (noun)	adv.	147	
τότε	then	adv.	160	

Word	Meaning	Type	Freq.	Derivatives
ἕως	(conj.) until [+gen] as far as	conj. prep.	146	
καθώς	as, even as, just as	conj.	182	
οὐδέ	and not, not even, neither, nor	conj.	143	

Word	Meaning	Type	Freq.	Derivatives
ἰδού	look!, behold!	interj.	200	

Word	Meaning	Type	Freq.	Derivatives
ἁμαρτία, -ας, ἡ	sin	noun	173	
βασιλεία, -ας, ἡ	kingdom	noun	162	*basilica*
δόξα, -ης, ἡ	glory	noun	166	*doxology*
ἔθνος, -ους, τό	(sg.) nation; (pl.) Gentiles	noun	162	*ethnic*
ἔργον, -ου, τό	work, deed, action	noun	169	*ergonomic*
ὄχλος, -ου, ὁ	crowd, multitude	noun	175	

Word	Meaning	Type	Freq.	Derivatives
ἄν	-ever; if, would, might (conditional, untranslatable particle)	partic.	166	

Word	Meaning	Type	Freq.	Derivatives
ὑπέρ	(+gen.) in behalf of (+acc.) above	prep.	150	*hyperbole*

Table 55: Prepositions Spatial Translation Chart

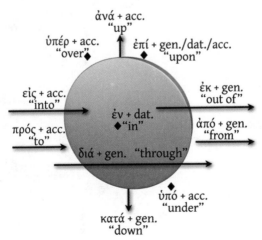

Chapter 7 Exercises

LEARNING ACTIVITY 1: VOCABULARY (1 HOUR)

Be sure to review previous vocabulary as well as learn the new.

Completed: _____ Yes _____ No

LEARNING ACTIVITY 2: READING PRACTICE (30 MINUTES)

Take 15 minutes to practice your Greek reading using the Greek audio Bible resource in Logos. For another 15 minutes, practice reading 1 John 1:1–10. (Remember, it is okay not to fully understand what you are reading.)

Completed: _____ Yes _____ No

LEARNING ACTIVITY 3: TEXTBOOK READING (1 HOUR)

Read chapter 7 of the textbook.

Completed: _____ Yes _____ No

LEARNING ACTIVITY 4: PREPOSITIONS
(30–45 MINUTES RECOMMENDED)

Chapter 7 has a spatial prepositions chart. This is a good way to learn the basic meanings of prepositions. Make a few photocopies of the following image and practice filling it out from memory until you can do it correctly.

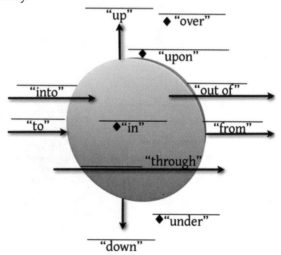

LEARNING ACTIVITY 5: VERB TENSES
(30–60 MINUTES RECOMMENDED)

Take some time to review the indicative verb system. Sing along with the songs below over and over until you have memorized them.

◢ Recommended for learning the indicative mood: ◣
The Singing Grammarian: (1) Present Active Indicative, (2) Present Middle and Passive, (3) Future Active and Middle, (4) Secondary Endings-Imperfect Tense, (5) Aorist Active and Middle, (6) Liquid Verbs, (7) Passives, (8) (Plu)Perfect, and (9) MI Verbs Songs.

Completed: _____Yes _____No

LEARNING ACTIVITY 6: IDENTIFYING CLAUSES AND PHRASES
(4–5 HOURS RECOMMENDED)

The following section is 1 John 1:1–4 and has been divided into clauses, with sentence breaks, preposition phrases, and verbs indicated. For each question below, add a translation and examine each clause and phrase to determine its type and/or function.

Ὃ ἦν ἀπ᾽ ἀρχῆς,|| ὃ ἀκηκόαμεν,|| ὃ ἑωράκαμεν τοῖς ὀφθαλμοῖς

_____

ἡμῶν,|| ὃ ἐθεασάμεθα || καὶ αἱ χεῖρες ἡμῶν ἐψηλάφησαν περὶ

_____

τοῦ λόγου τῆς ζωῆς || - καὶ ἡ ζωὴ ἐφανερώθη,|| καὶ ἑωράκαμεν

_____

καὶ μαρτυροῦμεν καὶ ἀπαγγέλλομεν ὑμῖν τὴν ζωὴν τὴν αἰώνιον

_____

|| ἥτις ἦν πρὸς τὸν πατέρα || καὶ ἐφανερώθη ἡμῖν - || ὃ

_____

ἑωράκαμεν καὶ ἀκηκόαμεν,||[ἀπαγγέλλομεν καὶ ὑμῖν,]|| ἵνα καὶ

_____

ὑμεῖς κοινωνίαν {ἔχητε} μεθ᾽ ἡμῶν.||| καὶ ἡ κοινωνία δὲ ἡ ἡμετέρα

_____

<u>μετὰ τοῦ πατρὸς</u> καὶ <u>μετὰ τοῦ υἱοῦ αὐτοῦ Ἰησοῦ Χριστοῦ.</u>||| καὶ

ταῦτα γράφομεν ἡμεῖς, || ἵνα ἡ χαρὰ ἡμῶν {ᾖ} {πεπληρωμένη}.

1. Using your bible software, put the translation of 1 Jn 1:1–4 below the Greek. Do not be a slave to your preferred English translation, though it is okay if you mostly follow it. But try to offer an exaggerated translation of the verbs. The {curly bracket words} are types of words you have not yet learned about, so take the translation directly from your preferred English version.

2. There are six underlined word groups.[1] These are phrases. Identify what type of phrase each one is, and working alongside an English translation explain how you think each phrase is functioning.

    _____

    _____

    _____

    _____

    _____

    _____

3. There are 15 sections divided by vertical lines. All of the vertical lines divide clauses. The ||| indicate the three sentences in the section.[2] The |[ ]| dividers indicate the independent clause in the sentence. Answer the questions for each clause:

    1. What type of clause is this, independent or dependent? How do you know? _____

        _____

    2. What type of clause is this, independent or dependent? How do you know? _____

        _____

___

1. Remember a word group can be just one word.
2. Remember, a Greek sentence has (at least) one independent clause and as many dependent clauses as it wants.

3. What type of clause is this, independent or dependent? How
    do you know? _____

    _____

4. What type of clause is this, independent or dependent? How
    do you know? _____

    _____

5. What type of clause is this, independent or dependent? How
    do you know? _____

    _____

6. What type of clause is this, independent or dependent? How
    do you know? _____

    _____

7. a. What type of clause is this, independent or dependent?
       How do you know? _____

       _____

    b. This clause has three verbs. How can this be, when the
       normal rule for clauses is one verb per clause? _____

       _____

8. What type of clause is this, independent or dependent? How
    do you know? _____

    _____

9. What type of clause is this, independent or dependent? How
    do you know? _____

    _____

10. a. What type of clause is this, independent or dependent?
       How do you know? _____

       _____

       _____

b. This clause has two verbs. How can this be, when the normal rule for clauses is one verb per clause? _____

_____

11. a. What type of clause is this, independent or dependent? How do you know? _____

_____

b. How did I know that this is the independent clause? ____

_____

12. What type of clause is this, independent or dependent? How do you know? _____

_____

13. a. What type of clause is this, independent or dependent? How do you know? _____

_____

b. This clause (a sentence on its own) has no verb. How can this be? _____

_____

14. What type of clause is this, independent or dependent? How do you know? _____

_____

15. What type of clause is this, independent or dependent? How do you know? _____

_____

Okay, now it is your turn. It is a good idea to photocopy the following page as you work through separating the section into clauses. Do the following:

i. Translate, focusing on an exaggerated translation of the verbs (work on accurately translating the verbs without worrying about a smooth or economical English style. Ignore the {curly words}).

ii.   Underline the phrases (hint, there are 3 of them).

iii. Break the passage up with vertical lines into clauses—go ahead and use Logos resources to help (clausal outlines, Cascadia Greek New Testament, or propositional outlines). Name the types of clauses and how you know below.

_____

_____

_____

_____

_____

_____

_____

_____

Καὶ τῇ ἡμέρᾳ τῇ τρίτῃ γάμος ἐγένετο ἐν Κανὰ τῆς

_____

Γαλιλαίας, καὶ ἦν ἡ μήτηρ τοῦ Ἰησοῦ ἐκεῖ· ἐκλήθη δὲ καὶ

_____

ὁ Ἰησοῦς καὶ οἱ μαθηταὶ αὐτοῦ εἰς τὸν γάμον. καὶ

_____

{ὑστερήσαντος οἴνου} λέγει ἡ μήτηρ τοῦ Ἰησοῦ πρὸς αὐτόν·

_____

οἶνον οὐκ ἔχουσιν. [καὶ] λέγει αὐτῇ ὁ Ἰησοῦς· τί ἐμοὶ καὶ

_____

σοί, γύναι; οὔπω ἥκει ἡ ὥρα μου. (John 2:1–4)

_____

LEARNING ACTIVITY 7: REVIEW (30 MINUTES RECOMMENDED)

You've just spent a good amount of time learning a lot of new things. Take 30 minutes to do one final read through of the chapter to solidify the knowledge, and make sure you can answer all of the questions in the *Least You Need to Know* section. Use the online flashcards link in the chapter to quiz yourself on the questions.

Completed: _____ Yes _____ No

7.9 THE SECOND TIME AROUND Second time around users should focus on preposition functions, as well as the phrases and clauses section. In particular, take time to memorize the particular dependent clause introducers.

ADVANCED EXERCISES (CH. 7)

Learning Activity 1: Vocabulary (1 hour)

Learn your assigned vocabulary list from Appendix A. Be sure to review previous vocabulary as well as learn the new. Knowledge of this new vocabulary is assumed in the translation work.

Completed: _____ Yes _____ No

Learning Activity 2: Reading (1 hour)

Read chapter 7 of the textbook again.

Completed: _____ Yes _____ No

Learning Activity 4: Parsing Practice (1.5 hours)

Drill yourself using either ParseGreek or Paradigms Master Pro.

- For ParseGreek, choose any vocabulary range in conjunction with chapters 2–6 grammar concepts.

- For Paradigms Master Pro, review nouns and verbs.

Completed: _____ Yes _____ No

Learning Activity 5: Syntax Review (1.5 hours)
Take time to *thoroughly* review the 1 John 1:1–4 syntax sheet provided at the back of this book. Take time to recognize how each dependent clause and phrase is introduced. In addition, be prepared to label how each phrase and dependent clause is functioning (noun, adjective, or adverb).

Learning Activity 6: Translation and Syntax Work (4 hours)
The following sentences have already occurred in previous round 2 exercises. With the following sentences, students should do the following:

1. Use a parallel line (/) to break up the clauses, and circle the main verb of each clause.

2. Underline any phrase and label its usage (noun, adjective, adverb).

3. [Bracket] any dependent clauses and label its usage (noun, adjective, adverb).

4. Use a double parallel line (//) to identify sentence breaks.

5. Draw a square box around the main verb of each sentence (i.e., the main verb of the independent clause).

6. Note that participles and infinitives are identified for you.

ἀλλὰ λέγω, Ἰσραὴλ οὐκ ἔγνω (understand); πρῶτος Μωϋσῆς λέγει· ἐγὼ παραζηλώσω (will make jealous) ὑμᾶς ἐπ᾽ οὐκ ἔθνει (Rom 10:19)

_____

_____

_____

μετὰ δὲ πολὺν χρόνον (long time) ἔρχεται ὁ κύριος τῶν δούλων ἐκείνων καὶ συναίρει (settled) λόγον μετ᾽ αὐτῶν. (Matt 25:19)

_____

_____

_____

αὕτη δέ ἐστιν ἡ <u>κρίσις</u> (judgment) ὅτι τὸ φῶς <u>ἐλήλυθεν</u> (has come) εἰς τὸν κόσμον καὶ ἠγάπησαν οἱ ἄνθρωποι μᾶλλον τὸ <u>σκότος</u> (darkness) ἢ τὸ φῶς (John 3:19)

_____

_____

_____

Καὶ <u>ἀπεσταλμένοι ἦσαν</u> (they had been sent) ἐκ τῶν Φαρισαίων. καὶ ἠρώτησαν αὐτὸν καὶ εἶπαν αὐτῷ· τί οὖν βαπτίζεις εἰ σὺ οὐκ εἶ ὁ χριστὸς οὐδὲ Ἠλίας (Elijah) οὐδὲ ὁ προφήτης; <u>ἀπεκρίθη</u> (lex = <u>ἀποκρίνομαι</u>) αὐτοῖς ὁ Ἰωάννης <u>λέγων</u> (saying)· ἐγὼ βαπτίζω ἐν ὕδατι· μέσος ὑμῶν <u>ἕστηκεν</u> (lex = <u>ἵστημι</u>) ὃν ὑμεῖς οὐκ οἴδατε (John 1:24–26)

_____

_____

_____

καὶ ὁ <u>Κορνήλιος</u> (Cornelius) ἔφη· ἀπὸ τετάρτης <u>ἡμέρας</u> (days) <u>μέχρι</u> (until) ταύτης τῆς ὥρας ἤμην τὴν <u>ἐνάτην</u> (nine) <u>προσευχόμενος</u> (I was praying) ἐν τῷ οἴκῳ μου, καὶ ἰδοὺ ἀνὴρ <u>ἔστη</u> (lex = <u>ἵστημι</u>) ἐνώπιόν μου ἐν <u>ἐσθῆτι λαμπρᾷ</u> (dazzling clothes) (Acts 10:30)

_____

_____

_____

CHAPTER 8

Participles Made Simple

What's the Point: Many a grammarian has echoed the sentiments that the mastery of the Greek participle is mastery of Greek itself. Participles are robust in their meaning and usage—it often takes many words in English to translate what a participle is doing. One out of every four verb forms is a participle; they are everywhere! Because of their frequency and complexity of usage, it would be better to start working with participles earlier, except a student needs many other pieces in place first, because participles are part verb and part adjective. Let the fun begin!

A participle is a hybrid word, part adjective and part verb. Its meaning is derived from its verb stem, so its lexical form is a verb. But while its stem is a verb, its adjective nature shows by taking declension endings.

8.1 PARTICIPLE DESCRIPTION

Once we stray outside of the indicative mood, the number of Greek tenses that occur reduces significantly. In the NT, participles only occur in present (3,687), aorist (2,289), perfect (673), and future (13) tenses. Because of the scarcity of future participles, we will focus only on the other three tenses. The action described by an aorist participle usually occurs prior to the main verb's action. The action described by a present participle usually occurs at the same time as the main verb's action. The action described by a perfect participle usually occurs prior to the main verb's action. The action of a future participle usually occurs after the main verb's action.

Are these funky hybrid words in English, too? Of course they are. *Participles describe an action happening in and around the main verb.* Examine the following examples:

- The dog barked at the car.

  □ "bark" is the verb of the clause.

- The barking dog ran after the car.

  □ "ran" is the main verb of the clause.
  □ Notice how the verb "bark" is no longer the main verb. "-ing" has been added to the verb and paired with "dog" to act like an adjective.
  □ In the scene that has been portrayed, there are two actions happening in the scene, but only one is the main action (main verb). Other actions happening in and around the main verb will often use a participle to describe these peripheral actions in the clause.

8.2
HOW PARTICIPLES ARE FORMED

The following table breaks down how participles are formed. See commentary on the table below.

Table 56: Participle Formation

verb parts					adjective parts (case, gender, number)		
tense		voice			masc.	fem.	neut.
					declension use		
Present	First principal part	active	οντ	ουσ (fem. and dat. pl)	third	first	third
		mid/pass	ομεν		second	first	second
Aorist (NO augment)	Third principal part *(first aor. ends with σα, second aor. does not)*	active	ντ	σ (fem. and dat. pl)	third	first	third
		middle	μεν		second	first	second

	Sixth principal part *(ends with* θε*)*[1]	passive	ντ	ισ (fem. and dat. pl)	third	first	third
Perfect	Fourth and fifth principal part *(WITH reduplication)*	active	κοτ	κυι (fem.)	third	first	third
		mid/pass	μεν		second	first	second

While this table may not look too complicated, it amounts to A LOT of participle forms because of the declension endings a participle can take. The following tables shows all possible participle forms of λύω (see the discussion below the tables).

Bear in mind the following points as you compare the full paradigm of λύω as a participle (comparing it with the table above):

1. A participle's parsing information is: tense, voice, part of speech (participle), case, gender, number, lexical form. For example, the first participle in Table 57 above is parsed as perfect, active, participle, nominative, masculine, singular, λύω.

2. The most difficult participle form to recognize is the nominative, masculine, singular form, because the case ending is ς, which is a bully and changes things.

   a. For present active, the ς case ending kicks out the τ from the voice suffix, slips on the ν, and as it leaves it lengthens the ο to an ω; i.e., ο̲ν̲τ̲ς̲ becomes ω̲ν̲.

   b. A similar thing happens to the perfect active; the τ drops out and lengthens the ο to an ω (i.e., κ̲ο̲τ̲ς̲ becomes κ̲ω̲ς̲).

   c. For aorist active and passive the ς case ending kicks out the ντ voice suffix all together (see §2.7.3) (i.e., ν̲τ̲ς̲

1. Remember from the indicative mood that some verbs drop the *theta* (θ).

becomes ς). For the aorist passive, the ε at the end of the tense will lengthen to ει (i.e., θεντς becomes θεις).

3. Present participle voice suffixes begin with an *omicron* (ο). This is actually a connecting vowel. The important thing to know is that this can cause contraction with contract verbs (review contract verbs in §5.3.2).

4. Remember the phrase μεν *are in the middle*. Notice how μεν is always the middle voice suffix for every tense.

5. Present and aorist active as well as aorist passive have different voice suffixes for feminine participles. For present and aorist active, the suffix also applies to masculine and neuter dative plural forms.

6. Aorist participles:

   a. If you remember from the aorist indicative, *epsilon* (ε) augment is one of the markers of the tense. The augment DOES NOT occur with aorist participles.

   b. If you remember from the aorist active and middle indicative, σα was the suffix for the aorist tense; σα still indicates aorist here (and the *sigma* [σ] may slip away).

   c. If you remember from the aorist passive indicative, θη was the suffix. For the participle, it is only slightly different: θε.

7. Perfect participles:

   a. Reduplication was the marker of the perfect tense in the indicative mood. It still indicates perfect for participles.

   b. Perfect active and middle indicative verbs had a κ in its suffix. A κ occurs in the perfect participle suffix as well.

   c. The perfect active dative plural participle loses the τ from the suffix and replaces it with a σ. (I've told you before, the *sigma* is sinister!)

Remember, in the approach of *Biblical Greek Made Simple* you don't need to memorize this. This is about understanding what you see as you come across participles in the NT, so this is for reference. As you look at the following tables, compare with the formations table and points above to understand the participle forms.

Table 57: Present Tense λύω Participles

First Principal Part: λύω		active			middle/passive		
		masc.	*fem.*	*neut.*	*masc.*	*fem.*	*neut.*
sg.	*nom.*	λύων	λύουσα	λῦον	λυόμενος	λυομένη	λυόμενον
	gen.	λύοντος	λυούσης	λύοντος	λυομένου	λυομένης	λυομένου
	dat.	λύοντι	λυούσῃ	λύοντι	λυομένῳ	λυομένη	λυομένῳ
	acc.	λύοντα	λύουσαν	λῦον	λυόμενον	λυομένην	λυόμενον
pl.	*nom.*	λύοντες	λύουσαι	λύοντα	λυόμενοι	λυόμεναι	λυόμενα
	gen.	λυόντων	λυουσῶν	λυόντων	λυομένων	λυομένων	λυομένων
	dat.	λύουσιν	λυούσαις	λύουσιν	λυομένοις	λυομέναις	λυομένοις
	acc.	λύοντας	λυούσας	λύοντα	λυομένους	λυομένας	λυόμενα

Table 58: Aorist Tense λύω Participles

Third Principal Part: ἐλύσα		active			middle		
		masc.	*fem.*	*neut.*	*masc.*	*fem.*	*neut.*
sg.	*nom.*	λύσας	λύσασα	λῦσαν	λυσάμενος	λυσαμένη	λυσάμενον
	gen.	λύσαντος	λυσάσης	λύσαντος	λυσαμένου	λυσαμένης	λυσαμένου
	dat.	λύσαντι	λυσάσῃ	λύσαντι	λυσαμένῳ	λυσαμένη	λυσαμένῳ
	acc.	λύσαντα	λύσασαν	λῦσαν	λυσάμενον	λυσαμένην	λυσάμενον
pl.	*nom.*	λύσαντες	λύσασαι	λύσαντα	λυσάμενοι	λυσάμεναι	λυσάμενα
	gen.	λυσάντων	λυσασῶν	λυσάντων	λυσαμένων	λυσαμένων	λυσαμένων
	dat.	λύσασιν	λυσάσαις	λύσασιν	λυσαμένοις	λυσαμέναις	λυσαμένοις
	acc.	λύσαντας	λυσάσας	λύσαντα	λυσαμένους	λυσαμένας	λυσάμενα

Sixth Principal Part: ἐλύθην		passive		
		masc.	*fem.*	*neut.*
sg.	*nom.*	λυθείς	λυθεῖσα	λυθέν
	gen.	λυθέντος	λυθείσης	λυθέντος
	dat.	λυθέντι	λυθείσῃ	λυθέντι
	acc.	λυθέντα	λυθεῖσαν	λυθέν
pl.	*nom.*	λυθέντες	λυθεῖσαι	λυθέντα
	gen.	λυθέντων	λυθεισῶν	λυθέντων
	dat.	λυθεῖσιν	λυθείσαις	λυθεῖσι(ν)
	acc.	λυθέντας	λυθείσας	λυθέντα

Table 59: Perfect Tense λύω Participles

		Fourth Principal Part λελύκα			Fifth Principal Part λελύμαι		
		active			middle/passive		
		masc.	*fem.*	*neut.*	*masc.*	*fem.*	*neut.*
sg.	*nom.*	λελυκώς	λελυκυῖα	λελυκός	λελυμένος	λελυμένη	λελυμένον
	gen.	λελυκότος	λελυκυίας	λελυκοτος	λελυμένου	λελυμένης	λελυμένου
	dat.	λελυκότι	λελυκυίᾳ	λελυκότι	λελυμένῳ	λελυμένῃ	λελυμένῳ
	acc.	λελυκότα	λελυκυῖαν	λελυκός	λελυμένον	λελυμένην	λελυμένον
pl.	*nom.*	λελυκότες	λελυκυῖαι	λελυκότα	λελυμένοι	λελυμέναι	λελυμένα
	gen.	λελυκότων	λελυκυιῶν	λελυκότων	λελυμένων	λελυμένων	λελυμένων
	dat.	λελυκόσιν	λελυκυίαις	λελυκόσι(ν)	λελυμένοις	λελυμέναις	λελυμένοις
	acc.	λελυκότας	λελυκυίας	λελυκότα	λελυμένους	λελυμένας	λελυμένα

The next chapter will deal in depth with what participles can do and how they are translated. This chapter will only highlight how the participle functions adjectivally, since it is part adjective.

Since a participle is a verbal adjective, it can do the things an adjective can do:

1. A participle can be in full concord with a nearby noun that it is paired with and attribute value to the noun. If the noun has an article, so will the participle. If the noun doesn't have an article, the participle may or may not have the article. For example: τίς ὑπέδειξεν ὑμῖν φυγεῖν ἀπὸ τῆς μελλούσης ὀργῆς; (Matt 3:7) is *who told you to free from* the coming *wrath*. (This is like "the barking dog" example above.)

2. All by itself and <u>with an article</u>, a participle functions as a substantive. For example: ὁ λύων is *the one who is loosing* or *the man who is loosing*. Remember that the gender and number of a substantive adjective affects the translation—the same goes for participles. For example: ἐξῆλθεν ὁ σπείρων τοῦ σπείρειν (Matt 13:3) is a sower *went out to sow.*

3. As a substantive, a nominative participle can be the object[1] of an equative verb. This includes being the object in a verbless clause (remember that a verbless clause assumes the copulative εἰμί). For example: ποῦ ἐστιν ὁ τεχθεὶς βασιλεὺς τῶν Ἰουδαίων; (Matt 2:2) is translated *who is* the one born *king of the Jews?* The verb here is ἐστιν (a form of εἰμί), with the participle acting as the object of εἰμί.

---

1. The proper term is predicate nominative.

8.3.2
Participle Acting
Like a Verb

Although very rare in the New Testament, there are times when a participle can act as the main verb of a sentence. In these instances where the participle is acting as a finite verb, it will be translated as an indicative or imperative.

8.4
THE LEAST YOU
NEED TO KNOW

You should be able to clearly and accurately answer these questions. Use the flashcards at http://quizlet.com/_7tfy6 to memorize the answers:

- What is a participle?

- What three tenses most frequently occur as participles?

- What are all of the components in participle parsing?

- What is the indicator for an aorist active or middle participle?

- What is the indicator for an aorist passive participle?

- What is the indicator for a perfect active or middle/passive participle?

- What is the present active voice suffix for participles?

- What is the aorist active voice suffix for participles?

- What is the aorist passive voice suffix for participles?

- What is the perfect active voice suffix for participles?

- What does it mean when a participle has an article?

- What is the most difficult participle form to recognize? Why?

- What is the suffix for all middle(/passive) participles?

- When a participle is acting like an adjective, what things can it do?

- A nominative participle with an equative verb may be doing what?

Utilizing the Logos help file, Logos forums, Logos wiki, and videos provided, users should take the time, this chapter, to learn:

8.5

GREEK@LOGOS

- Use the Passage Guide

  ▫ See the article on the Passage Guide at https://support.logos.com

- Topic Guide

  ▫ See the article on the Topic Guide at https://support.logos.com

8.6

VOCABULARY

Word	Meaning	Type	Freq.	Derivatives
ἄλλος, -η, -ον	other, another	adj.	155	allegory
πρῶτος, -η, -ον	first, earlier; foremost	adj. adv.	155	

Word	Meaning	Type	Freq.	Derivatives
πάλιν	again	adv.	141	palindrome

Word	Meaning	Type	Freq.	Derivatives
καρδία, -ας, ἡ	heart	noun	156	cardiac
λαός, -ου, ὁ	people, crowd	noun	142	laity
πόλις, -εως, ἡ	city	noun	162	metropolis
προφήτης, -ου, ὁ	prophet	noun	144	
σάρξ, σαρκός, ἡ	flesh, body	noun	147	sarcophogus
σῶμα, -ματος, τό	body	noun	142	psychosomatic
χάρις, -ιτος, ἡ	grace, favor	noun	155	Eucharist

Word	Meaning	Type	Freq.	Derivatives
ὅστις, ἥτις, ὅτι	whoever/whichever/ whatever; everyone, which	pron.	153	

Word	Meaning	Type	Freq.	Derivatives
ἀγαπάω	I love, cherish	verb	143	
ἀγαπάω, ἀγαπήσω, ἠγάπησα, ἠγάπηκα, ἠγάπημαι, ἠγαπήθην				
ἀφίημι	I let go, leave, permit, divorce, forgive	verb	143	
ἀφίημι (ἀφίω, ἀφέω), ἀφήσω, ἀφῆκα, ——, ἀφέωμαι, ἀφέθην				
ἐγείρω	I raise up, wake	verb	144	
ἐγείρω, ἐγερῶ, ἤγειρα, ——, ἐγήγερμαι, ἠγέρθην				
ζάω	I live	verb	140	
ζάω, ζήσω, ἔζησα, ——, ——, ——				

Chapter 8 Exercises

LEARNING ACTIVITY 1: VOCABULARY (1 HOUR)
Be sure to review previous vocabulary as well as learn the new.
Completed: _____ Yes _____ No

LEARNING ACTIVITY 2: NOUN ENDINGS AND PARTICIPLES
(30–45 MINUTES RECOMMENDED)
Take some time to remind yourself of the declension endings, as participles use them. Then work on memorizing *and understanding* the Participles Song. Listen to it over and over until you have it memorized.

◢ Recommended for learning declension endings: ◣
The Singing Grammarian: (1) First Declension, (2) Second Declension, (3) Third Declension Songs, and (4) The Participles Song.

Completed: _____ Yes _____ No

LEARNING ACTIVITY 3: READ (1 HOUR RECOMMENDED)
Read chapter 8.
Completed: _____ Yes _____ No

LEARNING ACTIVITY 4: PARTICIPLE PARSING
(1–2 HOURS RECOMMENDED)
Go ahead and *use your Bible software* to help you parse these (you will need to type them in Greek to find them).

1. Circle the inflected ending on each word.

2. Underline the principal part portion of each word.

3. Identify what declension ending the word uses, and what principal part the word is built off of.

4. Parse.

1. *λύσασα* (*example*)

   a. declension: first declension. third principal part (ἔλυσα)

   b. parsing: aorist, active, participle, nominative, feminine, singular, λύω.

2. ἰδών

   a. declension: _____

   b. parsing: _____

3. ἐλθών

   a. declension: _____

   b. parsing: _____

4. ἀκούσαντες

   a. declension: _____

   b. parsing: _____

5. λαβών

   a. declension: _____

   b. parsing: _____

6. γενομένης

   a. declension: _____

   b. parsing: _____

7. πορευθέντες

   a. declension: _____

   b. parsing: _____

8. πέμψας

   a. declension: _____

   b. parsing: _____

9. ῥηθέν

   a. declension: _____

   b. parsing: _____

10. γεγραμμένον

    a. declension: _____

    b. parsing: _____

11. γεγραμμένα

    a. declension: _____

    b. parsing: _____

LEARNING ACTIVITY 5: PARTICIPLE AS ADJECTIVE
(3–4 HOURS RECOMMENDED)

Go through the following sentences. (1) Write out the participle, (2) parse it (use Bible software if you are stumped, but understand how they are formed from the chapter), and (3) working with the top portion of the participle flowchart (table 60, page 200), label how each participle is functioning.

1. ὁ πιστεύων εἰς αὐτὸν οὐ κρίνεται· (John 3:18)

   Participle: _____

   Parsing: _____

   Function: _____

2. ὁ πέμψας με ἀληθής ἐστιν (John 8:26)

   Participle: _____

   Parsing: _____

   Function: _____

3. τὸ γεγεννημένον ἐκ τῆς σαρκὸς σάρξ ἐστιν, καὶ τὸ γεγεννημένον ἐκ τοῦ πνεύματος πνεῦμά ἐστιν. (John 3:6)

Participle: _____

Parsing: _____

Function: _____

4. εἶπεν τῷ παραλελυμένῳ (Luke 5:24)

Participle: _____

Parsing: _____

Function: _____

5. τὸ πνεῦμά ἐστιν τὸ ζῳοποιοῦν (John 6:63)

Participle: _____

Parsing: _____

Function: _____

6. Ἰησοῦς ἐστιν ὁ ποιήσας αὐτὸν ὑγιῆ (John 5:15)

Participle: _____

Parsing: _____

Function: _____

7. οὗτοί εἰσιν οἱ ἀκούσαντες (Luke 8:14)

Participle: _____

Parsing: _____

Function: _____

8. οὐ τιμᾷ τὸν πατέρα τὸν πέμψαντα αὐτόν. (John 5:23)

Participle: _____

Parsing: _____

Function: _____

9. ἡ οἰκονομία τοῦ μυστηρίου τοῦ ἀποκεκρυμμένου ἀπὸ τῶν αἰώνων
   (Eph 3:9)

   Participle: _____

   Parsing: _____

   Function: _____

10. ἀλλ' ἐπὶ τῷ θεῷ τῷ ἐγείροντι τοὺς νεκρούς (2Cor 1:9)

    Participle: _____

    Parsing: _____

    Function: _____

11. ἀδελφοὶ ἠγαπημένοι ὑπὸ κυρίου (2Thess 2:13)

    Participle: _____

    Parsing: _____

    Function: _____

12. κληθήσονται υἱοὶ θεοῦ ζῶντος (Rom 9:26)

    Participle: _____

    Parsing: _____

    Function: _____

13. πιστεύσασιν ἐπὶ τὸν κύριον Ἰησοῦν Χριστόν (Acts 11:17)

    Participle: _____

    Parsing: _____

    Function: _____

14. χρυσίον πεπυρωμένον ἐκ πυρός (Rev 3:18)

    Participle: _____

    Parsing: _____

    Function: _____

15. καὶ ὁ ζῶν, καὶ ἐγενόμην νεκρὸς καὶ ἰδοὺ ζῶν εἰμι εἰς τοὺς αἰῶνας τῶν αἰώνων καὶ ἔχω τὰς κλεῖς τοῦ θανάτου καὶ τοῦ ᾅδου (Rev 1:18)

Participle: _____

Parsing: _____

Function: _____

Second Participle: _____

Parsing: _____

Function: _____

16. καὶ ἡ γυνὴ ἦν περιβεβλημένη πορφυροῦν καὶ κόκκινον (Rev 17:4)

Participle: _____

Parsing: _____

Function: _____

17. Ζῶν γὰρ ὁ λόγος τοῦ θεοῦ καὶ ἐνεργής (Heb 4:12)

Participle: _____

Parsing: _____

Function: _____

18. ἡ ὁδὸς ἡ ἀπάγουσα εἰς τὴν ζωὴν καὶ ὀλίγοι εἰσὶν οἱ εὑρίσκοντες αὐτήν (Matt 7:14)

Participle: _____

Parsing: _____

Function: _____

Second Participle: _____

Parsing: _____

Function: _____

19. πυρράζει γὰρ στυγνάζων ὁ οὐρανός (Matt 16:3)

    Participle: _____

    Parsing: _____

    Function: _____

20. καὶ μακαρία ἡ πιστεύσασα (Luke 1:45)

    Participle: _____

    Parsing: _____

    Function: _____

LEARNING ACTIVITY 6: REVIEW (30 MINUTES RECOMMENDED)

You've just spent a good amount of time learning a lot of new things. Take 30 minutes to do one final read through of the chapter to solidify the knowledge, and make sure you can answer all of the questions in the *Least You Need to Know* section. Use the online flashcards link in the chapter to quiz yourself on the questions.

Completed: _____ Yes _____ No

The Second Time Around focuses heavily on the formation of participles. Memorize not only the participle formation tables, but also how to reproduce the λύω participle paradigm in full.

8.7

THE SECOND TIME AROUND

ADVANCED EXERCISES (CH. 8)

Learning Activity 1: Vocabulary (1 hour)

Learn List 8 vocabulary from Appendix A. Be sure to review previous vocabulary as well as learn the new. Knowledge of this new vocabulary is assumed in the translation work.

Learning Activity 2: Reading (1 hour)

Read chapter 8 of the textbook again.

Completed: _____ Yes _____ No

Learning Activity 3: Memorize Declension Endings (15–30 minutes)
Review first, second, and third declension endings, as participles use the declension endings. Use *The Singing Grammarian* as help, and practice filling in the paradigms from memory using the practice tables.
Completed: _____ Yes _____ No

Learning Activity 4: Parsing Practice (1.5 hours)
Drill yourself using either ParseGreek or Paradigms Master Pro

- For ParseGreek, choose any vocabulary range in conjunction with chapter 8 grammar concepts

- For Paradigms Master Pro, work on **All Verbs: Participles**.

Completed: _____ Yes _____ No

Learning Activity 5: Parsing Work (1.5–2 hours)

1. λέγων _____

2. λέγοντες _____

3. ἀποκριθείς _____

4. ἰδών _____

5. ἐλθών _____

6. ἔχοντες _____

7. ὤν _____

8. ἀναστάς _____

9. γενομένης _____

10. ἀκούσας _____

11. γενόμενος _____

12. λέγοντος _____

13. εἰδότες _____

14. λέγουσα _____

15. ὄντα _____

16. γεγραμμένον _____

17. πορευθέντες _____

18. ὄντας _____

19. γνούς _____

20. ἔχοντι _____

21. πιστεύουσιν _____

22. προσκαλεσάμενος _____

23. λαλοῦντος _____

24. λαβόντες _____

Learning Activity 6: Translation (3.5 hours)

Translate the following sentences. Be ready to parse any participles that appear in the sentences. The following sentences assume knowledge of all words occurring up to 43 times (chs. 1–11 and lists 1–8). For difficult forms, consult the morphological information in Logos Bible Software.

ὅτι ἐν αὐτῷ κατοικεῖ πᾶν τὸ πλήρωμα (fullness) τῆς θεότητος (deity) σωματικῶς (bodily), καὶ ἐστὲ ἐν αὐτῷ πεπληρωμένοι, ὅς ἐστιν ἡ κεφαλὴ πάσης ἀρχῆς καὶ ἐξουσίας. (Col 2:9–10)

_____

_____

_____

_____

_____

_____

_____

πᾶς γὰρ ὁ αἰτῶν λαμβάνει καὶ ὁ ζητῶν εὑρίσκει καὶ <u>τῷ κρούοντι</u> (the one who knocks) ἀνοιγήσεται. ἢ τίς ἐστιν ἐξ ὑμῶν ἄνθρωπος, ὃν αἰτήσει ὁ υἱὸς αὐτοῦ ἄρτον, μὴ λίθον <u>ἐπιδώσει</u> (will give) αὐτῷ; (Matt 7:8-9)

_____

_____

_____

_____

_____

_____

οὐ γὰρ ὑμεῖς ἐστε οἱ λαλοῦντες ἀλλὰ τὸ πνεῦμα τοῦ πατρὸς ὑμῶν τὸ λαλοῦν ἐν ὑμῖν. Παραδώσει δὲ ἀδελφὸς ἀδελφὸν εἰς θάνατον καὶ πατὴρ τέκνον, καὶ <u>ἐπαναστήσονται</u> (will rise) τέκνα ἐπὶ <u>γονεῖς</u> (parents) καὶ <u>θανατώσουσιν</u> (will put to death) αὐτούς. καὶ ἔσεσθε <u>μισούμενοι</u> (periphrastic ptc. "hated") ὑπὸ πάντων διὰ τὸ ὄνομά μου· <u>ὁ δὲ ὑπομείνας</u> (the one who endures) εἰς <u>τέλος</u> (end) οὗτος σωθήσεται. (Matt 10:20-22)

_____

_____

_____

_____

_____

ἰδόντες δὲ <u>ἐγνώρισαν</u> (made known) περὶ τοῦ ῥήματος τοῦ λαληθέντος αὐτοῖς περὶ τοῦ παιδίου τούτου. καὶ πάντες οἱ ἀκούσαντες <u>ἐθαύμασαν</u> (were amazed) περὶ τῶν λαληθέντων ὑπὸ τῶν <u>ποιμένων</u> (shepherds) πρὸς αὐτούς· ἡ δὲ Μαριὰμ πάντα <u>συνετήρει</u> (treasured) τὰ <u>ῥήματα</u> (lex = <u>ῥῆμα</u>) ταῦτα <u>συμβάλλουσα</u> (pondered) ἐν τῇ καρδίᾳ αὐτῆς. (Luke 2:17-19)

_____

_____

_____

_____

_____

Participle Functions Made Simple

What's the Point: The difficulty with participles is not only how they are formed, but also how they can function. Participles can do such a wide range of things that they can be daunting. But because participles are so numerous, you cannot ignore them.

9.1 WHAT A PARTICIPLE CAN DO

The following information covers the most common uses of the participle. In the future as you work with Greek and your preferred English translation, consult Wallace's *Greek Grammar Beyond the Basics* when you are struggling over what a participle is doing, or questioning the decision of an English translation.

9.1.1 Periphrastic Participle

Periphrastic means to combine words to form a single idea. In Greek, εἰμί is a word that sometimes needs a verbal idea to convey one verb idea. It is no different in English. Sometimes "I am" can be the verb in a clause all by itself, and other times it works with a participle to convey one verbal idea. So for example, "I am hungry" or "I am a teacher" has "I am" as the verb working on its own. But "he is kicking the ball" has "is" working with the participle "kicking" to form one verbal idea. You may be wondering why Greek didn't just use a regular indicative verb to indicate the same thing as a periphrastic construction, like "he kicks the ball." Good question! Periphrastic constructions are somewhat redundant but do add overemphasis for effect. One thing to note is that because εἰμί is working as a package, it is no longer considered an equative verb.

Periphrastic participles are almost always nominative, and regularly follow the εἰμί form. They combine with εἰμί to work in present, imperfect, future, and perfect tenses:

- Present periphrastic construction: present εἰμί + present participle

  □ ὅ ἐστιν μεθερμηνευόμενον Κρανίου Τόπος (Mark 15:22)
    which <u>is</u> *translated* place of the skull.

- Imperfect periphrastic construction: imperfect εἰμί + present participle[1]

  □ ἦν προσδεχόμενος τὴν βασιλείαν τοῦ θεοῦ (Mark 15:43)
    <u>he was</u> *waiting* for the kingdom of God.

- Future periphrastic construction: future εἰμί + present participle

  □ ἔσεσθε μισούμενοι ὑπὸ πάντων διὰ τὸ ὄνομά μου (Matt 10:22)
    <u>you will be</u> *hated* by all because of my name.

- Perfect periphrastic construction: present εἰμί[2] + perfect participle

  □ χάριτί ἐστε σεσῳσμένοι διὰ πίστεως (Eph 2:8)
    by grace <u>you</u> *have* <u>been</u> *saved* through faith.

9.1.2
Genitive Absolute

A genitive absolute participle clause stands "absolutely alone" within the sentence. This type of phrase is very similar to using parentheses in English sentences. The participle will always be in the genitive case, and will have a noun or pronoun in concord. The genitive (pro) noun it is with will be unrelated to any other noun in the sentence. *When you see a genitive absolute, say "when."* For example: ἐξελθόντων αὐτῶν ἀπὸ Βηθανίας ἐπείνασεν (Mark 11:12) is translated as *when they came* from Bethany, he was hungry.

9.1.3
Adverbial Participle

Most participles act adverbially, and when a participle does act adverbially it will *always be anarthrous.*[3] Remember that participles give you information about other actions happening in and around the main verb's action. Although it is one word in Greek, an adverbial

---

1. Remember that there are no imperfect participles.   3. This means it has no article.
2 Remember that there are no perfect forms of εἰμί.

participle is often translated with a whole clause in English. It is also not always easy to translate the tense of a participle (present participles will sometimes be translated as a past tense rather than a durative). Furthermore, *context determines the function*. There are times in the NT when it is unclear what an adverbial participle is trying to indicate. Remember also that participles are part of a phrase (§7.4.1), and a phrase can have more than one word. Often a participle may have its own object or other nouns working within the phrase.

The following is a list of the types of adverbial information a participle can convey. The listing of functions is in order of regularity (i.e., temporal is the dominant function). In the sentence examples, the participle phrases are underlined, the participle is red, and the participle's translation is *italicized*.

1. SIMULTANEOUS TEMPORAL ACTION: A participle can indicate an action happening at the same time as the main verb's action. The participle will always be in the present tense.

   ◦ Περιπατῶν δὲ παρὰ τὴν θάλασσαν τῆς Γαλιλαίας εἶδεν δύο ἀδελφούς (Matt 4:18)
   While he walked by the sea of Galilee he saw two brothers.

2. PRECEDING TEMPORAL ACTION: A participle can indicate an action that happened prior to the main verb's action. The participle will always be in the aorist tense.

   ◦ Τότε Ἡρῴδης λάθρᾳ καλέσας τοὺς μάγους ἠκρίβωσεν παρ' αὐτῶν τὸν χρόνον . . . (Matt 2:7)
   Then *after he* secretly *called* the magi, Herod learned from them the time . . .

3. PURPOSE or RESULT: A participle can indicate the purpose or result of the main verb's action.

   ◦ τοῦτο δὲ ἔλεγεν πειράζων αὐτόν (John 6:6)
   But he was saying this *in order to test* him.

▫ πατέρα ἴδιον ἔλεγεν τὸν θεὸν ἴσον ἑαυτὸν ποιῶν τῷ θεῷ (John 5:18)
He was also calling God his own Father, *thereby making* himself equal to God.

4. CAUSE: A participle can indicate the action which caused the main verb's action.

▫ οἱ πατριάρχαι ζηλώσαντες τὸν Ἰωσὴφ ἀπέδοντο εἰς Αἴγυπτον (Acts 7:9)
Because the patriarchs *were jealous* of Joseph, they sold him into Egypt.

5. CONDITION: A participle can indicate a conditional action that needs to happen before the main verb's action occurs.

▫ θερίσομεν μὴ ἐκλυόμενοι (Gal 6:9)
We will reap *if we do not give up.*

6. CONCESSION: A concessive participle introduces an (inconvenient) action that is occurring, but the main verb's action is still happening in spite of the participle's action.

▫ γνόντες τὸν θεὸν οὐχ ὡς θεὸν ἐδόξασαν (Rom 1:21)
Although they knew God, they did not honor him as God.

7. MEANS: A participle can indicate the action that provides the means for the main verb's action.

▫ οἵτινες ὅλους οἴκους ἀνατρέπουσιν διδάσκοντες . . . αἰσχροῦ (Titus 1:11)
they are upsetting whole families *by teaching* shameful things

8. MANNER: A participle can indicate the manner in which the main verb's action is occurring.

▫ ἐπορεύοντο χαίροντες (Acts 5:41)
They went *with rejoicing.*

9. REDUNDANT: A participle can indicate action related to the main verb's action, but it is not essential to the main

verb's action. Because the participle is redundant, either it OR the main verb is left untranslated. In the example below, the participle is translated; the main verb is not.

▫ <u>ἀποκριθεὶς</u> δὲ ὁ Ἰησοῦς εἶπεν πρὸς αὐτόν (Matt 3:15)
But Jesus *answered* him.

In the *Biblical Greek Made Simple* approach, you do not need to determine participle function and translation on your own. What you do need to do is understand how and why modern translators come to the decisions they have (and decide if you agree!). Translation is interpretation, and in the case of adverbial participles you will find that you may disagree at times with English translations. The following flowchart is a "determination device" for participles. As you come across Greek participles in the NT and study them in conjunction with English translation(s), take the time to see how the participle has flowed through the flowchart. The following points are items to note as you use and study the flowchart:

**9.2
UNDERSTANDING
PARTICIPLE
FUNCTION AND
TRANSLATION**

- A participle with an article instantly means its adjectival quality has kicked in.

- A nominative participle (with or without an article) that is in a clause with an equative verb or in a verbless clause will be the predicate nominative OR a periphrastic construction with a form of εἰμί.

- A genitive participle that has a (pro)noun in concord nearby (and that genitive is not connected to any other noun), is likely a genitive absolute.

- An anarthrous[1] participle is most often an adverbial participle. But, an anarthrous participle in concord with a nearby noun may be acting like an indefinite attributive adjective.

- The adverbial functions in the flowchart are listed in order of frequency (i.e., temporal functions are the most common).

---

1. Anarthrous means no article.

- Remember, the flowchart does not cover everything a participle can do. Consult Wallace's *Greek Grammar Beyond the Basics* to understand the other minor functions.

Table 60: Participle Flowchart

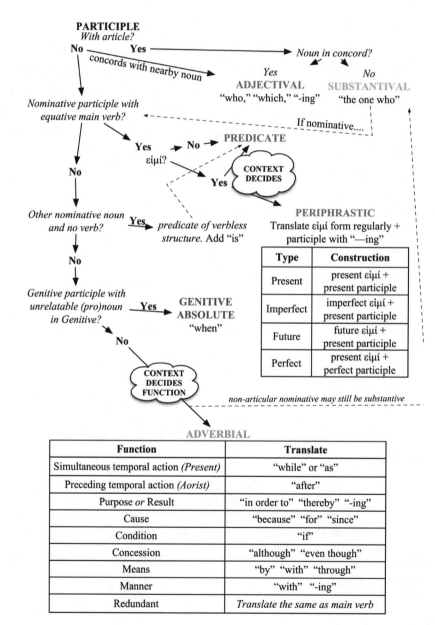

Because an adverbial participle is describing an action happening in and around the main verb, it only makes sense that there is someone or something doing the action. At times, the way a participle indicates who did the action is by placing the participle in concord with a noun in the clause, or in concord with the "built-in" pronoun of the main verb. A pronoun, not present in the Greek, is often added to the English translation of these types of participles to indicate the doer of the participle action. The following examples (taken from §9.1), highlight how the participle is in concord with a substantive in the clause. The participle is in red, the phrase is underlined, the participle translation is *italicized*, and the pronoun provided in English (but not present in Greek) is **bold**.

9.2.1
The Subject of an
Adverbial Participle

- <u>Περιπατῶν δὲ παρὰ τὴν θάλασσαν τῆς Γαλιλαίας</u> εἶδεν δύο ἀδελφούς (Matt 4:18)

  While **he** walked by the sea of Galilee he saw two brothers.

  - Participle Parsing: pres., act., ptc., nom., masc., sg., περιπατέω.
  - There are three "actors" in this section: the sea (acc., fem., sg.), brothers (acc., masc., pl.), and the built-in subject of the verb εἶδεν (third-person singular). This built-in pronoun is the subject of the clause.
  - This means the participle's parsing matches the built-in he/she/it of the main verb. That is why "he" is supplied in the translation of the participle.

- Τότε Ἡρῴδης <u>λάθρᾳ καλέσας τοὺς μάγους</u> ἠκρίβωσεν παρ᾽ αὐτῶν τὸν χρόνον . . . (Matt 2:7)

  Then *after* **he** secretly *called* the magi, Herod learned from them the time . . .

  - Participle Parsing: aor., act., ptc., nom., masc., sg., καλέω.
  - There are two "actors" in this section: Herod (nom., masc., sg.) and the Magi (acc., masc., pl.). In this case the built-in pronoun is not necessary because the Greek has provided the subject (Herod).

- □ This means the participle's parsing matches Herod. That is why "he" is supplied in the translation of the participle.

- θερίσομεν μὴ ἐκλυόμενοι (Gal 6:9)

  We will reap *if **we** do not give up.*

  - □ Participle Parsing: pres., m/p., ptc., nom., masc., pl., ἐκλύω.
  - □ There is only one "actor" in this section, the "we" built into the main verb θερίσομεν (which is first-person plural).
  - □ The participle's parsing matches the built-in pronoun. That is why "we" is supplied in the translation of the participle.

- γνόντες τὸν θεὸν οὐχ ὡς θεὸν ἐδόξασαν (Rom 1:21)

  *Although **they** knew God, they did not honor him as God.*

  - □ Participle Parsing: aor., act., ptc., nom., masc., pl., γινώσκω.
  - □ There are two "actors" in this section: God (acc., masc., sg.) and the built-in subject of the verb (third-person pl.).
  - □ This means the participle's parsing matches the built-in subject of the verb. That is why "they" is supplied in the translation of the participle.

9.2.2
The Tense of a
Participle

As mentioned before, a present-tense participle *usually* indicates an action concurrent with the main verb, while aorist and perfect-tense participles *usually* indicates action prior to the action of the main verb.

The tense of participles is yet another example of how it is often difficult to translate Greek into good English. Often present participles end up being translated as past tense. Notice this example:

- Περιπατῶν δὲ παρὰ τὴν θάλασσαν τῆς Γαλιλαίας εἶδεν δύο ἀδελφούς (Matt 4:18)

  *While **he** walked by the sea of Galilee he saw two brothers.*

  - □ Participle Parsing: pres., act., ptc., nom., masc., sg., περιπατέω.
  - □ The participle is present and would more accurately be translated as *while walking* by the sea . . .

You should be able to clearly and accurately answer these questions. Use these flashcards http://quizlet.com/_7tfyd to memorize the answers:

9.3

THE LEAST YOU NEED TO KNOW

- What is a periphrastic participle?

- How is a present periphrastic construction made?

- How is an imperfect periphrastic construction made?

- How is a future periphrastic construction made?

- How is a perfect periphrastic construction made?

- What is a genitive absolute? How do you translate it?

- What is an adverbial participle?

- What function is an anarthrous participle usually performing?

- How is the subject of an adverbial participle determined?

- What does a present tense participle usually indicate?

- What does an aorist tense participle usually indicate?

- What does a perfect tense participle usually indicate?

Utilizing the Logos help file, Logos forums, Logos wiki, and videos provided, users should take the time this chapter to learn:

9.4

GREEK@LOGOS

- How to use the Exegetical Guide

  - See the article on the Exegetical Guide at https://support.logos.com

- How to use the Sermon Starter Guide

  - See the article on the Sermon Starter Guide at https://support.logos.com

- How to save and access your layouts

  - See the article on Layouts at https://support.logos.com

9.5

VOCABULARY

Word	Meaning	Type	Freq.	Derivatives
ἀμήν	amen, truly	partic.	129	Amen
δύο	two	adj.	135	duo
νεκρός, -ά, -όν	dead	adj.	128	*necrosis*
ὅταν	whenever	conj.	123	
αἰών, -ῶνος, ὁ	age, eternity	noun	122	eon
ἀρχιερεύς, -έως, ὁ	chief priest, high priest	noun	122	
δοῦλος, -ου, ὁ	slave, servant	noun	124	
δύναμις, -εως, ἡ	power, ability	noun	119	*dynamite*
ζωή, -ῆς, ἡ	life	noun	135	zoology
θάνατος, -ου, ὁ	death	noun	120	eu*thanasia*
φωνή, -ῆς, ἡ	sound	noun	139	*phone*
σύν	(+dat.) with	prep.	128	*syn*thesis
ἀποστέλλω	I send (away)	verb	132	*apostle*
ἀποστέλλω, ἀποστελῶ, ἀπέστειλα, ἀπέσταλκα, ἀπέσταλμαι, ἀπεστάλην				
βάλλω	I throw	verb	122	*ballistic*
βάλλω, βαλῶ, ἔβαλον, βέβληκα, βέβλημαι, ἐβλήθην				
βλέπω	I see	verb	133	
βλέπω, βλέψω, ἔβλεψα, ——, ——, ——				
παραδίδωμι	I entrust, hand over, betray	verb	119	
παραδίδωμι, παραδώσω, παρέδωκα, παραδέδωκα, παραδέδομαι, παρεδόθην				

Chapter 9 Exercises

LEARNING ACTIVITY 1: VOCABULARY (1 HOUR)

Be sure to review previous vocabulary as well as learn the new.

Completed: _____ Yes _____ No

LEARNING ACTIVITY 2: NOUN ENDINGS AND PARTICIPLES
(15 MINUTES RECOMMENDED)

Make sure you have the Participles Song memorized.

◢ Recommended for learning declension endings: ◤
The Singing Grammarian: The Participles Song.

Completed: _____ Yes _____ No

LEARNING ACTIVITY 3: READING (30–60 MINUTES
RECOMMENDED)

Read through chapter 9.

Completed: _____ Yes _____ No

LEARNING ACTIVITY 4: PARTICIPLE FUNCTION
(2–3 HOURS RECOMMENDED)

The following 17 verses each have a participle functioning in a particular way. All of these functions are represented on the Participle Flowchart. **For each verse**, you will provide a translation, parsing of the participle, and decide which function the participle is performing. In the line in which you declare participle function, *explain the steps through the flowchart that brings you to that decision.* (Go ahead and use Bible software for help.)

(1) adjectival, (2) substantival, (3) predicate of equative verb, (4) predicate of verbless clause, (5) genitive absolute, (6) present periphrastic, (7) imperfect periphrastic, (8) future periphrastic, (9) perfect periphrastic, (10) adverbial/simultaneous temporal, (11) adverbial/preceding temporal, (12) adverbial/purpose or result, (13) adverbial/cause, (14) adverbial/condition, (15) adverbial/concession, (16) adverbial/means, (17) adverbial/manner, (18) adverbial/redundant.

1. τὸ ὕδωρ τὸ ζῶν (John 4:11)

    a. Participle parsing: _____
        _____

    b. Translation: _____
        _____

    c. Participle function: _____
        _____

2. Καὶ πορευομένων αὐτῶν ἐν τῇ ὁδῷ εἶπέν τις πρὸς αὐτόν· (Luke 9:57)

    a. Participle parsing: _____
        _____

    b. Translation: _____
        _____

    c. Participle function: _____
        _____

3. Ἀκούοντα δὲ τὰ ἔθνη ἔχαιρον καὶ ἐδόξαζον τὸν λόγον τοῦ κυρίου
    (Acts 13:48)

    a. Participle parsing: _____
        _____

    b. Translation: _____
        _____

    c. Participle function: _____
        _____

4. ἦν γὰρ διδάσκων αὐτούς (Matt 7:29)

    a. Participle parsing: _____
        _____

    b. Translation: _____
        _____

    c. Participle function: _____
        _____

5. θερίσομεν μὴ ἐκλυόμενοι (Gal 6:9)

   a. Participle parsing: _____

   _____

   b. Translation: _____

   _____

   c. Participle function: _____

   _____

6. καὶ ἐγένετο νεφέλη ἐπισκιάζουσα αὐτοῖς (Mark 9:7)

   a. Participle parsing: _____

   _____

   b. Translation: _____

   _____

   c. Participle function: _____

   _____

7. καὶ νηστεύσας ἡμέρας τεσσεράκοντα καὶ νύκτας τεσσεράκοντα
   (Matt 4:2)

   a. Participle parsing: _____

   _____

   b. Translation: _____

   _____

   c. Participle function: _____

   _____

8. Τῇ γὰρ χάριτί ἐστε σεσιῳσμένοι διὰ πίστεως· (Eph 2:8)

   a. Participle parsing: _____

   _____

   b. Translation: _____

   _____

   c. Participle function: _____

   _____

9. οἱ πατριάρχαι ζηλώσαντες τὸν Ἰωσὴφ ἀπέδοντο εἰς Αἴγυπτον (Acts 7:9)

    a. Participle parsing: _____

    _____

    b. Translation: _____

    _____

    c. Participle function: _____

    _____

10. θεὸς γάρ ἐστιν ὁ ἐνεργῶν ἐν ὑμῖν (Phil 2:13)

    a. Participle parsing: _____

    _____

    b. Translation: _____

    _____

    c. Participle function: _____

    _____

11. ἥμαρτον παραδοὺς αἷμα ἀθῷον (Matt 27:4)

    a. Participle parsing: _____

    _____

    b. Translation: _____

    _____

    c. Participle function: _____

    _____

12. ἔσεσθε γὰρ εἰς ἀέρα λαλοῦντες. (1 Cor 14:9)

    a. Participle parsing: _____

    _____

    b. Translation: _____

    _____

    c. Participle function: _____

    _____

13. ζῶν γὰρ ὁ λόγος τοῦ θεοῦ (Heb 4:12)

    a. Participle parsing: _____

    _____

    b. Translation: _____

    _____

    c. Participle function: _____

    _____

14. Μαρία δὲ εἱστήκει πρὸς τῷ μνημείῳ ἔξω κλαίουσα (John 20:11)

    a. Participle parsing: _____

    _____

    b. Translation: _____

    _____

    c. Participle function: _____

    _____

15. εὑρήκαμεν τὸν Μεσσίαν, ὅ ἐστιν μεθερμηνευόμενον χριστός. (John 1:41)

    a. Participle parsing: _____

    _____

    b. Translation: _____

    _____

    c. Participle function: _____

    _____

16. γνόντες τὸν θεὸν οὐχ ὡς θεὸν ἐδόξασαν (Rom 1:21)

    a. Participle parsing: _____

    _____

    b. Translation: _____

    _____

    c. Participle function: _____

    _____

17. ἀποκριθεὶς ὁ Ἰησοῦς εἶπεν· ἐξομολογοῦμαί σοι, πάτερ (Matt 11:25)

   a. Participle parsing: _____

       _____

   b. Translation: _____

       _____

   c. Participle function: _____

       _____

18. πᾶς ὁ πίνων ἐκ τοῦ ὕδατος τούτου διψήσει πάλιν (John 4:13)

   a. Participle parsing: _____

       _____

   b. Translation: _____

       _____

   c. Participle function: _____

       _____

LEARNING ACTIVITY 5: BIBLE SOFTWARE WORK (2.5–3.5 HOURS RECOMMENDED)

Τῇ ἐπαύριον πάλιν εἱστήκει ὁ Ἰωάννης καὶ ἐκ τῶν μαθητῶν

_____

αὐτοῦ δύο καὶ ἐμβλέψας τῷ Ἰησοῦ περιπατοῦντι λέγει·ἴδε ὁ

_____

ἀμνὸς τοῦ θεοῦ. καὶ ἤκουσαν οἱ δύο μαθηταὶ αὐτοῦ λαλοῦντος

_____

καὶ ἠκολούθησαν τῷ Ἰησοῦ. στραφεὶς δὲ ὁ Ἰησοῦς καὶ

_____

θεασάμενος αὐτοὺς ἀκολουθοῦντας λέγει αὐτοῖς· τί ζητεῖτε; οἱ

_____

δὲ εἶπαν αὐτῷ· ῥαββί, ὃ λέγεται μεθερμηνευόμενον διδάσκαλε,

_____

ποῦ μένεις; λέγει αὐτοῖς· {ἔρχεσθε καὶ ὄψεσθε}. ἦλθαν οὖν καὶ

_____ Come and see. _____

εἶδαν ποῦ μένει καὶ παρ᾽ αὐτῷ ἔμειναν τὴν ἡμέραν ἐκείνην·

_____

ὥρα ἦν ὡς δεκάτη. Ἦν Ἀνδρέας ὁ ἀδελφὸς Σίμωνος Πέτρου εἷς

_____

ἐκ τῶν δύο τῶν ἀκουσάντων παρὰ Ἰωάννου καὶ

_____

ἀκολουθησάντων αὐτῷ· (John 1:35–40)

_____

(1) Underline all verbs and circle the participles in the passage above.

(2) In the provided lines, provide an exaggerated translation (i.e., work on accurately translating verbs, cases, and participles without worrying about a smooth or terse English style).

(3) Write out each participle in the passage, parse it, and describe its function.

1. Participle 1: _____

   a. parsing: _____

   b. function: _____

2. Participle 2: _____

   a. parsing: _____

   b. function: _____

3. Participle 3: _____

    a. parsing: _____

    b. function: _____

4. Participle 4: _____

    a. parsing: _____

    b. function: _____

5. Participle 5: _____

    a. parsing: _____

    b. function: _____

6. Participle 6: _____

    a. parsing: _____

    b. function: _____

7. Participle 7: _____

    a. parsing: _____

    b. function: _____

8. Participle 8: _____

    a. parsing: _____

    b. function: _____

9. Participle 9: _____

    a. parsing: _____

    b. function: _____

10. Read about ἐμβλέπω *and* θεάομαι in Louw-Nida as well as a theological dictionary (NIDNTTE, EDNT, or little Kittel). Both of these words are used in the passage. After reading about these words,

describe the significance of the how the words are used in the passage: _____

_____

_____

_____

_____

Where is the only other place ἐμβλέπω is used in the Gospel of John? _____

_____

LEARNING ACTIVITY 6: REVIEW (30 MINUTES RECOMMENDED)

You've just spent a good amount of time learning a lot of new things. Take 30 minutes to do one final read through of the chapter to solidify the knowledge, and make sure you can answer all of the questions in the *Least You Need to Know* section. Use the online flashcards link in the chapter to quiz yourself on the questions.

Completed: _____ Yes _____ No

9.6 THE SECOND TIME AROUND

The second time around is all about practice in working with participles. Through the exercises, continually focus on how the participle flows through the participle flowchart. You would also do well to try your best to memorize the flowchart and try and recreate it from memory.

ADVANCED EXERCISES (CH. 9)

Learning Activity 1: Vocabulary (1 hour)

Learn your assigned vocabulary list from Appendix A. Be sure to review previous vocabulary as well as learn the new. Knowledge of this new vocabulary is assumed in the translation work.

Completed: _____ Yes _____ No

Learning Activity 2: Reading (1 hour)

Read chapter 9 of the textbook again.

Completed: _____ Yes _____ No

Learning Activity 3: Memorize Participle Flowchart (1.5 hours)

Using the blank flowchart in the practice tables, memorize the participle flowchart by filling it out from memory.

Completed: _____ Yes _____ No

Learning Activity 4: Parsing Practice (1.5 hours)

Drill yourself using either ParseGreek or Paradigms Master Pro

- For ParseGreek, choose any vocabulary range in conjunction with chapter <u>8</u> grammar concepts

- For Paradigms Master Pro, work on **All Verbs: Participles**.

Completed: _____ Yes _____ No

Learning Activity 5: Translation (4 hours)

Be ready to parse any participles that appear in the sentences *and identify their functions using the participle flowchart.* The following sentences assume knowledge of all words occurring up to 40 times (chs. 1–11 and lists 1–9).

Καὶ ἐλθόντος αὐτοῦ εἰς τὸ ἱερὸν προσῆλθον αὐτῷ διδάσκοντι οἱ ἀρχιερεῖς καὶ οἱ πρεσβύτεροι τοῦ λαοῦ λέγοντες· <u>ἐν ποίᾳ</u> (by what) ἐξουσίᾳ ταῦτα ποιεῖς; καὶ τίς σοι ἔδωκεν τὴν ἐξουσίαν ταύτην; ἀποκριθεὶς δὲ ὁ Ἰησοῦς εἶπεν αὐτοῖς· ἐρωτήσω ὑμᾶς κἀγὼ λόγον ἕνα, <u>ὃν ἐὰν εἴπητέ</u> (if you tell) μοι κἀγὼ ὑμῖν ἐρῶ <u>ἐν ποίᾳ</u> (by what) ἐξουσίᾳ ταῦτα ποιῶ· (Matt 21:23–24)

_____

_____

_____

_____

_____

_____

Καὶ καταβαινόντων αὐτῶν ἐκ τοῦ ὄρους ἐνετείλατο (ordered) αὐτοῖς ὁ Ἰησοῦς λέγων· μηδενὶ εἴπητε (tell) τὸ ὅραμα (the vision) ἕως οὗ ὁ υἱὸς τοῦ ἀνθρώπου ἐκ νεκρῶν ἐγερθῇ. Καὶ ἐπηρώτησαν αὐτὸν οἱ μαθηταὶ λέγοντες· τί οὖν οἱ γραμματεῖς λέγουσιν ὅτι Ἡλίαν (Elijah) δεῖ ἐλθεῖν (must come) πρῶτον; ὁ δὲ ἀποκριθεὶς εἶπεν· Ἡλίας (Elijah) μὲν ἔρχεται καὶ ἀποκαταστήσει (will restore) πάντα· λέγω δὲ ὑμῖν ὅτι Ἡλίας (Elijah) ἤδη ἦλθεν, καὶ οὐκ ἐπέγνωσαν αὐτὸν ἀλλὰ ἐποίησαν ἐν αὐτῷ ὅσα ἠθέλησαν· οὕτως καὶ ὁ υἱὸς τοῦ ἀνθρώπου μέλλει πάσχειν (to suffer) ὑπ᾽ αὐτῶν. (Matt 17:9–12)

_____

_____

_____

_____

_____

οὕτως γὰρ ἠγάπησεν ὁ θεὸς τὸν κόσμον, ὥστε τὸν υἱὸν τὸν μονογενῆ (only begotten) ἔδωκεν, ἵνα πᾶς ὁ πιστεύων εἰς αὐτὸν μὴ ἀπόληται ἀλλ᾽ ἔχῃ ζωὴν αἰώνιον. ὁ πιστεύων εἰς αὐτὸν οὐ κρίνεται· ὁ δὲ μὴ πιστεύων ἤδη κέκριται, ὅτι μὴ πεπίστευκεν εἰς τὸ ὄνομα τοῦ μονογενοῦς (only begotten) υἱοῦ τοῦ θεοῦ. αὕτη δέ ἐστιν ἡ κρίσις ὅτι τὸ φῶς ἐλήλυθεν εἰς τὸν κόσμον καὶ ἠγάπησαν οἱ ἄνθρωποι μᾶλλον τὸ σκότος (darkness) ἢ τὸ φῶς· ἦν γὰρ αὐτῶν πονηρὰ τὰ ἔργα. (John 3:16, 18–19)

_____

_____

_____

_____

_____

ἦλθεν γὰρ Ἰωάννης μήτε (neither) ἐσθίων μήτε (nor) πίνων, καὶ λέγουσιν· δαιμόνιον ἔχει. ἦλθεν ὁ υἱὸς τοῦ ἀνθρώπου ἐσθίων καὶ πίνων, καὶ λέγουσιν· ἰδοὺ ἄνθρωπος φάγος (glutton) καὶ οἰνοπότης (drunkard) (Matt 11:18–19)

_____

_____

_____

_____

ἀποκριθεὶς δὲ ὁ Ἰησοῦς εἶπεν πρὸς αὐτόν· <u>ἄφες ἄρτι</u> (let it be now), οὕτως γὰρ <u>πρέπον</u> (proper) ἐστὶν ἡμῖν <u>πληρῶσαι</u> (to fulfill) πᾶσαν δικαιοσύνην. τότε ἀφίησιν αὐτόν. βαπτισθεὶς δὲ ὁ Ἰησοῦς <u>εὐθὺς</u> (immediately) ἀνέβη ἀπὸ τοῦ ὕδατος· καὶ ἰδοὺ ἠνεῴχθησαν αὐτῷ οἱ οὐρανοί, καὶ εἶδεν τὸ πνεῦμα τοῦ θεοῦ καταβαῖνον <u>ὡσεὶ περιστερὰν</u> (like a dove) καὶ ἐρχόμενον ἐπ᾽ αὐτόν· (Matt 3:15–16)

_____

_____

_____

_____

_____

_____

CHAPTER 10

Nonindicative Verbs Made Simple

What's the Point: Wandering outside of the indicative mood takes us into the realm of possibility. When a command is given, request is made, or a possibility is discussed, verbs in the subjunctive, imperative, and optative are used. About 3,556 of these nonindicative verbs occur, which is almost one in four verbs in the New Testament.

Indicative verbs are finite verbs that have a proper subject. Finite verbs are the main verb in their clause. This is in contrast to participles and infinitives, which are not true verbs, but verbals. These verbs will have a proper subject and be the main verb in their clause. Whereas the indicative mood *indicates* reality, nonindicative moods do not indicate reality, just possibility in varying degrees.

10.1

INTRODUCTION

Compare the following sentences:

- I am going to have pizza for supper. (indicative)

- You should have pizza for supper. (subjunctive)

- I may have pizza for supper. (subjunctive)

- Do not have pizza for supper! (imperative)

- Mom, please make pizza for supper. (imperative)

- If I just so happen to have pizza for supper, I'll let you know. (optative)

Only the first sentence expresses certainty of action, all of the remaining sentences have varying degrees of probability regarding the action of having pizza for supper. If these sentences were in

Greek, the first sentence would use the indicative mood, because it is the only sentence that represents certainty. Whereas the Greek indicative mood expresses certainty about the action of the verb, the nonindicative moods express probability. The subjunctive mood expresses something that is probable. The imperative mood is used to express commands or requests. The optative mood expresses an action that is only remotely possible.

10.2
SUBJUNCTIVE
MOOD

The subjunctive mood expresses probability. In other words, Greek uses the subjunctive mood to indicate an action that will probably happen. In English we also have this mood, and most often express it with words like "may," "might," "should," "could," "when," "whenever," or "if." These are the words that will be used when translating the subjunctive mood as well. Sometimes an English translator will have to supply one of these words to the translation, but quite often the Greek will have one of these words in the sentence already. Like the indicative mood, the subjunctive is a "true" verb—it will have a subject and be the main verb in its clause (most often, dependent clauses). Subjunctive verb parsing will be the same as indicative verbs—tense, voice, mood, person, number, lexical form.

10.2.1
How the Subjunctive
is Formed

The subjunctive occurs primarily in the present and aorist tenses. Of the 1,868 subjunctive verbs, only 10 of them are perfect tense, and 7 are future tense.

The primary marker of the subjunctive mood is a lengthened connecting vowel. Whereas in the indicative mood the connecting vowel is *epsilon* (ε) or *omicron* (ο), in the subjunctive the connecting vowel is *eta* (η) or *omega* (ω).

Table 61: Subjunctive Formation

tense		connecting vowel		inflected endings
Present	First principal part	active	ω/η	primary active
		mid/pass	ω/η	primary middle/passive
Aorist (NO augment)	Third principal part (*first aor. ends with σ,*[1] *second aor. does not*)	active	ω/η	primary active
		middle	ω/η	primary middle/passive
	Sixth principal part (*ends with* θ)[2]	passive	ω/η	primary active

As you may notice from the formation table, the subjunctive can be tricky to spot in Greek because it is often similar to the indicative. Like the infinitive and participle, second aorist forms end up looking just like present tense, but with a different stem.

An additional difficulty with the subjunctive is the lengthened connecting vowel. If you remember from our discussion of contract verbs (§5.3.2), stems that end with a vowel lengthen. This means that indicative contract verbs and subjunctive verbs are sometimes identical. In the *Biblical Greek Made Simple* approach, you do not need to worry about identifying these troublesome forms, just know that they exist and let your Bible software do the work for you.

As with all other verb forms, the usual quirks of Greek appear in the subjunctive: contract verbs contract (and thus look identical), liquid verbs cause *sigmas* to disappear, the aorist *sigma* will interact with stop consonants, and the *theta* of the aorist passive can also interact with a stop consonant.

---

1. Remember that σα has been the regular indicator of the aorist in the other verb forms.

2. Remember from the indicative mood that some verbs drop the *theta* (θ).

Table 62: λύω Subjunctive Paradigm

Parts		First λύω		Third ἔλυσα				Sixth ἐλύθην
tense and voice		present active	present m/p	aorist active	second aorist active	aorist middle	second aorist middle	aorist passive
sg	1	λύω	λύωμαι	λύσω	λάβω	λύσωμαι	λάβωμαι	λυθῶ
	2	λύῃς	λύῃ	λύσῃς	λάβῃς	λύσῃ	λάβῃ	λυθῇς
	3	λύῃ	λύηται	λύσῃ	λάβῃ	λύσηται	λάβηται	λυθῇ
pl	1	λύωμεν	λυώμεθα	λύσωμεν	λάβωμεν	λυσώμεθα	λαβώμεθα	λυθῶμεν
	2	λύητε	λύησθε	λύσητε	λάβητε	λύσησθε	λάβησθε	λυθῆτε
	3	λύωσι	λύωνται	λύσωσι	λάβωσι	λύσωνται	λάβωνται	λυθῶσι

Table 63: εἰμί Subjunctive Paradigm[1]

person and number		present	translation
sg	first	ὦ	I might be
	second	ἦς	you might be
	third	ᾖ	he/she/it might be
pl	first	ὦμεν	we might be
	second	ἦτε	y'all might be
	third	ὦσι (ν)	they might be

10.2.2 Understanding Subjunctive Translation and Function

The tense of a subjunctive retains its essential difference (internal aspect vs. external aspect) although when it comes to translating, the present and aorist subjunctive often end up being translated the same.

As mentioned previously, sometimes the Greek sentence will have a word that provides the necessary context for it to convey possible reality (like "if," "whenever," etc.). At other times the translator needs

1. Notice how the subjunctive forms of εἰμί are identical to the present active subjunctive forms of λύω, without the λυ.

to provide one of the many words that will make the reality possible ("could," "might," etc.). For the most part, when a subjunctive is the main verb of an independent clause, then the translator needs to add a helper word. *Most subjunctives, though, live in dependent clauses.* Remember that dependent clauses function like an adjective, adverb, or noun for the independent clause. Dependent clauses, particularly those with a subjunctive verb, frequently are introduced by particular words.

The following table summarizes most of the subjunctive functions and translation, with examples following.

Table 64: Subjunctive Function Table

	Function	Cue	Translation
Independent clause	hortatory *to exhort or command*	first-person plural	"let us"
	deliberative *asks a question*	interrogative pronoun, ποῦ, and/or question mark (;)	"shall we . . . ?"
	emphatic negation *a decisive negation*	aorist with οὐ μή	"never"
	prohibitive *a negative command*	aorist with μή	"do not"
Dependent clause	purpose or result *purpose/result of the independent clause*	ἵνα or ὅπως	"(in order) to" "as a result"
	indefinite relative *acts as a noun or as an adjective*	indefinite relative pronoun or relative pronoun (ὅς, ἥ, ὅν) sometimes followed by ἄν or [independent clause lacks substantive]	"who(ever)," etc. *[acts as subject or object]* "may," "might," etc.
	temporal *tells when the main verb action will occur*	ὅταν, ἕως, ἄχρι, μέχρι	*translate cue word*
	conditional	ἐάν	*translate cue word*

10.2.2.1

*Subjunctive in
Independent Clauses*

1. HORTATORY: A hortatory subjunctive offers an exhortation or command. The subjunctive verb will usually be a first-person plural verb, and is usually translated with "let us."

   □ <u>διέλθωμεν</u> εἰς τὸ πέραν (Mark 4:35)
   <u>Let us go</u> to the other side.

2. DELIBERATIVE: A deliberative subjunctive asks a question, real or rhetorical. The subjunctive will frequently be introduced with an interrogative pronoun, and the NT editors will add the question mark (;). Translation is usually "shall we . . . ?"

   □ μὴ μεριμνήσητε λέγοντες· τί <u>φάγωμεν</u>; (Matt 6:31)
   Do not be anxious, saying, '*What* <u>should we eat</u>?'

3. EMPHATIC NEGATION: An aorist subjunctive with οὐ μή is a decisive negation, usually translated as "never . . . !"

   □ οἱ λόγοι μου οὐ μὴ <u>παρέλθωσιν</u> (Matt 24:35)
   My words will *never* <u>pass away</u>.

4. PROHIBITIVE: An aorist subjunctive with μή is a negative command, usually translated as "do not."

   □ μὴ <u>φοβηθῇς</u> παραλαβεῖν Μαρίαν τὴν γυναῖκά σου (Matt 1:20)
   Do not <u>be afraid</u> to take Mary as your wife.

10.2.2.2

*Subjunctive in
Dependent Clauses*

1. PURPOSE or RESULT: As with infinitives and participles, purpose or result is sometimes hard to differentiate. The subjunctive dependent clause will be introduced by ἵνα or ὅπως. ἵνα is usually translated as "so that" or "(in order) to."

   □ προσηνέχθησαν αὐτῷ παιδία ἵνα τὰς χεῖρας <u>ἐπιθῇ</u> αὐτοῖς (Matt 19:13)
   Children were brought to him *in order that* <u>he might lay</u> his hands on them.

2. INDEFINITE RELATIVE: An indefinite relative dependent clause functions as the subject or object of the independent clause.

    ◦ [ὃς δ' ἂν <u>πίῃ</u> ἐκ τοῦ ὕδατος] οὗ ἐγὼ δώσω αὐτῷ, οὐ μὴ διψήσει εἰς τὸν αἰῶνα (John 4:14)
       [But *whoever* <u>drinks</u> of the water] that I will give him will never thirst again.

3. TEMPORAL: A subjunctive in a temporal dependent clause tells when the main verb object will occur.

    ◦ τὸν θάνατον τοῦ κυρίου καταγγέλλετε ἄχρι οὗ <u>ἔλθῃ</u> (1 Cor 11:26)
       you do proclaim the Lord's death *until* <u>he comes</u>.

10.2.3 Conditional Sentences

Whenever you see the word "if" in an English or Greek sentence, you are entering a conditional sentence, and expecting a "then" independent clause to follow. "If" indicates possibility, thus subjunctive verbs are often found in conditional sentences.

There is a further element of logic in Greek conditional sentences that is not present in English conditional sentences, and this logic is difficult to add to an English translation (yet another great reason to know how to work with Greek!). Greek conditional sentences are complex beasts, but basically the grammar of a conditional sentence determines whether or not the conditional sentence is already determined to be true or false. In English we assume "if" sentences are up in the air, but not so in Greek.

1. When the "if" verb is indicative in Greek, the sentence is NOT up in the air—the writer/speaker assumes the sentence to be true or false already.

    a. It is assumed false if the tense is imperfect, aorist, or pluperfect.

    b. It is assumed true if the tense is any of the remaining indicative tenses.

2. When the "if" verb is subjunctive, the assumption is then undetermined but possible (like an English conditional sentence).

3. When the "if" verb is optative, the assumption is undetermined but only remotely possible (like an English conditional sentence).

Observe the following sentences:

- εἰ [if] γὰρ <u>ἐπιστεύετε</u> Μωϋσεῖ, ἐπιστεύετε ἂν ἐμοί (John 5:46)

  If you <u>believed</u> Moses, [then] you would believe me.

  - The verb in the "if" dependent clause is imperfect indicative. Indicative = determined. Imperfect = false.
  - *In other words*, the assumption is that they *do not believe* Moses. The translation could be "If you believed Moses, then you would believe me—but you didn't, so you don't."

- εἰ [if] δὲ ἐν πνεύματι θεοῦ ἐγὼ <u>ἐκβάλλω</u> τὰ δαιμόνια, ἄρα ἔφθασεν ἐφ᾽ ὑμᾶς ἡ βασιλεία τοῦ θεοῦ. (Matt 12:28)

  But if it is by the Spirit of God that <u>I cast out</u> demons, then the kingdom of God has come to you.

  - Whereas in the English translation you may be wondering if Jesus is casting out demons by the Spirit of God, the Greek is crystal clear. The "if" verb in the dependent clause is present indicative. Indicative = determined. Present = true.
  - *In other words*, the assumption is that *it is* by the Spirit of God that Jesus casts out demons.

- καὶ εἶπεν αὐτῷ· ταῦτά σοι πάντα δώσω, ἐὰν [if] πεσὼν <u>προσκυνήσῃς</u> μοι. (Matt 4:9)

  And he said to him, "All these I will give you, if you will <u>fall down</u> and worship me."

  - The verb in the "if" dependent clause is subjunctive. Subjunctive = possible.

      ▫   *In other words*, there is no assumption on the devil's part here. The conditional sentence indicates only the possibility that Jesus might fall down and worship him.

The imperative mood expresses probability, but in a different way than the subjunctive. The imperative is used primarily to express commands or requests. This means that the imperative only expresses the will or desire of the speaker—the ball is in the court of the person receiving the command or request. For the most part, an imperative going from a superior to an inferior is a command, and an imperative going from an inferior to a superior is a request. Like the indicative and subjunctive, the imperative is a "true" verb—it will have a subject and be the main verb in its clause. Imperative verb parsing will be the same as indicative verbs—tense, voice, mood, person, number, lexical form.

10.3

IMPERATIVE

The imperative occurs primarily in the present and aorist tenses. Of the 1,636 imperative verbs, only 4 of them are perfect tense. The imperative also has no first-person forms.

10.3.1

How the Imperative is Formed

    The primary marker of the imperative mood is a unique set of endings. Whereas the indicative and subjunctive used primary and secondary endings, imperative has its own set of endings.

Table 65: Imperative Endings

Person		Active set	Middle/Passive set
singular	second	-(ε), ς, θι/τι, ον	σο, (ου), αι
	third	τω	σθω
plural	second	τε	σθε
	third	τωσαν	σθωσαν

    Like participles and the subjunctive, second aorist forms end up looking just like present tense, but with a different stem. If you recall the primary active endings, you will notice that the second-person plural (active) ending is identical. This results in identical forms of verbs, with context being the only indicator of whether or not a verb is an indicative or an imperative. The other difficult factor with imperatives is the second-person singular forms of verbs, which vary in their endings.

Table 66: Imperative Formation

tense		connecting vowel		inflected endings
Present	first principal part	active	ε	active set
		mid/pass	ε	middle/passive set
Aorist (NO augment)	third principal part (*first aor. ends with* σα, *second aor. does not*)	active	second aor: ε	active set
		middle	second aor: ε	middle/passive set
	sixth principal part (*ends with* θη)	passive	-	active set

As with all other verb forms, the usual quirks of Greek appear in the imperative: contract verbs contract, liquid verbs cause *sigmas* to disappear, the aorist *sigma* will interact with stop consonants, the θ of the aorist passive may drop out. Remember, in the *Biblical Greek Made Simple* approach, you don't need to worry about memorizing these endings, just be familiar with them and understand how imperatives are formed.

Table 67: λύω Imperative Paradigm

Parts		First λύω		Third ἔλυσα				Sixth ἐλύθην
tense and voice		present active	present m/p	aorist active	second aorist active	aorist middle	second aorist middle	aorist passive
sg	second	λῦε	λύου	λῦσον	λάβε	λῦσαι	λαβοῦ	λύθητι
	third	λυέτω	λυέσθω	λυσάτω	λαβέτω	λυσάσθω	λαβέσθω	λυθήτω
pl	second	λύετε	λύεσθε	λύσατε	λάβετε	λύσασθε	λάβεσθε	λύθητε
	third	λυέτωσαν	λυέσθωσαν	λυσάτωσαν	λαβέτωσαν	λυσάσθωσαν	λαβέσθωσαν	λυθήτωσαν

Table 68: εἰμί Imperative Paradigm

person		present	translation
sg	second	ἴσθι	you be!
	third	ἔστω (ἤτω)	let him/her/it be!
pl	second	ἔστε	y'all be!
	third	ἔστωσαν	let them be!

As with the subjunctive, the nuance of the aorist or present tense imperative is often difficult to translate into English. Remember that aorist represents external aspect and that present represents internal aspect. This means that an aorist imperative is generally commanding the action as a whole, while the present commands an action in progress.

10.3.2
Understanding
Imperative
Translation and
Function

1. COMMAND: The most common function of the imperative is to issue a command, usually from a superior to an inferior.

   □ ἀκολούθει μοι (Mark 2:14)
   Follow me!

   □ εἰ τις ὑμῶν λείπεται σοφίας, αἰτείτω παρὰ τοῦ . . . θεοῦ (Jas 1:5)
   If anyone of you lacks wisdom, let him ask of God.

      - Notice that the English translation of this third-person imperative sounds more like a suggestion in English, but it is a command in Greek.

2. PROHIBITION: A prohibition is also a command, but it is a command NOT to do something. The negative μή will occur with the imperative.

   □ μὴ μεθύσκεσθε οἴνῳ (Eph 5:18)
   Do not get drunk with wine.

3. REQUEST: An imperative becomes a request when spoken from an inferior to a superior. Whereas God frequently

speaks with imperatives to command, imperatives occur in prayers (and elsewhere) to make requests.

- <u>ἐλθέτω</u> ἡ βασιλεία σου· <u>γενηθήτω</u> τὸ θέλημά σου (Matt 6:10–11)

Let your kingdom <u>come</u>, <u>let</u> your will <u>be done</u>.

10.4
OPTATIVE

The optative mood is one step further away from possibility than the subjunctive—it is the subjunctive's weaker brother. There are only 68 optative verbs in the NT, that's less than 1% of the verbs in the NT. They are translated in a similar way to the subjunctive. Since the optative occurs so infrequently, it is best to simply consult Wallace's *Greek Grammar Beyond the Basics* when you run into an optative.

The optative occurs only in the present and aorist tenses. The active endings are a bit like μι verb endings, and a bit like secondary endings—we'll call them μι-ish endings. The marker of the optative is an iota (ι) after the stem or connecting vowel; think of it as the *oiptative* mood.

Table 69: Optative Formation

tense		connecting vowel		optative marker	optative endings
Present	first principal part	active	o	ι	μι-ish endings
		mid/pass	o	ι	secondary middle/passive
Aorist (NO augment)	third principal part (*first aor. ends with* σα,[1] *second aor. does not*)	active	2Aor: o	ι	μι-ish endings
		middle	2Aor: o	ι	secondary middle/passive
	sixth principal part (*ends with* θε)[2]	passive	-	ιη	secondary active

1. Remember that σα has been the regular indicator of the aorist in the other verb forms.

2. Remember from the indicative mood that some verbs drop the *theta* (θ).

Table 70: λύω Optative Paradigm

Parts		First λύω		Third ἐλύσα				Sixth ἐλύθην
tense and voice		present active	present m/p	aorist active	second aorist active	aorist middle	second aorist middle	aorist passive
sg	first	λύοιμι	λυοίμην	λύσαιμι	λάβοιμι	λυσαίμην	λαβοίμην	λυθείην
	second	λύοις	λύοιο	λύσαις	λάβοις	λύσαιο	λάβοιο	λυθείης
	third	λύοι	λύοιτο	λύσαι	λάβοι	λύσαιτο	λάβοιτο	λυθείη
pl	first	λύοιμεν	λυοίμεθα	λύσαιμεν	λάβοιμεν	λυσαίμεθα	λαβοίμεθα	λυθείημεν
	second	λύοιτε	λύοισθε	λύσαιτε	λάβοιτε	λύσαισθε	λάβοισθε	λυθείητε
	third	λύοιεν	λύοιντο	λύσαιεν	λάβοιεν	λύσαιντο	λάβοιντο	λυθείησαν

You should be able to clearly and accurately answer these questions. Use these flashcards http://quizlet.com/_7tfyk to memorize the answers:

- What are the three nonindicative moods?

- What do the three nonindicative moods indicate?

- What tenses occur in the nonindicative moods?

- What does the subjunctive mood indicate?

- What kinds of words in English are used to translate a subjunctive?

- What is the grammatical marker of the subjunctive?

- What kind of clause are most subjunctives found in?

- What is a conditional sentence?

- What does it mean to say a Greek conditional sentence has been determined?

- How does Greek show that a conditional sentence has been undetermined?

- How does Greek show that a conditional sentence is possible?

- How does Greek show that a conditional sentence is only remotely possible?

- What is the most common function of the imperative mood?

- What is the grammatical marker of the imperative?

- What does the optative mood indicate?

- What is the grammatical marker of the optative?

10.6
GREEK@LOGOS

Utilizing the Logos help file, Logos forums, Logos wiki, and videos provided, users should take the time this chapter to learn:

- How to use the Timeline

  - See the article on the Timeline tool at https://support.logos.com

- How to use the Bible Sense Lexicon

  - See the article on the Bible Sense Lexicon at https://support.logos.com (*Note: the Bible Sense Lexicon decides the semantic domain of each word for you. While this is an incredibly useful tool, it is still important for you to be able to do this for yourself, which is why this resource is only being introduced now.*)

10.7

VOCABULARY

Word	Meaning	Type	Freq.	Derivatives
ἴδιος, -α, -ον	one's own; his/her/its	adj.	114	*idiom*
μόνος, -η, -ον	alone, only	adj.	114	*monologue*
ὅλος, -η, -ον	(adj.) whole, complete; (adv.) entirely	adj.	109	*whole*
ἀγάπη, -ης, ἡ	love	noun	116	
βασιλεύς, -έως, ὁ	king	noun	115	*basilica*
ἐκκλησία, -ας, ἡ	assembly, church, congregation	noun	114	*ecclesiology*
οἶκος, -ου, ὁ	house, home	noun	114	*ecology*
ὅσος, -α, -ον	as great as, as many as, as much, how much	pron.	110	
ἀπέρχομαι	I depart, go away	verb	117	
ἀπέρχομαι, ἀπελεύσομαι, ἀπῆλθον, ἀπελήλυθα, ——, ——				
ἀποθνήσκω	I die, am about to die, am freed from	verb	111	
ἀποθνήσκω, ἀποθανοῦμαι, ἀπέθανον, ——, ——, ——				
ζητέω	I seek, desire	verb	117	
ζητέω, ζητήσω, ἐζήτησα, ἐζήτηκα, ——, ἐζητήθην				
κρίνω	I judge, decide, prefer	verb	114	*critic*
κρίνω, κρινῶ, ἔκρινα, κέκρικα, κέκριμαι, ἐκρίθην				
μέλλω	I am about to, intend	verb	109	
μέλλω, μελλήσω, ἔμελλον, ——, ——, ——				
μένω	I remain, live, abide, stay	verb	118	
μένω, μενῶ, ἔμεινα, μεμένηκα, ——, ——				
παρακαλέω	I call, urge, exhort, comfort, beseech	verb	109	*paraclete*
παρακαλέω, ——, παρεκάλεσα, ——, παρακέκλημαι, παρεκλήθην				

Chapter 10 Exercises

LEARNING ACTIVITY 1: VOCABULARY (1 HOUR)
Be sure to review previous vocabulary as well as learn the new.
Completed: _____ Yes _____ No

LEARNING ACTIVITY 2: SUBJUNCTIVE AND IMPERATIVE (15–30 MINUTES RECOMMENDED)
Take some time to become as familiar as possible with the imperative and subjunctive. Sing along with the songs below over an over until you have memorized them.

◢ Recommended for learning
about the imperative and subjunctive moods: ◣
The Singing Grammarian: (1) The Subjunctive Song,
(2) The Imperative Song.

Completed: _____ Yes _____ No

LEARNING ACTIVITY 3: CHAPTER READING (30–60 MINUTES RECOMMENDED)
Read through the chapter.
Completed: _____ Yes _____ No

LEARNING ACTIVITY 4: SUBJUNCTIVE AND IMPERATIVE FORMATION (1.5–2 HOURS RECOMMENDED)
Photocopy the following page. Using just your mind and the textbook, take the following subjunctive and imperative forms of λύω and place them into the table, then check your work. Do it numerous times until you can do it correctly.

There are also several forms that are identical to indicative forms of λύω. Circle the items in the tables below that are identical to indicative forms.

λυθῶμεν, λύου, λυέτω, λύω, λυέσθωσαν, λυθῇ, λύῃς, λύῃ, λύθητι,
λύωμεν, λύσωσι, λυθῶ, λύητε, λυέτωσαν, λυσάσθω, λυθήτω,
λῦσον, λύωσι, λυσάσθωσαν, λύεσθε, λυσάτω, λύωνται, λύσατε,
λύσωμεν, λύωμαι, λύσησθε, λῦσαι, λύῃ, λύηται, λυθῇς, λύησθε,
λύσω, λύσῃ, λύσητε, λύσωμαι, λυέσθω, λύσῃ, λύσηται, λυθῆτε,
λυσώμεθα, λύετε, λύθητε, λύσωνται, λυώμεθα, λυθήτωσαν,
λύσασθε, λυθῶσι, λύσῃς, λῦε, λυσάτωσαν

Subjunctive

tense and voice		present active	present m/p	aorist active	aorist m/p	aorist passive
sg	first					
	second					
	third					
pl	first					
	second					
	third					

Imperative

tense and voice		present active	present m/p	aorist active	aorist m/p	aorist passive
sg	second					
	third					
pl	second					
	third					

LEARNING ACTIVITY 5: SUBJUNCTIVE AND IMPERATIVE FUNCTION (1–1.5 HOURS RECOMMENDED)

Identify the functions of the subjunctive and imperative verbs in the following verses.

1. <u>ἆρον</u> τὸν κράβαττόν σου καὶ περιπάτει (John 5:11)

   a. Parsing: _____

   _____

b. Function: _____

_____

c. How do you know this is the function? _____

_____

2. οἱ μαθηταὶ τῷ Ἰησοῦ λέγοντες· ποῦ θέλεις <u>ἑτοιμάσωμέν</u> σοι φαγεῖν τὸ πάσχα; (Matt 26:17)

a. Parsing: _____

_____

b. Function: _____

_____

c. How do you know this is the function? _____

_____

3. ταῦτα δὲ γέγραπται ἵνα <u>πιστεύ[σ]ητε</u> ὅτι Ἰησοῦς ἐστιν ὁ χριστός (John 20:31)

a. Parsing: _____

_____

b. Function: _____

_____

c. How do you know this is the function? _____

_____

4. πώρωσις ἀπὸ μέρους τῷ Ἰσραὴλ γέγονεν ἄχρι οὗ τὸ πλήρωμα τῶν ἐθνῶν <u>εἰσέλθῃ</u> (Rom 11:25)

a. Parsing: _____

_____

b. Function: _____

_____

c. How do you know this is the function? _____

_____

5. Ἐν τῷ μεταξὺ ἠρώτων αὐτὸν οἱ μαθηταὶ λέγοντες· ῥαββί, <u>φάγε</u>. (John 4:31)

   a. Parsing: _____

   _____

   b. Function: _____

   _____

   c. How do you know this is the function? _____

   _____

6. μακάριος ἀνὴρ οὗ οὐ μὴ <u>λογίσηται</u> κύριος ἁμαρτίαν (Rom 4:8)

   a. Parsing: _____

   _____

   b. Function: _____

   _____

   c. How do you know this is the function? _____

   _____

7. Μὴ <u>ἀγαπᾶτε</u> τὸν κόσμον μηδὲ τὰ ἐν τῷ κόσμῳ. (1 John 2:15)

   a. Parsing: _____

   _____

   b. Function: _____

   _____

   c. How do you know this is the function? _____

   _____

8. ὃς ἐὰν οὖν <u>λύσῃ</u> μίαν τῶν ἐντολῶν τούτων τῶν ἐλαχίστων . . . (Matt 5:19)

   a. Parsing: _____

   _____

   b. Function: _____

   _____

c. How do you know this is the function? _____

_____

9. μὴ <u>σφραγίσῃς</u> τοὺς λόγους τῆς προφητείας τοῦ βιβλίου τούτου
(Rev 22:10)

a. Parsing: _____

_____

b. Function: _____

_____

c. How do you know this is the function? _____

_____

LEARNING ACTIVITY 6: BIBLE SOFTWARE WORK
(3–3.5 HOURS RECOMMENDED)

In the provided lines, provide an exaggerated translation (i.e., work on accurately translating verbs, cases, and participles without worrying about a smooth or economical English style).

Μὴ ταρασσέσθω ὑμῶν ἡ καρδία· πιστεύετε εἰς τὸν θεὸν καὶ εἰς

_____

ἐμὲ πιστεύετε. ἐν τῇ οἰκίᾳ τοῦ πατρός μου μοναὶ πολλαί εἰσιν·

_____

εἰ δὲ μή, εἶπον ἂν ὑμῖν ὅτι πορεύομαι {ἑτοιμάσαι} τόπον ὑμῖν;
_____ to prepare _____

καὶ ἐὰν πορευθῶ καὶ ἑτοιμάσω τόπον ὑμῖν, πάλιν ἔρχομαι καὶ

_____

παραλήμψομαι ὑμᾶς πρὸς ἐμαυτόν, ἵνα ὅπου εἰμὶ ἐγὼ καὶ

_____

ὑμεῖς ἦτε. καὶ ὅπου [ἐγὼ] ὑπάγω οἴδατε τὴν ὁδόν. (John 14:1–4)

Using your Bible software, identify all subjunctive and imperative verbs in the above section to fill the lists below. In the "function" line, also describe why you know that is the function. After you are done, create a translation above.

1. nonindicative verb 1: _____

   a. parsing: _____
   _____

   b. function: _____
   _____

2. nonindicative verb 2: _____

   a. parsing: _____
   _____

   b. function: _____
   _____

3. nonindicative verb 3: _____

   a. parsing: _____
   _____

   b. function: _____
   _____

4. nonindicative verb 4: _____

   a. parsing: _____
   _____

   b. function: _____
   _____

5. Word Study: Read about τἀράσσω in Louw-Nida and a theological dictionary.

   a. Using your Bible software, find where else this occurs in the NT: _____

   _____

   _____

   b. Which Gospel uses this word the most? _____

   c. Take a few minutes to look at how this word is used in John.

   d. Given your reading of the lexicon and theological dictionary, as well as how it is used in John, describe the significance of this word in the Gospel of John, and our passage in particular:

   _____

   _____

   _____

   _____

   _____

   _____

   _____

LEARNING ACTIVITY 7: REVIEW (30 MINUTES RECOMMENDED)
You've just spent a good amount of time learning a lot of new things. Take 30 minutes to do one final read through of the chapter to solidify the knowledge, and make sure you can answer all of the questions in the *Least You Need to Know* section. Use the online flashcards link in the chapter to quiz yourself on the questions.
Completed: _____ Yes _____ No

10.8
THE SECOND
TIME AROUND
Second time around students should focus on the formation tables so that the λύω subjunctive and imperative paradigms can be created from memory. The optative is so infrequent that you do not need to focus on it, even in the second time around.

ADVANCED EXERCISES (CH. 10)

Learning Activity 1: Vocabulary (1 hour)
Learn your assigned vocabulary list from Appendix A. Be sure to review previous vocabulary as well as learn the new. Knowledge of this new vocabulary is assumed in the translation work.
Completed: _____ Yes _____ No

Learning Activity 2: Reading (1 hour)
Read chapter 10 of the textbook again.
Completed: _____ Yes _____ No

Learning Activity 3: Memorize Paradigms (30 minutes)
Memorize the subjunctive and imperative paradigms using *The Singing Grammarian* songs. Practice filling in the paradigms from memory using the practice tables.
Completed: _____ Yes _____ No

Learning Activity 4: Parsing Practice (1.5 hours)
Drill yourself using either ParseGreek or Paradigms Master Pro

- For ParseGreek, choose any vocabulary range in conjunction with chapter 10 grammar concepts

- For Paradigms Master Pro,
  Verbs by moods: All verbs–Subjunctives and Imperatives

Completed: _____ Yes _____ No

Learning Activity 5 Parsing Work (1.5 hours)

1. γένηται _____

   _____

2. ᾖ _____

   _____

3. εἴπῃ _____

   _____

4. ὕπαγε _____

_____

5. ποιήσω _____

_____

6. γίνεσθε _____

_____

7. ἔχητε _____

_____

8. εἴπωμεν _____

_____

9. ποιεῖτε _____

_____

10. ἀκούσωσιν _____

_____

11. εἰδῆτε _____

_____

12. πορεύου _____

_____

13. εἰδότες _____

_____

14. παραδοῖ _____

_____

15. ἄφες _____

_____

16. εἰσέλθῃ _____

_____

17. δῶμεν _____

_____

18. γράψον _____

_____

19. πληρωθῇ _____

_____

20. εἴπατε _____

_____

21. ἀποθάνῃ _____

_____

22. γένοιτο _____

_____

Learning Activity 6: Translation (3.5 hours)

Translate the following sentences. Be ready to parse any nonindicative verbs that appear in the sentences and identify their functions. The following sentences assume knowledge of all words occurring up to 37 times (chs. 1–11 and lists 1–10). For difficult forms, consult the morphological information in Logos Bible Software.

Καὶ ἐγένετο ἐν τῷ εἶναι αὐτὸν (while he was) ἐν τόπῳ τινὶ προσευχόμενον, ὡς ἐπαύσατο (he had finished), εἶπέν τις τῶν μαθητῶν αὐτοῦ πρὸς αὐτόν· κύριε, δίδαξον ἡμᾶς προσεύχεσθαι (to pray), καθὼς καὶ Ἰωάννης ἐδίδαξεν τοὺς μαθητὰς αὐτοῦ. εἶπεν δὲ αὐτοῖς· ὅταν προσεύχησθε λέγετε·

Πάτερ, ἁγιασθήτω (hallowed) τὸ ὄνομά σου·

ἐλθέτω ἡ βασιλεία σου·

τὸν ἄρτον ἡμῶν τὸν ἐπιούσιον (daily) δίδου ἡμῖν τὸ καθ' ἡμέραν·

καὶ ἄφες ἡμῖν τὰς ἁμαρτίας ἡμῶν,

καὶ γὰρ αὐτοὶ ἀφίομεν παντὶ ὀφείλοντι (indebted) ἡμῖν·

καὶ μὴ εἰσενέγκῃς (bring) ἡμᾶς εἰς πειρασμόν (temptation). (Luke 11:1–4)

_____

_____

_____

_____

Ἐγόγγυζον (complained) οὖν οἱ Ἰουδαῖοι περὶ αὐτοῦ ὅτι εἶπεν· ἐγώ εἰμι ὁ ἄρτος ὁ καταβὰς ἐκ τοῦ οὐρανοῦ, καὶ ἔλεγον· οὐχ οὗτός ἐστιν Ἰησοῦς ὁ υἱὸς Ἰωσήφ (Joseph), οὗ ἡμεῖς οἴδαμεν τὸν πατέρα καὶ τὴν μητέρα; πῶς νῦν λέγει ὅτι ἐκ τοῦ οὐρανοῦ καταβέβηκα; ἀπεκρίθη Ἰησοῦς καὶ εἶπεν αὐτοῖς· μὴ γογγύζετε (complain) μετ' ἀλλήλων. (John 6:41–43)

_____

_____

_____

_____

οὕτως ὀφείλουσιν (ought) καὶ οἱ ἄνδρες ἀγαπᾶν (to love) τὰς ἑαυτῶν γυναῖκας ὡς τὰ ἑαυτῶν σώματα. ὁ ἀγαπῶν τὴν ἑαυτοῦ γυναῖκα ἑαυτὸν ἀγαπᾷ. Οὐδεὶς γάρ ποτε (ever) τὴν ἑαυτοῦ σάρκα ἐμίσησεν ἀλλὰ ἐκτρέφει (he nourishes) καὶ θάλπει (cares) αὐτήν, καθὼς καὶ ὁ Χριστὸς τὴν ἐκκλησίαν, ὅτι μέλη (members) ἐσμὲν τοῦ σώματος αὐτοῦ. ἀντὶ τούτου (for this reason) καταλείψει (will leave) ἄνθρωπος [τὸν] πατέρα καὶ [τὴν] μητέρα καὶ προσκολληθήσεται (will be joined) πρὸς τὴν γυναῖκα αὐτοῦ, καὶ ἔσονται οἱ δύο εἰς σάρκα μίαν. τὸ μυστήριον (mystery) τοῦτο μέγα ἐστίν· ἐγὼ δὲ λέγω εἰς Χριστὸν καὶ εἰς τὴν ἐκκλησίαν. πλὴν (however) καὶ ὑμεῖς οἱ καθ' ἕνα, ἕκαστος τὴν ἑαυτοῦ γυναῖκα οὕτως ἀγαπάτω ὡς ἑαυτόν, ἡ δὲ γυνὴ ἵνα φοβῆται τὸν ἄνδρα. (Eph 5:28–33)

_____

_____

_____

_____

_____

Infinitives Made Simple

What's the Point: While not quite as difficult or frequent as participles, infinitives are nonetheless another verbal form that is peppered throughout the NT. One out of every ten verb forms is an infinitive, so they occur quite often. Because infinitives are another hybrid form, this time part verb and part noun, they can function in numerous ways.

11.1 INFINITIVE DESCRIPTION

An infinitive is another hybrid word, part noun and part verb. Its meaning is derived from its verb stem, so its lexical form is a verb. Infinitives have their own unique set of endings (a small set), and are limited primarily to present tense (994) and aorist tense (1,242; 393 of these are second aorist forms). There are 49 perfect tense infinitives, and 5 future infinitives.[1]

Are these funky hybrid words in English too? Of course they are. *Like participles, infinitives describe action happening in and around the main verb.* Like a participle, the verbal part of an infinitive will often act adverbially or work with the main verb. Other times, an infinitive's noun characteristics will make the infinitive function as a substantive, usually the subject or object of the main verb. Like nouns, an infinitive can have an article, but *they only ever take neuter singular articles.* An infinitive in English usually has "to" in front of it, for example, "to go." This is often, but not always, a good way to translate a Greek infinitive.

11.2 HOW INFINITIVES ARE FORMED

Infinitives are indeclinable verbal forms, so they do not take primary or secondary endings like indicative verbs. They also do not take case

---

1. Four of the five future infinitives are ἔσεσθαι, the future infinitive form of εἰμί.

endings like participles. The simplicity of infinitives makes them easy to spot, although like participles they can do many things.

The following table breaks down how infinitives are formed, with commentary on the table below.

Table 71: Infinitive Formation

Tense			Voice						
				connecting vowel + ending = final ending					paradigm
Present	first principal part	active	ε	+	εν	=	ειν	λύειν
		mid/pass	ε	+	σθαι	=	εσθαι	λύεσθαι
Aorist (NO augment)	third principal part (*first aor. ends with* σα, *second aor. does not*)	active	-	+	ι	=	σαι	λῦσαι
		active (second aor.)	ε	+	εν	=	ειν	βαλεῖν
		middle	-	+	σθαι	=	σασθαι	λύσασθαι
		middle (second aor.)	ε	+	σθαι	=	εσθαι	βαλέσθαι
	sixth principal part (*ends with* θη)	passive	-	+	ναι	=	θηναι	λυθῆναι
Perfect	fourth/fifth principal part (WITH *reduplication*)	active	-	+	κεναι[1]	=	κεναι	λελυκέναι
		mid/pass	-	+	σθαι	=	σθαι	λελύσθαι

Infinitive formation is relatively straightforward because infinitives do not have case endings like participles, or person and number like indicative verbs. Keep in mind the following points as you study the table above:

1. The parsing of infinitives is the simplest of all inflected forms; tense, voice, part of speech (i.e., infinitive), lexical form.

---

1. Remember that a *kappa* (κ) suffix is characteristic of the perfect tense.

2. Notice that σα is still the aorist active and middle indicator, and θη is the aorist passive indicator.

3. Second aorist forms are recognized by the altered stem. The endings of a second aorist form are just like the present tense.

4. For the aorist active and middle, remember that the *sigma* is slippery and may disappear in liquid verbs (see §1.3.1 and §1.3.2).

5. For the aorist passive, remember that the θ sometimes disappears (§4.3.1.4).

6. Notice that reduplication is still the indicator of the perfect tense, and active forms still have a κ(ε) in the ending.

7. Like any contract verb form, a vowel at the end of a stem can collide with the connecting vowel and cause changes.

8. εἰμί occurs in a single infinitive form, εἶναι. Like εἰμί anywhere else, it does not have voice. So εἶναι is parsed as present infinitive.

11.3
WHAT AN INFINITIVE CAN DO

An infinitive has a wide range of uses, so like participles it is wise to consult Wallace's *Greek Grammar Beyond the Basics* when you are struggling over what an infinitive is doing, or questioning the decision of an English translation. The following information covers the most common usages. The infinitive (and its article) will be red, with the infinitive phrase underlined. The infinitive's translation will be *italicized*.

11.3.1
Infinitive as Subject (Nominative)

When there is no subject in the clause, an infinitive (or the infinitive phrase) may be acting as the subject. The infinitive as subject will frequently have a nominative neuter singular article, but not always.

• Ἐμοὶ γὰρ <u>τὸ ζῆν</u> Χριστὸς καὶ <u>τὸ ἀποθανεῖν</u> κέρδος. (Phil 1:21)

  For me, *to live* is Christ and *to die* is gain.

- This verse is two verbless clauses (the assumed verb is ἔστιν, "is")
- In both clauses, the infinitive has the nominative neuter singular article.

11.3.2
Infinitive as Object (Accusative)

When there is no object in the clause, an infinitive (or the infinitive phrase) may be acting as the object. The infinitive as object will frequently have an accusative neuter singular article, but not always. When the infinitive is the object the usual infinitive translation (adding "to" before it) does not always work.

- ἤδη ποτὲ ἀνεθάλετε <u>τὸ ὑπὲρ ἐμοῦ φρονεῖν</u> (Phil 4:10)

now at last you have revived *concern* for me.

11.3.3
Appositional Infinitive or Epexegetical Infinitive (Accusative)

When a clause already has an object (an accusative noun) and you ALSO have an infinitive (or infinitive phrase) with an accusative neuter article, it is acting alongside the actual direct object. Occasionally, a genitive infinitive may also function in this manner. Apposition and epexegetical are two roles a second accusative in the sentence can perform. In general, they are giving you more information about the object. The difference is subtle and not always easy to distinguish; in general apposition renames the object, while epexegetical further defines it (it exegetes the object a little bit for you). Another thing to note is that an epexegetical infinitive is essential to the sentence, it can't be removed without losing something. An appositional infinitive, though, can usually be removed without loss of meaning. However, sometimes even these distinctions do not work well. Just remember, it is a second accusative in the clause tied to the actual object.

- Τοῦτο γάρ ἐστιν θέλημα τοῦ θεοῦ, ὁ ἁγιασμὸς ὑμῶν, <u>ἀπέχεσθαι ὑμᾶς ἀπὸ τῆς πορνείας</u> (1 Thess 4:3)

For this is the will of God, your holiness: that you *abstain* from fornication.

- "the will of God" is the object of the clause, while "your holiness" is an epexegetical noun.

- □ "that you abstain from fornication" is the infinitive phrase, functioning in apposition.

- δέδωκα ὑμῖν τὴν ἐξουσίαν <u>τοῦ πατεῖν</u> ἐπάνω ὄφεων καὶ σκορπίων (Luke 10:19)

  I have given you authority *to tread* on snakes and scorpions.

  - □ "authority" is the object of the clause
  - □ The infinitive phrase is epexegetical, describing the object more.

11.3.4 Infinitive in Indirect Discourse

Often an infinitive can follow a verb (including a participle) of perception (e.g., "I know") or communication (e.g., "they said"), thus being in a section of direct or indirect speech. This type of infinitive will be anarthrous (i.e., no article). When an infinitive is functioning in this way, it is usually translated the same as the main verb in the sentence, usually an indicative or an imperative. It may be translated with the typical infinitive "to" in front, it may use "that," or quotation marks may indicate the indirect discourse.

- ὁ λέγων <u>ἐν αὐτῷ μένειν</u> . . . (1 John 2:6)

  The one who says '*I remain* in him' . . .

  - □ In this example the communication verb is a participle.
  - □ Notice how an acceptable translation would also be "The one who says *that he remains* in him . . ."

- τίνα με λέγετε εἶναι; (Mark 8:29)

  who do you say *that I am*.

  - □ In this example the main verb is a communication word.
  - □ The infinitive εἶναι ("to be") is translated as a first-person indicative.

11.3.5 Complementary Infinitive

If someone said to you "I want," you would say, "you want what?!" The verb "I want" demands some help; "I want *to eat* supper." Notice how "I want" needs an infinitive to complete its thought. This is what is called a complementary infinitive. Numerous Greek (and English) verbs demand some help from a complementary infinitive.

- καὶ ἤρξαντο τίλλειν στάχυας καὶ ἐσθίειν (Matt 12:1)

  And they began *to pluck* heads of grain and *to eat.*

11.3.6
Adverbial Infinitive

Like participles, the predominant function of an infinitive is adverbial. Unlike a participle, though, the construction of an adverbial infinitive makes the type of adverbial function clear. Most adverbial infinitives are preceded by the accusative neuter singular article (τό) AND a preposition. An adverbial infinitive can also be preceded by a conjunction. Occasionally just the infinitive by itself, or the infinitive with a genitive article can also act adverbially.

1. PURPOSE or RESULT: An infinitive or infinitive phrase can indicate the purpose or result of the main verb's action. These two functions are very closely linked and sometimes hard to tell apart. Words like *to, so that, in order to,* or *as a result* are often used to translate. The constructions can be: (1) just the infinitive, (2) τοῦ + infinitive, (3) εἰς τό + infinitive, or (4) ὥστε + infinitive.

   ▫ Μὴ νομίσητε ὅτι ἦλθον <u>καταλῦσαι</u> <u>τὸν νόμον</u> (Matt 5:17)

     Do not think that I have come *(in order) to destroy* the law

   ▫ καὶ ἀπήγαγον αὐτὸν <u>εἰς τὸ</u> <u>σταυρῶσαι</u> (Matt 27:31)

     And they led him away *to crucify* him.

2. PURPOSE: While the previous constructions can all indicate the purpose or result of the main verb, there are two particular constructions that indicate purpose. Words like *to, so that,* and *in order to* are often used to translate. The constructions can be: (1) πρὸς τό + infinitive or (2) ὡς + infinitive.[1]

---

1. ὡς + infinitive can also indicate result, but this is rare.

- ἐγὼ δὲ λέγω ὑμῖν ὅτι πᾶς ὁ βλέπων γυναῖκα <u>πρὸς τὸ</u> <u>ἐπιθυμῆσαι</u> . . . (Matt 5:28)

  But I say to you that anyone who looks at a woman *in order to lust* . . .

3. CAUSE: The infinitive phrase διὰ τό + infinitive will indicate *the cause of the main verb*. The translation is relatively straightforward, just translate διά as it should be: *because.*

   - καὶ εὐθέως ἐξανέτειλεν <u>διὰ τὸ μὴ</u> <u>ἔχειν</u> βάθος γῆς (Matt 13:5)

     And they sprang up quickly, *because they had* no depth of soil.

4. TIME: ANTECEDENT: The infinitive phrase μετὰ τό + infinitive can indicate an action that occurred *prior to* the action of the main verb. The translation is straightforward, simply translate μετὰ as it should be: *after.*

   - <u>μετὰ τὸ</u> <u>ἐγερθῆναί</u> <u>με</u> προάξω ὑμᾶς εἰς τὴν Γαλιλαίαν. (Matt 26:32)

     After I have been raised I will go before you into Galilee.

5. TIME: SIMULTANEOUS: The infinitive phrase ἐν τῷ + infinitive can indicate an action that occurs *at the same time as* the action of the main verb. The translation of this type uses *while* or *as.*

   - καὶ <u>ἐν τῷ</u> <u>σπείρειν</u> <u>αὐτὸν</u> ἃ μὲν ἔπεσεν παρὰ τὴν ὁδόν (Matt 13:4)

     And *while he sowed,* some seeds fell on the road.

6. TIME: SUBSEQUENT: The infinitive phrase can indicate an action that occurred <u>after</u> the action of the main verb. The construction will be (1) πρὸ τοῦ + infinitive, (2) πρὶν + infinitive, or (3) πρὶν ἤ + infinitive. The translation is straightforward, simply translate πρό or πρίν as they should be: *before.*

> □ ὁ πατὴρ ὑμῶν ὧν χρείαν ἔχετε πρὸ τοῦ ὑμᾶς αἰτῆσαι αὐτόν
> (Matt 6:8)
>
> Your Father knows what you need *before* you *ask* him.

**11.4
UNDERSTANDING
INFINITIVE
FUNCTION AND
TRANSLATION**

In the *Biblical Greek Made Simple* approach, you do not need to determine infinitive function and translation on your own. What you do need to do is understand how and why modern translators came to the decisions they have. Infinitive translation is more straightforward than participles, particularly adverbial participles. The following flowchart is a "determination device" for infinitives. As you come across Greek infinitives in the NT and study them in conjunction with English translation(s), take the time to see how the infinitive has flowed through the flowchart. The following points are items to note as you use and study the flowchart:

- A lone infinitive is the most flexible construction, as it can perform any function.

- Preposition + article + infinitive is the most common construction, and is ALWAYS adverbial.

- conjunction + infinitive is ALWAYS adverbial.

- If your infinitive has the article τό, your Bible software will parse it for you as nominative or accusative. This helps to determine if the infinitive is the subject (nominative), object (accusative), appositional (accusative), or epexegetical (accusative).

- While the standard "to _____" translation is adequate in some situations, it does not always work when bringing the infinitive into English. Sometimes the infinitive is translated more like an indicative, an imperative, or a participle.

- The adverbial functions in the flowchart are listed in order of frequency (i.e., purpose and result functions are the most common).

- Remember, the flowchart does not cover everything an infinitive can do. Consult Wallace's *Greek Grammar Beyond the Basics* to understand the other minor functions.

Table 72: Infinitive Flowchart

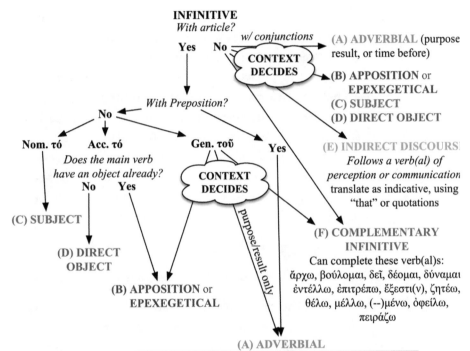

Adverbial Use	Constructions	Translation
purpose	just infinitive	"to"
or	εἰς τό + infinitive τοῦ + infinitive	"so that" "in order to"
result	ὥστε + infinitive	"as a result"
purpose	πρὸς τό + infinitive	"to" "so that"
	ὡς + infinitive	"in order to"
cause	διὰ τό + infinitive	"because"
time: antecedent	πρὸ τοῦ + infinitive πρίν (ἤ) + infinitive	"before"
time: simultaneous	ἐν τῷ + infinitive	"while" or "as"
time: subsequent	μετὰ τό + infinitive	"after"

11.4.1
The Sort-of-Subject
of an Infinitive

Because an adverbial infinitive is describing an action happening in and around the main verb, it only makes sense that there is someone or something doing the action at times. Like a participle, an infinitive is not a true verb, so it does not have a proper subject, but there is someone or something in the clause that is doing the action of the infinitive. This sort-of-subject will be an accusative noun or pronoun.[1] Sometimes it is the subject of the verbs, sometimes it is the object of the verb, for example: "I asked <u>him</u> *to go* wash his hands." Other times, though, the infinitive phrase will have an accusative acting as the sort-of-subject. Sometimes, an infinitive phrase will even have two accusatives, one acting as the sort-of-subject, and the other acting as the object of the infinitive. This accusative sort-of-subject is a time when an accusative (normally object) is translated as a nominative (normally subject). The following examples (taken from §11.3) highlight how the infinitive is connected to its sort-of-subject in the clause. The infinitive is in red, the phrase is <u>underlined</u>, its sort-of-subject will be blue, and the infinitive translation is *italicized*.

- *καὶ <u>ἐν τῷ σπείρειν αὐτὸν</u> ἃ μὲν ἔπεσεν παρὰ τὴν ὁδόν* (Matt 13:4)

   And *while* he *sowed*, some seeds fell on the road.

   ◦ The pronoun that is part of the infinitive phrase is in the accusative. The regular translation of αὐτόν would be "him," but because it is the sort-of-subject of the infinitive, it is translated as "he."

- *ὁ πατὴρ ὑμῶν ὧν χρείαν ἔχετε <u>πρὸ τοῦ ὑμᾶς αἰτῆσαι αὐτόν</u>* (Matt 6:8)

   Your Father knows what you need *before* you *ask* him.

   ◦ In this example there are two accusatives in the infinitive phrase. The first is the sort-of-subject, and the second is the object of the infinitive.

- *<u>μετὰ τὸ ἐγερθῆναί με</u> προάξω ὑμᾶς εἰς τὴν Γαλιλαίαν.* (Matt 26:32)

   After I *have been raised* I will go before you into Galilee.

---

1. It may also be a predicate nominative.

- □ Like the first example, the pronoun με is an accusative and would regularly be translated as "me." But because it is the sort-of-subject of the infinitive, it is translated as "I."

- καὶ ἀπήγαγον αὐτὸν <u>εἰς τὸ</u> <u>σταυρῶσαι</u> (Matt 27:31)

  And they led him away *to crucify* him.

  - □ Notice how in this translation there is no extra pronoun in the infinitive phrase. The object of the sentence is the sort-of-subject. To clarify this, most translations repeat the pronoun again at the end.

11.4.2
The Tense Of An Infinitive

As with participles, the tense of an infinitive is often hard to translate. Technically speaking, a present tense infinitive displays internal aspect, an aorist tense infinitive displays external aspect, and a perfect tense infinitive is stative.[1] However, when it comes to translating these aspectual differences of an infinitive into readable English, the tense does not usually come through. Present and aorist infinitives are usually translated the same, with perfect infinitives often having the word "have" or "had" in its translation. Remember, in the *Biblical Greek Made Simple* approach, you don't need to make these translation decisions, you just need to understand the choices modern English translations make, and understand what they have left out!

11.5
THE LEAST YOU NEED TO KNOW

You should be able to clearly and accurately answer these questions. Use these flashcards http://quizlet.com/_7tfyr to memorize the answers:

- What is an infinitive?

- What type of articles do infinitives take?

- What three tenses occur as infinitives?

- What are all of the components in infinitive parsing?

- What is the indicator for an aorist active or middle infinitive?

1. The aspect of the Greek tenses were discussed in §4.1.3.

- What is the indicator for an aorist passive infinitive?

- What is the indicator for a perfect active or middle/passive infinitive?

- What is the present active suffix for infinitives?

- What is the suffix for all middle/passive infinitives (except aorist passive)?

- What is a complementary infinitive?

- How are infinitives translated in indirect discourse?

- Why is an infinitive all by itself the most difficult to translate?

- An infinitive with an article and preposition is always performing what function?

- What is an infinitive phrase and what can it do?

- What is the "sort-of-subject" of an infinitive?

11.6
GREEK@LOGOS

Utilizing the Logos help file, Logos forums, Logos wiki, and videos provided, users should take the time in this chapter to learn:

- How to utilize Logos notes, highlighting, and clippings

  ▫ See the articles on Highlighting and Notes at https://support.logos.com

11.7

VOCABULARY

Word	Meaning	Type	Freq.	Derivatives
ἀγαθός, -ή, -όν	good, useful	adj.	102	
καλός, -ή, -όν	good, beautiful	adj.	100	calligraphy
ἐκεῖ	there, in that place	adv.	105	
ὅτε	when	conj.	103	
ἐξουσία, -ας, ἡ	authority, power	noun	102	
ὁδός, -οῦ, ἡ	way, road, journey; conduct	noun	100	odometer
ὀφθαλμός, -οῦ, ὁ	eye, sight	noun	100	ophthamology
ψυχή, -ῆς, ἡ	soul, life, self	noun	103	psychology
ὥρα, -ας, ἡ	hour; occasion, moment	noun	106	
πῶς	how?	partic.	103	
ἀλλήλων (-οις, -ους)	one other (of one another, to one another)	pron.	100	parallel
αἴρω	I raise, take up, take away	verb	101	aorta
αἴρω, ἀρῶ, ἦρα, ἦρκα, ἦρμαι, ἤρθην				
ἀνίστημι	I rise, get up; I raise	verb	108	
ἀνίστημι, ἀναστήσω, ἀνέστησα, ἀνέστηκα, ἀνέστημαι, ἀνεστάθην				
δεῖ	it is necessary	verb	101	
δεῖ [Imperfect, ἔδει]				
σῴζω (σώζω)	I save, heal, deliver, rescue	verb	106	
σῴζω (σώζω), σώσω, ἔσωσα, σέσωκα, σέσωμαι, ἐσώθην				
τίθημι	I put, place	verb	100	
τίθημι, θήσω, ἔθηκα, τέθεικα, τέθειμαι, ἐτέθην				

Chapter 11 Exercises

LEARNING ACTIVITY 1: VOCABULARY (1 HOUR)
Be sure to review previous vocabulary as well as learn the new.
Completed: _____Yes _____No

LEARNING ACTIVITY 2: INFINITIVE (15 MINUTES RECOMMENDED)
Take some time to become as familiar as possible with infinitive formation. Sing along with the song below over an over until you have memorized it.

◢ Recommended for learning about the infinitive: ◣
The Singing Grammarian: The Infinitives Song.

Completed: _____Yes _____No

LEARNING ACTIVITY 3: CHAPTER READING (30–60 MINUTES RECOMMENDED)
Read through the chapter.
Completed: _____Yes _____No

LEARNING ACTIVITY 4: INFINITIVE FORMATION (30 MINUTES RECOMMENDED)
Photocopy this page. Take the following forms of λύω and place them into the proper place in the infinitive paradigm table. Do it over and over until you can do it correctly and check your work with the textbook.

λύεσθαι, λελυκέναι, λύειν, λῦσαι, λυθῆναι, λελύσθαι, λύσασθαι

Present		Aorist			Perfect	
active	*mid/pass*	*active*	*middle*	*passive*	*active*	*mid/pass*

LEARNING ACTIVITY 5: INFINITIVE FUNCTION
(1–1.5 HOURS RECOMMENDED)

The following 14 verses each have an infinitive functioning in a particular way. All of these functions are represented on the Infinitive Flowchart. For each verse, you will provide a translation, parsing of the infinitive (use the software as needed), and decide which function the infinitive is performing. In the line in which you declare infinitive function, *explain the steps through the flowchart that brings you to that decision*—and don't be afraid to use English translations to help you decide.

(1) subject, (2) indirect discourse, (3) complementary infinitive, (4) adverbial/purpose or result, (5) adverbial/purpose, (6) adverbial/cause, (7) adverbial/antecedent, (8) adverbial/simultaneous, (9) adverbial/subsequent.

1. ἔρχονται Σαδδουκαῖοι πρὸς αὐτόν, οἵτινες λέγουσιν ἀνάστασιν μὴ εἶναι (Mark 12:18)

    a. Translation: _____

    _____

    b. Infinitive parsing: _____

    _____

    c. Infinitive function: _____

    _____

    _____

2. ἔπλησαν ἀμφότερα τὰ πλοῖα ὥστε βυθίζεσθαι αὐτά (Luke 5:7)

    a. Translation: _____

    _____

    b. Infinitive parsing: _____

    _____

    c. Infinitive function: _____

    _____

    _____

3. ἀλλ' ὁ πέμψας με βαπτίζειν ἐν ὕδατι (John 1:33)

    a. Translation: _____

    _____

    b. Infinitive parsing: _____

    _____

    c. Infinitive function: _____

    _____

    _____

4. ἀπ' ἄρτι λέγω ὑμῖν πρὸ τοῦ γενέσθαι (John 13:19)

    a. Translation: _____

    _____

    b. Infinitive parsing: _____

    _____

    c. Infinitive function: _____

    _____

    _____

5. γινώσκειν δὲ ὑμᾶς βούλομαι, ἀδελφοί, ὅτι . . . (Phil 1:12)

    a. Translation: _____

    _____

    b. Infinitive parsing: _____

    _____

    c. Infinitive function: _____

    _____

    _____

6. Ἰησοῦς οὐκ ἐπίστευεν αὐτὸν αὐτοῖς διὰ τὸ αὐτὸν γινώσκειν πάντας (John 2:24)

    a. Translation: _____

    _____

    b. Infinitive parsing: _____

        _____

    c. Infinitive function: _____

        _____

        _____

7. καὶ ἐγένετο ἐν τῷ σπείρειν ὃ μὲν ἔπεσεν παρὰ τὴν ὁδόν (Mark 4:4)

    a. Translation: _____

        _____

    b. Infinitive parsing: _____

        _____

    c. Infinitive function: _____

        _____

        _____

8. μετὰ δὲ τὸ παραδοθῆναι τὸν Ἰωάννην ἦλθεν ὁ Ἰησοῦς εἰς τὴν Γαλιλαίαν (Mark 1:14)

    a. Translation: _____

        _____

    b. Infinitive parsing: _____

        _____

    c. Infinitive function: _____

        _____

        _____

9. ὁ Πέτρος λέγει τῷ Ἰησοῦ· ῥαββί, καλόν ἐστιν ἡμᾶς ὧδε εἶναι (Mark 9:5)

    a. Translation: _____

        _____

    b. Infinitive parsing: _____

        _____

    c. Infinitive function: _____

        _____

**LEARNING ACTIVITY 6: BIBLE SOFTWARE WORK
(4.5–5.5 HOURS RECOMMENDED)**
(See instructions below.)

Ἦν δὲ ἄνθρωπος ἐκ τῶν Φαρισαίων, Νικόδημος ὄνομα αὐτῷ,

ἄρχων τῶν Ἰουδαίων· οὗτος ἦλθεν πρὸς αὐτὸν νυκτὸς καὶ

εἶπεν αὐτῷ· ῥαββί, οἴδαμεν ὅτι ἀπὸ θεοῦ ἐλήλυθας

διδάσκαλος· οὐδεὶς γὰρ δύναται ταῦτα τὰ σημεῖα <u>ποιεῖν</u> ἃ σὺ

ποιεῖς, ἐὰν μὴ ᾖ ὁ θεὸς μετ' αὐτοῦ. ἀπεκρίθη Ἰησοῦς καὶ εἶπεν

αὐτῷ· ἀμὴν ἀμὴν λέγω σοι, ἐὰν μή τις <u>γεννηθῇ</u> ἄνωθεν, οὐ

δύναται <u>ἰδεῖν</u> τὴν βασιλείαν τοῦ θεοῦ. λέγει πρὸς αὐτὸν [ὁ]

Νικόδημος· πῶς δύναται ἄνθρωπος <u>γεννηθῆναι</u> γέρων <u>ὤν</u>; μὴ

δύναται εἰς τὴν κοιλίαν τῆς μητρὸς αὐτοῦ δεύτερον <u>εἰσελθεῖν</u>

καὶ <u>γεννηθῆναι</u>; ἀπεκρίθη Ἰησοῦς· ἀμὴν ἀμὴν λέγω σοι, ἐὰν μή τις <u>γεννηθῇ</u> ἐξ ὕδατος καὶ πνεύματος, οὐ δύναται <u>εἰσελθεῖν</u>

εἰς τὴν βασιλείαν τοῦ θεοῦ. τὸ <u>γεγεννημένον</u> ἐκ τῆς σαρκὸς

σάρξ ἐστιν, καὶ τὸ <u>γεγεννημένον</u> ἐκ τοῦ πνεύματος πνεῦμά

ἐστιν. (John 3:1–6)

Fill in the information for the underlined verbs (which are either infinitives, subjunctives, or participles). In the "function" line, describe how you came to that decision.

1. verb 1: _____

   a. parsing: _____
          _____

   b. function: _____
          _____

2. verb 2: _____

   a. parsing: _____
          _____

   b. function: _____
          _____

3. verb 3: _____

   a. parsing: _____
          _____

   b. function: _____
          _____

4. verb 4: _____

   a. parsing: _____

       _____

   b. function: _____

       _____

5. verb 5: _____

   a. parsing: _____

       _____

   b. function: _____

       _____

6. verb 6: _____

   a. parsing: _____

       _____

   b. function: _____

       _____

7. verb 7: _____

   a. parsing: _____

       _____

   b. function: _____

       _____

8. verb 8: _____

   a. parsing: _____

       _____

   b. function: _____

       _____

9. verb 9: _____

   a. parsing: _____

       _____

b. function: _____

_____

10. verb 10: _____

a. parsing: _____

_____

b. function: _____

_____

11. verb 11: _____

a. parsing: _____

_____

b. function: _____

_____

12. verb 12: _____

a. parsing: _____

_____

b. function: _____

_____

13. Provide an exaggerated translation in the lines above. Focus on properly translating verb aspect and case/infinitive/participle/subjunctive usage, even if it means clunky english.

14. Most of us are familiar with the idea of being "born again." What you might not know is that some translations do not translate John 3:3 this way. Find out what word is translated "again" and read its entry in the *LALGNT* or *DBL Greek* lexicon.

a. Open the Information Pane. How do other English versions translate this? _____

_____

Search for the word in the Greek NT. Pay particular attention to how it is used in the Gospel of John.

b. In light of all of this, and considering the context of the passage, how do you prefer to translate this phrase? Explain why.

_____

_____

_____

_____

_____

_____

_____

15. Right-click on οἴδαμεν in John 3:2 (or if you have the information pane open, click on it). Notice that Logos indicates the likely Louw-Nida semantic domain (28.1). Read the Louw-Nida 28.1 entry. What are the implications for this passage?

_____

_____

_____

16. The verb γεννάω is used 5 times in this passage. Read about the word in *NIDNNTE, EDNT,* or *Little Kittel.* (1) Describe briefly the use of the word in the scriptures and (2) in view of what you read, what light does it shed on the current passage: _____

_____

_____

_____

_____

_____

_____

_____

_____

_____

LEARNING ACTIVITY 7: REVIEW (30 MINUTES RECOMMENDED)

You've just spent a good amount of time learning a lot of new things. Take 30 minutes to do one final read through of the chapter to solidify the knowledge, and make sure you can answer all of the questions in the *Least You Need to Know* section. Use the online flashcards link in the chapter to quiz yourself on the questions.

Completed: _____ Yes _____ No

11.8
THE SECOND
TIME AROUND

There are not many infinitive endings, so be sure the second time around that you have them memorized and can create a λύω table from memory. In addition, focus on the infinitive flowchart and analyze every infinitive you come across in exercises. Do your best to memorize the infinitive flowchart and practice creating it from memory.

ADVANCED EXERCISES (CH. 11)

Learning Activity 1: Vocabulary (1 hour)

Learn your assigned vocabulary list from Appendix A. Be sure to review previous vocabulary as well as learn the new. Knowledge of this new vocabulary is assumed in the translation work.

noteLearningList12(thefinallistofnewvocabulary)andLearning List 13 (Frequently used irregular forms) is highly recommended and will prepare you to read Greek using only your UBS Reader's Greek New Testament.

Completed: _____ Yes _____ No

Learning Activity 2: Reading (1 hour)

Read chapter 11 of the textbook again.

Completed: _____ Yes _____ No

Learning Activity 3: Memorize Infinitive Paradigms (15 minutes)

Memorize the infinitive paradigm, using *The Singing Grammarian* as help. Practice filling in the paradigms from memory using the practice tables.

Completed: _____ Yes _____ No

Learning Activity 4: Parsing Practice (1.5 hours)

Drill yourself using either ParseGreek or Paradigms Master Pro

- For ParseGreek, choose any vocabulary range in conjunction with ch.11 grammar concepts

- For Paradigms Master Pro, work on
  Verbs by moods: All verbs; Infinitives

Completed: _____ Yes _____ No

Learning Activity 5: Parsing Work (1.5 hours)

1. εἶναι _____

   _____

2. ποιῆσαι _____

   _____

3. ἐλθεῖν _____

   _____

4. ἰδεῖν _____

   _____

5. γενέσθαι _____

   _____

6. φαγεῖν _____

   _____

7. δοῦναι _____

   _____

8. ποιεῖν _____

   _____

9. λαβεῖν _____

   _____

10. λαλεῖν _____

    _____

11. λαλῆσαι _____

12. πορεύεσθαι _____

13. ἀποθανεῖν _____

14. ἀποκτεῖναι _____

15. γνῶναι _____

16. σῶσαι _____

17. ζῆν _____

18. παθεῖν _____

19. εἰδέναι _____

20. ἔρχεσθαι _____

Learning Activity 6: Translation (3.5–4 hours)

Translate the following sentences. Be ready to parse any infinitives that appear in the sentences and *identify their functions*. The following sentences assume knowledge of all words occurring up to 33 times (chs. 1–11 and lists 1–11). For difficult forms, consult the morphological information in Logos Bible Software.

Ἦσαν δὲ ἐν τῇ ὁδῷ ἀναβαίνοντες εἰς Ἱεροσόλυμα, καὶ ἦν <u>προάγων</u> (going before) αὐτοὺς ὁ Ἰησοῦς, καὶ <u>ἐθαμβοῦντο</u> (they were amazed), οἱ δὲ ἀκολουθοῦντες ἐφοβοῦντο. καὶ <u>παραλαβὼν</u> (lex = <u>παραλαμβάνω</u>) πάλιν τοὺς δώδεκα ἤρξατο αὐτοῖς λέγειν τὰ μέλλοντα αὐτῷ <u>συμβαίνειν</u> (to happen) ὅτι ἰδοὺ ἀναβαίνομεν εἰς Ἱεροσόλυμα, καὶ ὁ υἱὸς τοῦ ἀνθρώπου παραδοθήσεται τοῖς ἀρχιερεῦσιν καὶ τοῖς γραμματεῦσιν, καὶ <u>κατακρινοῦσιν</u> (will condemn) αὐτὸν θανάτῳ καὶ παραδώσουσιν αὐτὸν τοῖς ἔθνεσιν καὶ <u>ἐμπαίξουσιν</u> (will mock) αὐτῷ καὶ <u>ἐμπτύσουσιν</u> (will spit) αὐτῷ καὶ <u>μαστιγώσουσιν</u> (will flog) αὐτὸν καὶ ἀποκτενοῦσιν, καὶ μετὰ τρεῖς ἡμέρας ἀναστήσεται. (Mark 10:32–34)

_____

_____

_____

_____

_____

_____

Ἐγένετο δὲ ἐν σαββάτῳ <u>διαπορεύεσθαι αὐτὸν</u> (he was going through) διὰ <u>σπορίμων</u> (the grainfields), καὶ <u>ἔτιλλον</u> (plucked) οἱ μαθηταὶ αὐτοῦ καὶ ἤσθιον τοὺς <u>στάχυας</u> (heads of grain) <u>ψώχοντες</u> (rubbed) ταῖς χερσίν. τινὲς δὲ τῶν Φαρισαίων εἶπαν· τί ποιεῖτε ὃ οὐκ <u>ἔξεστιν</u> (lawful) τοῖς σάββασιν; καὶ ἀποκριθεὶς πρὸς αὐτοὺς εἶπεν ὁ Ἰησοῦς· οὐδὲ τοῦτο <u>ἀνέγνωτε</u> (read) ὃ ἐποίησεν Δαυὶδ ὅτε <u>ἐπείνασεν</u> (hungry) αὐτὸς καὶ οἱ μετ' αὐτοῦ ὄντες, ὡς εἰσῆλθεν εἰς τὸν οἶκον τοῦ θεοῦ καὶ τοὺς ἄρτους <u>τῆς προθέσεως</u> (of the presence) λαβὼν ἔφαγεν καὶ ἔδωκεν τοῖς μετ' αὐτοῦ, οὓς οὐκ <u>ἔξεστιν</u> (lawful) φαγεῖν εἰ μὴ μόνους <u>τοὺς ἱερεῖς</u> (the priests); (Luke 6:1–4)

_____

_____

_____

_____

_____

_____

Ἐγώ εἰμι ὁ ποιμήν (shepherd) ὁ καλὸς καὶ γινώσκω τὰ ἐμὰ καὶ γινώσκουσί με τὰ ἐμά, καθὼς γινώσκει με ὁ πατὴρ κἀγὼ γινώσκω τὸν πατέρα, καὶ τὴν ψυχήν μου τίθημι ὑπὲρ τῶν προβάτων. καὶ ἄλλα πρόβατα ἔχω ἃ οὐκ ἔστιν ἐκ τῆς αὐλῆς (fold) ταύτης· κἀκεῖνα δεῖ με ἀγαγεῖν καὶ τῆς φωνῆς μου ἀκούσουσιν, καὶ γενήσονται μία ποίμνη (flock), εἷς ποιμήν (shepherd). διὰ τοῦτό με ὁ πατὴρ ἀγαπᾷ ὅτι ἐγὼ τίθημι τὴν ψυχήν μου, ἵνα πάλιν λάβω αὐτήν. οὐδεὶς αἴρει αὐτὴν ἀπ' ἐμοῦ, ἀλλ' ἐγὼ τίθημι αὐτὴν ἀπ' ἐμαυτοῦ. ἐξουσίαν ἔχω θεῖναι αὐτήν, καὶ ἐξουσίαν ἔχω πάλιν λαβεῖν αὐτήν· ταύτην τὴν ἐντολὴν ἔλαβον παρὰ τοῦ πατρός μου. (John 10:14–18)

_____

_____

_____

_____

_____

_____

_____

CHAPTER 12

Where Do I Go From Here?

I f you've made it this far, your brain probably hurts—but it was worth it. The goal of the *Biblical Greek Made Simple* approach is to make the original language of the NT accessible to you without compromising a proper understanding of the grammar, while utilizing the latest tools. You may have heard your professor say, "a little bit of Greek is a dangerous thing." Just go on YouTube and you'll swiftly find that many preachers and teachers who do not really know Greek (or Hebrew) frequently use it and make mistakes. It was necessary to cover all of the basics in order to help you realize the complex machine that is Koine Greek. You hopefully realize now that working with the Greek NT alongside your preferred English translation is and will be incredibly rewarding for your study of the NT for life. No English translation is perfect and even the best translations lose something in their interpretive choices.

For those of you who have completed this book, you understand Greek and can work with it using your Bible software. Picking up and reading a Greek NT on its own is a different beast altogether— you are not yet equipped for that. With another few months of hard work, though, you can get to the point where you can start reading sections of the Greek NT with a nice Greek NT like *The UBS Greek New Testament: A Reader's Edition*. Here are some suggestions if you want to go beyond:

**12.1
GOING BEYOND**

1. Each chapter has a *Second Time Around* section at the end of the chapter. You will need to go through each chapter again, and this section will give you some tips on what

to focus on and offer some advanced information when necessary.

2. Additional exercises for another 11 weeks are included at the end of each chapter.

3. Practice parsing: I recommend ParseGreek for iOS and Android. If you do not have an iOS or Android device, then use the Mac/PC program called *Paradigms Master Pro*. The additional exercises will ask you to work with these programs.

4. Increase your vocabulary. Many of the popular full-year introductory grammars aim to teach you all words that occur 50 times or more. The first pass through this text has taught you all words that occur 100 times or more plus all proper nouns that occur 50 times, a total of 161 words. To get to 50 times or more, you need to learn 149 more words. I would actually recommend going a little bit further, to all words that occur 30 times or more, which would be 300 words more—461 words all together. I recommend this because the *Reader's Greek New Testament* (recommended above) works on the assumption that you know words occurring up to 30 times. To aid in your vocabulary acquisition, I have assembled 12 lists of words in Appendix A, placed into groups of about 25. A 13th list provides some of the highest frequency irregular verb forms.

5. STOP using your Bible software and start practicing reading. If you want to get to the point of reading Greek on your own, it is time to flex your brain muscle more. In addition to this grammar I also recommend the *Reader's Greek New Testament* mentioned above.

6. Print the following table out and practice filling out different words from memory.

**PRACTICE
TABLES**

Table 12.1: First Declension Endings (Normal)

	singular				plural			
	end of stem	*inflection*	**final form(s)**		*end of stem*	*inflection*	**final form**	
nominative	α/η	+	=		α/η	+	=	
genitive	α/η	+	=		α/η	+	=	
dative	α/η	+	=		α/η	+	=	
accusative	α/η	+	=		α/η	+	=	

Table 12.2: First Declension Endings (Second Type)

	singular				plural			
	end of stem	*inflection*	**final form(s)**		*end of stem*	*inflection*	**final form**	
nominative	α/η	+	=		α/η	+	=	
genitive	α/η	+	=		α/η	+	=	
dative	α/η	+	=		α/η	+	=	
accusative	α/η	+	=		α/η	+	=	

Table 12.3: Second Declension Endings (Mostly Masculine)

	singular				plural			
	end of stem	*inflection*	**final form(s)**		*end of stem*	*inflection*	**final form**	
nominative	ο	+	=		ο	+	=	
genitive	ο	+	=		ο	+	=	
dative	ο	+	=		ο	+	=	
accusative	ο	+	=		ο	+	=	

Table 12.4: Second Declension Endings (Neuter)

	singular			plural		
	end of stem	inflection	**final form(s)**	end of stem	inflection	**final form**
nominative	o	+	=	o	+	=
genitive	o	+	=	o	+	=
dative	o	+	=	o	+	=
accusative	o	+	=	o	+	=

Table 12.5: Verb Inflection Endings

	Primary		*Secondary*	
	Active	**Middle/Passive**	**Active**	**Middle/Passive**
	final ending	*μι verbs*		
1 sg				
2 sg				
3 sg				
1 pl				
2 pl				
3 pl				

Table 12.6: Indicative Slot Machine

principal part	tense & voice							
1st								
2nd								
3rd								
4th								
5th								
6th								

composes the principal part

Table 12.7: Indicative Tables

Parts	First				Second	
tense and voice	present active	present m/p	imperfect active	imperfect m/p	future active	future middle
1 sg						
2 sg						
3 sg						
1 pl						
2 pl						
3 pl						

Parts	Third		Fourth	Fifth	Sixth	
tense and voice	aorist active	aorist middle	perfect active	perfect middle	aorist passive	future passive
1 sg						
2 sg						
3 sg						
1 pl						
2 pl						
3 pl						

Parts	First λύω				Second λύσω	
tense and voice	present active	present m/p	imperfect active	imperfect m/p	future active	future middle
1 sg	λυ	λυ	λυ	λυ	λυ	λυ
2 sg	λυ	λυ	λυ	λυ	λυ	λυ
3 sg	λυ	λυ	λυ	λυ	λυ	λυ
1 pl	λυ	λυ	λυ	λυ	λυ	λυ
2 pl	λυ	λυ	λυ	λυ	λυ	λυ
3 pl	λυ	λυ	λυ	λυ	λυ	λυ

Parts	Third ἔλυσα		Fourth λέλυκα	Fifth λέλυμαι	Sixth ἐλύθην	
tense and voice	*aorist active*	*aorist middle*	*perfect active*	*perfect middle*	*aorist passive*	*future passive*
1 sg	λυ	λυ	λυ	λυ	λυ	λυ
2 sg	λυ	λυ	λυ	λυ	λυ	λυ
3 sg	λυ	λυ	λυ	λυ	λυ	λυ
1 pl	λυ	λυ	λυ	λυ	λυ	λυ
2 pl	λυ	λυ	λυ	λυ	λυ	λυ
3 pl	λυ	λυ	λυ	λυ	λυ	λυ

Table 12.8: Article Table

	Masculine		Feminine		Neuter	
	singular	*plural*	*singular*	*plural*	*singular*	*plural*
nominative						
genitive						
dative						
accusative						

Table 12.9: Noun Table

	singular	**plural**
nominative		
genitive		
dative		
plural		

Table 12.10: Participle Tables

PRESENT		active			middle / passive		
		masc.	*fem.*	*neut.*	*masc.*	*fem.*	*neut.*
sg.	*nom.*						
	gen.						
	dat.						
	acc.						
pl.	*nom.*						
	gen.						
	dat.						
	acc.						
AORIST		active			middle		
		masc.	*fem.*	*neut.*	*masc.*	*fem.*	*neut.*
sg.	*nom.*						
	gen.						
	dat.						
	acc.						
pl.	*nom.*						
	gen.						
	dat.						
	acc.						
					passive		
					masc.	*fem.*	*neut.*
sg.	*nom.*						
	gen.						
	dat.						
	acc.						
pl.	*nom.*						
	gen.						
	dat.						
	acc.						

PERFECT		Fourth Principal Part λελύχα			Fifth Principal Part λελύμαι		
		active			middle / passive		
		masc.	*fem.*	*neut.*	*masc.*	*fem.*	*neut.*
sg.	*nom.*						
	gen.						
	dat.						
	acc.						
pl.	*nom.*						
	gen.						
	dat.						
	acc.						

Table 12.11: Subjunctive Tables

Parts		First λύω		Third ἐλύσα		Sixth ἐλύθην
tense and voice		*present active*	*present m/p*	*aorist active*	*aorist m/p*	*aorist passive*
sg	first					
	second					
	third					
pl	first					
	second					
	third					

Table 12.12: Imperative Tables

Parts		First λύω		Third ἐλύσα		Sixth ἐλύθην
tense and voice		present active	present m/p	aorist active	aorist m/p	aorist passive
sg	second					
	third					
pl	second					
	third					

Table 12.13: Infinitive Table

Present		Aorist			Perfect	
active	mid/pas	active	middle	passive	active	mid/pas

Table 12.14: Blank Participle Flowchart

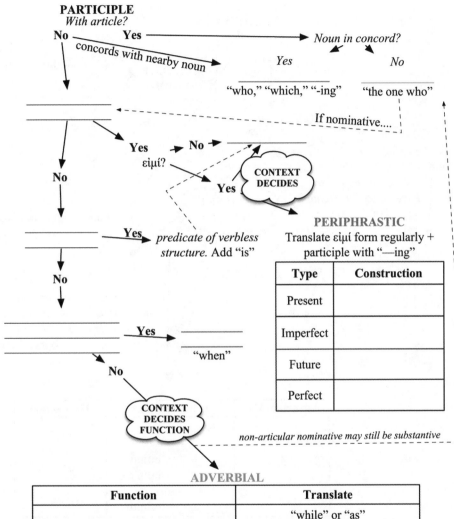

PARTICIPLE
With article?

No ——— **Yes** ———————————————→ *Noun in concord?*

concords with nearby noun →   *Yes*   *No*

"who," "which," "-ing"   "the one who"

If nominative....

No → **No** →

Yes
εἰμί?

No   **CONTEXT DECIDES**

Yes

PERIPHRASTIC
Translate εἰμί form regularly +
participle with "—ing"

Yes *predicate of verbless structure. Add "is"*

No

Type	Construction
Present	
Imperfect	
Future	
Perfect	

Yes ————
"when"

No

CONTEXT DECIDES FUNCTION

non-articular nominative may still be substantive

ADVERBIAL

Function	Translate
	"while" or "as"
	"after"
	"in order to" "thereby" "-ing"
	"because" "for" "since"
	"if"
	"although" "even though"
	"by" "with" "through"
	"with" "-ing"
	Translate the same as main verb

Table 12.15: Blank Infinitive Flowchart

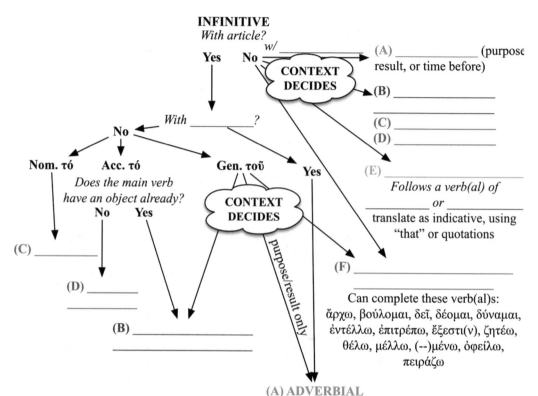

INFINITIVE
With article?

Yes   **No**

w/ _____ → (A) _____ (purpose
                  result, or time before)

CONTEXT DECIDES

(B) _____
    _____
(C) _____
(D) _____

With _____?

No

Nom. τό   **Acc. τό**   **Gen. τοῦ**   **Yes**

*Does the main verb
have an object already?*
No   **Yes**

CONTEXT DECIDES

(E) _____
Follows a verb(al) of
_____ *or* _____
translate as indicative, using
"that" or quotations

(C) _____

(D) _____
    _____

purpose/result only

(B) _____
    _____

(F) _____
    _____
Can complete these verb(al)s:
ἄρχω, βούλομαι, δεῖ, δέομαι, δύναμαι,
ἐντέλλω, ἐπιτρέπω, ἔξεστι(ν), ζητέω,
θέλω, μέλλω, (--)μένω, ὀφείλω,
πειράζω

(A) ADVERBIAL

Adverbial Use	Constructions	Translation
purpose	just _____	"to"
	-------	"so that"
or	_____ + infinitive	"in order to"
	_____ + infinitive	
result	-------	"as a result"
	_____ + infinitive	
purpose	_____ + infinitive	"to"
	-------	"so that"
	_____ + infinitive	"in order to"
cause	_____ + infinitive	"because"
time: before	_____ + infinitive	"before"

	_____ + infinitive	
time: during	_____ + infinitive	"while" or "as"
time: after	_____ + infinitive	"after"

Table 12.16: Subjunctive Function Table

	Function	Cue	Translation
Independent clause	hortatory *to exhort or command*		
	deliberative *asks a question*		
	emphatic negation *a decisive negation*		
	prohibitive *a negative command*		
Dependent clause	purpose or result *purpose/result of* *the independent clause*		
	indefinite relative *acts as a noun or as an adjective*		
	temporal *tells when the main* *verb action will occur*		
	conditional		

CHAPTER 13

Appendices

frequency: 99–90 **List 1**

Word	Meaning	Type	Freq.
αἷμα, -ματος, τό	blood	noun	97
ἀκολουθέω	I follow, accompany	verb	90
ἀπόλλυμι	I destroy, kill; I perish, die	verb	90
ἄρτος, -ου, ὁ	bread, loaf, food; burden	noun	97
γεννάω	I bear, beget, produce	verb	97
διδάσκω	I teach	verb	97
δικαιοσύνη, -ης, ἡ	righteousness, justice	noun	92
εἰρήνη, -ης, ἡ	peace, health	noun	92
ἐνώπιον	(+gen.) before, in front of	preposition	94
ἕτερος, -α, -ον	other, another, different	adjective	98
ἔτι	yet, still	adverb	93
θάλασσα, -ης, ἡ	sea, lake	noun	91
κάθημαι	I sit (down), live	verb	91
μηδείς, μηδεμία, μηδέν	no one, nothing	adjective	90
οἰκία, -ας, ἡ	house, home	noun	93
περιπατέω	I walk (around), live	verb	95
πίπτω	I fall	verb	90
πούς, ποδός, ὁ	foot	noun	93
τέκνον, -ου, τό	child, descendent	noun	99
τόπος, -ου, ὁ	place, position; opportunity	noun	94
φοβέω (mid. φοβέομαι)	I fear	verb	95

List 2   frequency: 89–79

Word	Meaning	Type	Freq.
ἀναβαίνω	I go up, come up, rise up, advance	verb	82
ἀπόστολος, -ου, ὁ	apostle	noun	80
ἄρχομαι (ἄρχω)	I begin; I rule over	verb	86
δίκαιος, -α, -ον	right, righteous, just	adjective	79
ἕκαστος, -η, -ον	each, every	adjective	82
ἐκβάλλω	I cast out, send out, drive out	verb	81
ἑπτά (indecl.)	seven	adjective	88
καιρός, -ου, ὁ	(appointed) time, season	noun	85
καταβαίνω	I come down, go down	verb	81
μᾶλλον	more, rather	adverb	81
μήτηρ, μητρός, ἡ	mother	noun	83
ὅπου (ποῦ)	where, whereas	conjunction	82
οὔτε	neither	conjunction	87
πέμπω	I send	verb	79
πληρόω	I fill, fulfill, complete	verb	86
προσέρχομαι	I come to	verb	86
προσεύχομαι	I pray	verb	85
ὑπάγω	I depart, go away; I draw off	verb	79
ὥστε	therefore, so that, in order that	conjunction	83

frequency: 78–70   **List 3**

Word	Meaning	Type	Freq.
αἰτέω	I ask, demand	verb	70
αἰώνιος, -ος, -ον	eternal	adjective	71
ἀνοίγω	I open, unlock, disclose	verb	77
ἀποκτείνω (ἀποκτέννω)	to kill	verb	74
βαπτίζω	I baptize, wash, dip, immerse	verb	77
δώδεκα (indecl.)	twelve	adjective	75
ἐμός, -ή, -όν	my, mine	adjective	76
ἔσομαι	I shall be (future of εἰμί)	verb	
εὐαγγέλιον, -ου, τό	good news, gospel	noun	76
ἱερόν, -οῦ, τό	temple	noun	72
κεφαλή, -ῆς, ἡ	head	noun	75
μαρτυρέω	I bear witness, testify	verb	76
πίνω	I drink	verb	73
πονηρός, -ά, -όν	evil, bad, wicked	adjective	78
πρόσωπον, -ου, τό	face, appearance, presence	noun	76
πῦρ, πυρός, τό	fire	noun	71
σημεῖον, -ου, τό	sign, miracle	noun	77
στόμα, -ματος, τό	mouth	noun	78
τηρέω	I keep, guard, observe	verb	70
ὕδωρ, ὕδατος, τό	water	noun	76
φῶς, φωτός, τό	light	noun	73
χαίρω	I rejoice	verb	74

List 4   frequency: 69–62

Word	Meaning	Type	Freq.
ἄγω	I bring, lead, arrest	verb	67
ἀπολύω	I release, divorce	verb	66
γραμματεύς, -έως, ὁ	scribe, secretary	noun	63
δαιμόνιον, -ου, τό	demon	noun	63
δοκέω	I think, suppose, seem	verb	62
εἴτε	(even) if; whether . . . or, or, either/or	conjunction	65
ἐντολή, -ῆς, ἡ	commandment, law	noun	67
ἔξω	[adv.] without; (+gen.) out, outside	adverb; preposition	63
ἐρωτάω	I ask, request, entreat	verb	63
θέλημα, -ματος, τό	will, desire, wish	noun	62
θρόνος, -ου, ὁ	throne, seat	noun	62
Ἰσραήλ, ὁ	Israel	noun	68
καρπός, -ου, ὁ	fruit, crop, result	noun	66
ὄρος, -ους, τό	mountain, high hill	noun	63
πιστός, -ή, -όν	faithful, believing; reliable	adjective	67
πλοῖον, -ου, τό	boat, ship	noun	67
πρεσβύτερος, -α, -ον	older; elder	adjective	66
ῥῆμα, -ματος, τό	word, thing	noun	68
σάββατον, -ου, τό	sabbath, week	noun	68
τρεῖς, τρεῖς, τρία	three	adjective	69
φέρω	I bear, carry, produce, bring	verb	66
φημί	I say, affirm	verb	66

frequency: 61–56   **List 5**

Word	Meaning	Type	Freq.
ἀγαπητός, -ή, -όν	beloved	adjective	61
ἀσπάζομαι	I greet, salute, welcome	verb	59
δέχομαι	I take, receive	verb	56
διδάσκαλος, -ου, ὁ	teacher	noun	59
δοξάζω	I praise, honor, glorify	verb	61
ἐπερωτάω	I ask (for), question, demand	verb	56
εὐθύς (εὐθέως)	immediately (adv.); straight (adj.)	adverb	59
ἤδη	now, already	adverb	61
θεωρέω	I look at, behold, see, observe	verb	58
ἱμάτιον, -ου, τό	garment, cloak, clothing	noun	60
κηρύσσω	I proclaim, preach	verb	61
λίθος, -ου, ὁ	stone	noun	59
μέσος, -η, -ον	middle; (prep +gen.) in the middle; (adv.) among	adjective	58
μηδέ	nor, and not, but not	conjunction	56
νύξ, νυκτός, ἡ	night	noun	61
προσκυνέω	I worship; I do obeisance	verb	60
συνάγω	I gather together, invite	verb	59
συναγωγή, -ῆς, ἡ	synagogue, meeting, gathering	noun	56
τοιοῦτος, -αύτη, -οῦτο(ν)	such, of such kind	pronoun	57
τρίτος, -η, -ον	third	adjective	56
ὑπάρχω	I am, exist; I possess	verb	60
χαρά, -ᾶς, ἡ	joy, delight, gladness	noun	59
ὧδε	here; in this way, so, thus	adverb	61

List 6   frequency: 55–50

Word	Meaning	Type	Freq.
ἄρα	then, therefore	particle	52
ἀρχή, -ῆς, ἡ	beginning, first; ruler	noun	55
γλῶσσα, -ης, ἡ	tongue, language	noun	50
γραφή, -ῆς, ἡ	written document, scripture	noun	50
δεξιός, -ά, -όν	right, right hand, right side	adjective	54
διό	therefore, for this reason	conjunction	53
ἐλπίς, -ίδος, ἡ	hope	noun	53
ἐπαγγελία, -ας, ἡ	promise	noun	52
ἔσχατος, -η, -ον	last, least, end	adjective	52
εὐαγγελίζω (mid. εὐαγγελίζομαι)	I bring good news, preach, announce	verb	54
κακός, -ή, -όν	evil, bad, wrong, harm	adjective	50
κράζω	I call out, cry out	verb	55
λοιπός, -ή, -όν	remaining; (adv.) henceforth, finally	adjective	55
μακάριος, -α, -ον	blessed, happy	adjective	50
ὅπως	how, (so) that, in order that	conjunction	53
οὐχί	not, no	particle	54
παιδίον, -ου, τό	child, infant	noun	52
παραβολή, -ῆς, ἡ	parable	noun	50
πείθω	I persuade, believe, trust	verb	52
πλείων, -ων, -ον	larger, more, greater (comparative of πόλυς)	adjective	55
σοφία, -ας, ἡ	wisdom	noun	51
σπείρω	I sow	verb	52
τυφλός, -ή, -όν	blind	adjective	50
χρόνος, -ου, ὁ	time	noun	54

frequency: 49–46   **List 7**

Word	Meaning	Type	Freq.
ἁμαρτωλός, -ός, -όν	sinner, sinful	adjective	47
ἀποδίδωμι	I give back, pay	verb	48
ἄχρι (ἄχρις)	(+gen.) until	conjunction, preposition	49
ἔμπροσθεν	(+gen.) before, in front of	adverb, preposition	48
ἔρημος, -ος, -ον	desolate, wilderness, desert	adjective	48
ἔτος, -ους, τό	year	noun	49
θηρίον, -ου, τό	wild animal	noun	46
καθίζω	I sit, set, place	verb	46
κρατέω	I grasp, am strong, take possession	verb	47
κρίσις -εως, ἡ	judgment, decision	noun	47
μείζων (μείζον)	greater, larger (comparative of μέγας)	adjective	48
μικρός, -ά, -όν	small, little; a little, a short time	adjective	46
οὐαί	woe! how terrible!	interjection	46
οὐκέτι	no longer	adverb	47
παραλαμβάνω	I take along, accept, receive	verb	49
ποῦ	where?	particle	48
πρό	(+gen.) before, above	preposition	47
προσφέρω	I bring, I offer	verb	47
σταυρόω	I crucify	verb	46
σωτηρία, -ας, ἡ	salvation, deliverance	noun	46
φανερόω	I reveal, make known	verb	49
φόβος, -ου, ὁ	fear, terror; reverence	noun	47
φυλακή, -ῆς, ἡ	guard, watch, prison	noun	47
χρεία, -ας, ἡ	need	noun	49

List 8   frequency: 45–43

Word	Meaning	Type	Freq.
ἁμαρτάνω	I sin	verb	43
ἀπαγγέλλω	I report, tell, bring news	verb	45
γενεά, -ᾶς, ἡ	generation	noun	43
δεύτερος, -α, -ον	second	adjective	43
δέω	I bind, stop	verb	43
διέρχομαι	I go/pass through	verb	43
διώκω	I pursue, persecute	verb	45
ἐπιγινώσκω	I know	verb	44
Ἡρῴδης, ου, ὁ	Herod	proper noun	43
θαυμάζω	I marvel, wonder	verb	43
θεραπεύω	I serve, heal	verb	43
θλῖψις, -ψεως, ἡ	affliction, trouble, tribulation, oppression	noun	45
Ἰουδαία, -ας, ἡ	Judea	proper noun	44
Ἰούδας, α, ὁ	Judas/Judah	proper noun	44
κατοικέω	I settle, dwell, inhabit	verb	44
ναός, -ου, ὁ	temple; palace	noun	45
ὅμοιος, -α, -ον	like, similar	adjective	45
σεαυτοῦ -ῆς	of yourself (sg.)	pronoun	43
σπέρμα, -ματος, τό	seed, offspring	noun	43
φωνέω	I call, to shout	verb	43

frequency: 42–40   **List 9**

Word	Meaning	Type	Freq.
ἀνάστασις, -εως, ἡ	standing up, resurrection	noun	42
ἄξιος, -α, -ον	worthy	adjective	41
ἐγγίζω	I bring near, come near	verb	42
ἐργάζομαι	I work	verb	41
ἑτοιμάζω	I prepare	verb	40
εὐλογέω	I bless	verb	41
Ἰάκωβος, -ου, ὁ	Jacob; James	proper noun	42
καινός, -ή, -όν	new	adjective	42
κλαίω	I weep, cry	verb	40
λογίζομαι	I count, think, calculate	verb	40
μέρος, -ους, τό	part	noun	42
μισέω	I hate	verb	40
μνημεῖον, -ου, τό	tomb, monument	noun	40
οἰκοδομέω	I build	verb	40
ὀλίγος, -η, -ον	little, few	adjective	40
πάντοτε	always	adverb	41
παρίστημι (παριστάνω)	I present, offer; (intrans.) I stand by	verb	41
πάσχω	I suffer	verb	42
σήμερον	today	adverb	41
τέλος, -ους, τό	end, goal; tribute	noun	40
τέσσαρες	four	adjective	41
τιμή, -ῆς, ἡ	honor	noun	41
χωρίς	separately (adv.) (+gen.) without	adverb; preposition	41

List 10   frequency: 39–37

Word	Meaning	Type	Freq.
ἅπτω (ἅπτομαί)	I touch, hold, grasp; I light, ignite	verb	39
ἄρχων, -χοντος, ὁ	ruler	noun	37
βούλομαι	I will, want	verb	37
διάβολος, -ος, -ον	enemy, adversary; devil	adj.	37
διακονέω	I serve, wait on	verb	37
δικαιόω	I justify, vindicate, pronounce righteous	verb	39
ἐκεῖθεν	from there	adv.	37
ἐμαυτοῦ -ῆς	of myself, my own	pron.	37
εὐχαριστέω	I give thanks	verb	38
θύρα, -ας, ἡ	door	noun	39
ἱκανός, -ή, -όν	sufficient, able, worthy	adj.	39
καλῶς	well, rightly	adv.	37
καυχάομαι	I boast, glory	verb	37
μαρτυρία, -ας, ἡ	testimony	noun	37
παραγίνομαι	I come, I appear	verb	37
πειράζω	I tempt, test	verb	38
πέντε (indecl.)	five	adj.	38
περισσεύω	I abound	verb	39
πλανάω	I deceive	verb	39
πράσσω	I do, I accomplish	verb	38
πρόβατον, -ου, τό	sheep	noun	39
ὑποτάσσω	I subject; I submit	verb	38

frequency: 36–33   **List 11**

Word	Meaning	Type	Freq.
ἀγρός, -οῦ, ὁ	field	noun	36
ἄπας, ἄπασα, ἄπαν	all, every	adjective	34
ἀρνέομαι	I deny	verb	33
ἄρτι	now	adverb	36
ἀσθενέω	I am weak	verb	33
βιβλίον, -ου, τό	scroll, papyrus strip	noun	34
βλασφημέω	I slander, blaspheme	verb	34
διαθήκη, -ης, ἡ	covenant	noun	33
διακονία, -ας, ἡ	service, ministry	noun	34
ἐκπορεύομαι	I go, come out	verb	33
ἐπιστρέφω	I turn back, return, turn	verb	36
εὐθέως	immediately, at once, suddenly	adverb	36
Ἰωσήφ, ὁ	Joseph	proper noun	35
μάρτυς, -υρος, ὁ	witness	noun	35
μέλος, -ους, τό	body part; musical part, melody	noun	34
μετανοέω	I repent	verb	34
μήτε	and not; neither . . . nor	conjunction	34
ναί	yes	particle	33
οἶνος, -ου, ὁ	wine	noun	34
ὀπίσω	back (adv.); (+gen.) after (prep.)	adverb; preposition	35
ὀργή, -ῆς, ἡ	wrath; anger	noun	36
οὖς, ὠτός, τό	ear	noun	36
ὀφείλω	I am obligated, I owe	verb	35
περιτομή, -ῆς, ἡ	circumcision	noun	36
ποῖος, -α, -ον	what kind of, which	pronoun	33
προσευχή, -ῆς, ἡ	prayer	noun	36
πτωχός, -ή, -όν	poor	adjective	34
Σατανᾶς, -ᾶ, ὁ	Satan	noun	36
ὑποστρέφω	I return	verb	35
Φίλιππος, -ου, ὁ	Philip	proper noun	36
ὥσπερ	as, just as	conjunction	36

List 12   frequency: 32–30

Word	Meaning	Type	Freq.
ἀγοράζω	I buy	verb	30
ἀκάθαρτος, -ος, -ον	unclean	adjective	32
ἀναγινώσκω	I read	verb	32
ἄνεμος, -ου, ὁ	wind	noun	31
ἀρνίον, -ου, τό	lamb, small lamb	noun	30
δείκνυμι (δείκνυω)	I show, explain	verb	30
διδαχή, -ῆς, ἡ	teaching	noun	30
δυνατός, -ή, -όν	possible, strong, able	adjective	32
ἐγγύς	(+gen.) near	adverb; preposition	31
ἐλπίζω	I hope	verb	31
ἔξεστι(ν)	it is right, possible	verb	31
ἐπικαλέω (ἐπικαλέομαι)	I call on	verb	30
ἐχθρός, -ά, -όν	hostile, enemy	adjective	32
ἥλιος, -ου, ὁ	sun	noun	32
ἱερεύς, -έως, ὁ	priest	noun	31
καθαρίζω	I cleanse	verb	31
ὁμοίως	likewise	adverb	30
παραγγέλλω	I command	verb	32
παρρησία, -ας, ἡ	boldness	noun	31
πλῆθος, -ους, τό	multitude	noun	31
πλήν	but, nevertheless (conj.) (+gen.) only, except	conjunction; preposition	31
ποτήριον, -ου, τό	cup	noun	31
σκότος, -ους, τό	darkness	noun	31
συνείδησις, -εως, ἡ	conscience	noun	30
συνέρχομαι	I come together; I go together	verb	30
ὑπομονή, -ῆς, ἡ	endurance; staying	noun	32
φαίνω	I appear, shine	verb	31
φυλάσσω	I guard, keep	verb	31
φυλή, -ῆς, ἡ	tribe	noun	31

Frequent Principal Parts of Irregular Verbs   **List 13**

Word	Meaning	Type
ἀκήκοα	I have heard (perfect of ἀκούω)	verb
ἀπέθανον	I died (aorist of ἀποθνῄσκω)	verb
γέγονα	I have become (perfect of γίνομαι)	verb
ἔβαλον	I threw (aorist of βάλλω)	verb
ἐγενόμην	I had been (aorist middle of γίνομαι)	verb
ἔγνων	I knew (aorist of γινώσκω)	verb
εἶδον	I saw (aorist of ὁράω)	verb
εἶπον	I said (aorist of λέγω)	verb
ἔλαβον	I took, received (aorist of λαμβάνω)	verb
ἐλήλυθα	I have come, gone (perfect of ἔρχομαι)	verb
ἐληλύθειν	I was coming (pluperfect of ἔρχομαι)	verb
ἔπεσον	I fall, fell (aorist of πίπτω)	verb
ἔπιον	I drank (aorist of πίνω)	verb
ἔσχον	I had (aorist of ἔχω)	verb
εὕρηκα	I have found (perfect of εὑρίσκω)	verb
εὗρον	I found (aorist of εὑρίσκω)	verb
ἔφαγον	I ate (aorist of ἐσθίω)	verb
ἤγαγον	I brought, lead (aorist of ἄγω)	verb
ἦλθον	I came, went (aorist of ἔρχομαι)	verb
ἤνεγκα	I brought, bore, carried (aorist of φέρω)	verb

APPENDIX B:
PRINCIPAL PARTS

All asterisked items indicate second aorist forms.

First	Second	Third	Fourth	Fifth	Sixth
ἀγαπάω	ἀγαπήσω	ἠγάπησα	ἠγάπηκα	ἠγάπημαι	ἠγαπήθην
ἄγω	ἄξω	ἤγαγον*	ἀγείοχα	ἦγμαι	ἤχθην
αἴρω	ἀρῶ	ἦρα	ἦρκα	ἦρμαι	ἤρθην
αἰτέω	αἰτήσω	ᾔτησα	ᾔτηκα	ᾔτημαι	ᾐτήθην
ἀκολουθέω	ἀκολουθήσω	ἠκολούθησα	ἠκολούθηκα	ἠκολούθημαι	ἠκολουθήθην
ἀκούω	ἀκούσω	ἤκουσα	ἀκήκοα	ἤκουσμαι	ἠκούσθην
ἀναβαίνω	ἀναβήσομαι	ἀνέβην*	ἀναβέβηκα	-	-
ἀνίστημι	ἀναστήσω	ἀνέστησα	ἀνέστηκα	ἀνέστημαι	ἀνεστάθην
ἀνοίγω	ἀνοίξω	ἀνέῳξα	ἀνέῳγα	ἀνέῳγμαι	ἀνεῴχθην
ἀπαγγέλλω	ἀπαγγελῶ	ἀπήγγειλα	-	ἀπήγγελμαι	ἀπηγγέλην
ἀπέρχομαι	ἀπελεύσομαι	ἀπῆλθον*	ἀπελήλυθα	-	-
ἀποθνήσκω	ἀποθανοῦμαι	ἀπέθανον*	-	-	-
ἀποκρίνομαι	-	ἀπεκρινάμην	-	-	ἀπεκρίθην
ἀποκτείνω	ἀποκτενῶ	ἀπέκτεινα	-	-	ἀπεκτάνθην
ἀπόλλυμι	ἀπολέσω	ἀπώλεσα	ἀπώλεκα	ἀπολώλεσμαι	ἀπωλέσθην
ἀπολύω	ἀπολύσω	ἀπέλυσα	-	ἀπολέλυμαι	ἀπελύθην
ἀποστέλλω	ἀποστελῶ	ἀπέστειλα	ἀπέσταλκα	ἀπέσταλμαι	ἀπεστάλην
ἄρχω	ἄρξω	ἦρξα	-	-	-
ἀσπάζομαι	-	ἠσπασάμην	-	-	-
ἀφίημι	ἀφήσω	ἀφῆκα	-	ἀφέωμαι	ἀφέθην
βάλλω	βαλῶ	ἔβαλον*	βέβληκα	βέβλημαι	ἐβλήθην
βαπτίζω	βαπτίσω	ἐβάπτισα	-	βεβάπτισμαι	ἐβαπτίσθην
βλέπω	βλέψω	ἔβλεψα	-	-	-
γεννάω	γεννήσω	ἐγέννησα	γεγέννηκα	γεγέννημαι	ἐγεννήθην
γίνομαι	γενήσομαι	ἐγενόμην*	γέγονα	γεγένημαι	ἐγενήθην
γινώσκω	γνώσομαι	ἔγνων*	ἔγνωκα	ἔγνωσμαι	ἐγνώσθην
γράφω	γράψω	ἔγραψα	γέγραφα	γέγραμμαι	ἐγράφην
δέχομαι	δέξομαι	ἐδεξάμην	-	δέδεγμαι	ἐδέχθην
διδάσκω	διδάξω	ἐδίδαξα	-	-	ἐδιδάχθην

First	Second	Third	Fourth	Fifth	Sixth
δίδωμι	δώσω	ἔδωκα	δέδωκα	δέδομαι	ἐδόθην
δοκέω	-	ἔδοξα	-		
δοξάζω	δοξάσω	ἐδόξασα	-	δεδόξασμαι	ἐδοξάσθην
δύναμαι	δυνήσομαι	-	-	δεδύνημαι	ἠδυνήθην
ἐγείρω	ἐγερῶ	ἤγειρα	-	ἐγήγερμαι	ἠγέρθην
εἰσέρχομαι	εἰσελεύσομαι	εἰσῆλθον*	εἰσελήλυθα	-	-
ἐκβάλλω	ἐκβαλῶ	ἐξέβαλον*	-	-	ἐξεβλήθην
ἐξέρχομαι	ἐξελεύσομαι	ἐξῆλθον*	ἐξελήλυθα	-	-
ἐπερωτάω	ἐπερωτήσω	ἐπηρώτησα	-	-	-
ἔρχομαι	ἐλεύσομαι	ἦλθον*	ἐλήλυθα	-	-
ἐρωτάω	ἐρωτήσω	ἠρώτησα	-	-	-
ἐσθίω	φάγομαι	ἔφαγον*	-	-	-
εὐαγγελίζω	εὐαγγελιῶ	εὐηγγέλισα	-	εὐηγγέλισμαι	εὐηγγελίσθην
εὑρίσκω	εὑρήσω	εὗρησα (εὗρον)*	εὕρηκα	-	εὑρέθην
ἔχω	ἕξω	ἔσχον*	ἔσχηκα	-	-
ζάω	ζήσω	ἔζησα	-	-	-
ζητέω	ζητήσω	ἐζήτησα	-	-	ἐζητήθην
θέλω	-	ἠθέλησα	-	-	-
θεωρέω	θεωρήσω	ἐθεώρησα	-	-	-
ἵστημι	στήσω	ἔστησα (ἔστην)	ἔστηκα	-	ἐστάθην
κάθημαι	καθήσομαι	-	-	-	-
καλέω	καλέσω	ἐκάλεσα	κέκληκα	κέκλημαι	ἐκλήθην
καταβαίνω	καταβήσομαι	κατέβην*	καταβέβηκα	-	-
κηρύσσω	κηρύξω	ἐκήρυξα	-	-	ἐκηρύχθην
κράζω	κράξω	ἔκραξα	κέκραγα	-	-
κρατέω	κρατήσω	ἐκράτησα	κεκράτηκα	κεκράτημαι	-
κρίνω	κρινῶ	ἔκρινα	κέκρικα	κέκριμαι	ἐκρίθην
λαλέω	λαλήσω	ἐλάλησα	λελάληκα	λελάλημαι	ἐλαλήθην
λαμβάνω	λήμψομαι	ἔλαβον*	εἴληφα		
λέγω	ἐρῶ	εἶπον*	εἴρηκα	εἴρημαι	ἐρρέθην
μαρτυρέω	μαρτυρήσω	ἐμαρτύρησα	μεμαρτύρηκα	μεμαρτύρημαι	ἐμαρτυρήθην

First	Second	Third	Fourth	Fifth	Sixth
μέλλω	μελλήσω	-	-	-	-
μένω	μενῶ	ἔμεινα	μεμένηκα	-	-
οἶδα	εἰδήσω	-	οἶδα (εἰδῆτε=subj.)		
ὁράω	ὄψομαι	εἶδον*	ἑώρακα (ἑόρακα)	-	ὤφθην
ὀφείλω	-	-	-	-	-
παραδίδωμι	παραδώσω	παρέδωκα	παραδέδωκα	παραδέδομαι	παρεδόθην
παρακαλέω	-	παρεκάλεσα	-	παρακέκλημαι	παρεκλήθην
πείθω	πείσω	ἔπεισα	πέποιθα	πέπεισμαι	ἐπείσθην
περιπατέω	περιπατήσω	περιεπάτησα	-	-	-
πίνω	πίομαι	ἔπιον*	πέπωκα	-	-
πίπτω	πεσοῦμαι	ἔπεσον* (ἔπεσα)	πέπτωκα	-	-
πιστεύω	πιστεύσω	ἐπίστευσα	πεπίστευκα	πεπίστευμαι	ἐπιστεύθην
πληρόω	πληρώσω	ἐπλήρωσα	-	πεπλήρωμαι	ἐπληρώθην
ποιέω	ποιήσω	ἐποίησα	πεποίηκα	πεποίημαι	-
πορεύομαι	πορεύσομαι	-	-	πεπόρευμαι	ἐπορεύθην
προσέρχομαι	-	προσῆλθον*	προσελήλυθα	-	-
προσεύχομαι	προσεύξομαι	προσηυξάμην	-	-	-
προσκυνέω	προσκυνήσω	προσεκύνησα	-	-	-
σπείρω	-	ἔσπειρα	-	ἔσπαρμαι	ἐσπάρην
συνάγω	συνάξω	συνήγαγον*	-	συνῆγμαι	συνήχθην
σῴζω (σώζω)	σώσω	ἔσωσα	σέσωκα	σέσωμαι	ἐσώθην
τηρέω	τηρήσω	ἐτήρησα	τετήρηκα	τετήρημαι	ἐτηρήθην
τίθημι	θήσω	ἔθηκα	τέθεικα	τέθειμαι	ἐτέθην
ὑπάγω	-	-	-	-	-
ὑπάρχω	-	-	-	-	-
φέρω	οἴσω	ἤνεγκα*	ἐνήνοχα	-	ἠνέχθην
φοβέω	-	-	-	-	ἐφοβήθην
χαίρω	χαρήσομαι	ἐχάρην (ἐχαίρησα)	-	-	ἐχάρην

Let God's word set the agenda   **APPENDIX C: A RUBRIC FOR PREPARING SERMONS AND BIBLE STUDIES UTILIZING THE ORIGINAL LANGUAGES**

Steps	Resources
Prayer and Observational Reading *Pray that the Holy Spirit will teach you. Read your passage over and over, observing details, flow, and repetition—aim for 15–30 observations. Avoid interpretation or application.*	• Your preferred English translation(s) of the Bible alongside the original text (Greek or Hebrew)
Create Exaggerated Translation *Create your own exaggerated translation. Focus on bringing out the declension usage, verb translation, participle/infinitive/subjunctive use, etc., in your translation.*	• Your own knowledge • Your preferred Greek or Hebrew lexicon • (Advanced) Wallace's *Greek Grammar Beyond the Basics* or Waltke and O'Connor's *Biblical Hebrew Syntax*[1]
Literary Context *Understand where and how your passage fits into the particular book. How does it fit into the story and move the story along? What is its genre and how does it affect how we understand it?*	• Outline of the Book • Read the whole book • Your preferred introduction to the biblical book • Fee and Stuart's *How to Read the Bible Book by Book*[2] • Introductory material in your preferred commentary
Canonical and Theological Context *Understand where the passage fits into the story of God's redemptive work in the Bible. If it deals with a particularly foundational doctrine, understand how this fits into Christian theology.*	• Dictionary of Biblical Theology • Your preferred systematic theology, biblical theology, and ethics textbooks • Class notes
Keywords *Focus on a few keywords from your passage which you've already identified in step 1. See how else your keywords are used in your particular book, in its testament, in the Bible.*	• Your preferred Greek or Hebrew lexicon • Your preferred Greek or Hebrew theological dictionary (*TDNT, NIDNTT, NIDOTTE, TLNT, TLOT, TWOT*) • Word searches in your Bible software
Historical and Cultural Context *Identify important people, places, and things that relate to your passage.*	• Good Bible dictionaries (e.g., InterVarsity Press "Black Dictionaries") • Bible atlases • Zondervan Background commentaries (*ZIBBCNT* and *ZIBBCOT*)
Cross References *Hear from the whole testimony of scripture on issues related to your passage.*	• Logos: *The Treasury of Scripture Knowledge* • Chain-reference or cross-reference Bible

1. Bruce Waltke and Michael O'Connor, *Introduction to Biblical Hebrew Syntax* (Winona Lake, IN: Eisenbrauns, 1990).

2. Gordon Fee and Douglas Stuart, *How to Read the Bible Book by Book* (Grand Rapids: Zondervan, 2014).

Steps	Resources
Parallel Passages *Compare the Gospels, Chronicles, Psalms*	• Logos: *Records of the Life of Jesus* • Chain-reference or cross-reference Bible
Learn from Others *Read and honor what other contemporaries say about your passage. Understand differences of opinion on the passage, and educate others about differences of opinion.*	• 2 or 3 technical commentaries ▫ www.bestcommentaries.com • Popular and academic level monographs
Learn from Church History *Read and honor how the church has read your passage through the centuries.*	• *Ancient Christian Commentary on Scripture*[1] • Apostolic Fathers, Ante-Nicene and Post-Nicene Fathers—Use scripture index or search. • Calvin, Luther, etc., commentaries
Application	

Bridge the Gap
What are the differences between the context of the passage and our own context?
What does the passage mean for our context?
	• NIV Application Commentaries (Zondervan)
	• 1 or 2 pastoral/devotional commentaries
	• Your own reflections
	• Other sermons on the subject
	    ▫ sermonaudio.com
	    ▫ soundfaith.com
	    ▫ sermoncentral.com
	    ▫ sermons.com
	    ▫ sermonindex.net
	    ▫ contemporary preachers you like

Other Resources (specifically for services)	
Related Songs	• Logos hymnal resource • Cyberhymnal.org • Scripture index of your church hymnal • You (or your worship leader) should tag modern songs by topic and scripture
Other Media	• Gracewaymedia.com (Logos tags these) • Sermonspice.com • Worshiphousemedia.com • Motionworship.com
Illustrations	• Logos: Encyclopedia of 7700 illustrations • www.sermonspice.com • www.bible.org/illustrations • www.preachingtoday.com

1. *Ancient Christian Commentary on Scripture*, ed. Thomas Oden (Downers Grove, IL: InterVarsity Press, 1998–2010).

Bauer, Walter, Frederick W. Danker, William Arndt, and F. Wilbur Gingrich, eds. *A Greek-English Lexicon of the New Testament and Other Early Christian Literature*. 3rd ed. Chicago: University of Chicago Press, 2000.

The BDAG lexicon is a highly respected Greek lexicon for the New Testament and other Christian literature. Some professors may want to utilize BDAG rather than the Louw-Nida lexicon used through the textbook, or some students may want to learn how to access another lexicon. This section covers BDAG in the same detail Louw-Nida was covered through the textbook.

13.1: Nouns in the BDAG Lexicon

The goal of the *Biblical Greek Made Simple* approach is to help you access the language using the best tools. One of the most important items in your toolkit when working with Greek is a lexicon.[1]

You will come to see that all translation is interpretation.[2] Simply take a look at the entry of a few different words in your lexicon and you will see that there can sometimes be numerous translation options for a single word.[3] This is why it is important to not only learn the main gloss while learning vocabulary, but also to be able to access a lexicon when looking closer at New Testament passages. A proper translation of a word is only yielded when the meaning of the word in *that specific* context in understood.

13.1.1: A Noun's Stem

Beyond giving you the various glosses for a noun, some of the first information a lexicon relates to a reader is the stem of a word and its gender. Remember, a noun's stem determines what declension endings a word uses. The biggest reason readers need a lexicon to help them with identifying a stem is because of third declension nouns (those that end in a consonant); remember that the lexical form (nominative singular) of a third declension noun does not show the stem the way first and second declension nominative singular nouns do (those pesky consonant interactions). A lexicon will help you identify

---

1. To read more about the BDAG lexicon, I encourage you to read this online essay by Rodney Decker: www.ntresources.com/documents/UsingBDAG.pdf

2. That's why not every English translation is the same and why it is important for you to be able to work with the primary language of the New Testament.

3. These options for translating a word are often called glosses.

the stem by showing you the genitive singular ending directly after the word is introduced (see examples below).

13.1.2: A Noun's Gender

Chapter 6 introduced the Greek article (the word "the"), which was in chapter 1's vocabulary. Three forms are important to understand now as you begin your work in the BDAG lexicon. The masculine singular form of "the" is ὁ. The feminine singular form of "the" is ἡ. The neuter singular form of "the" is τό. In a lexicon, after a noun and its genitive ending, an article[1] will occur to indicate the gender of the noun (see examples below).

13.1.3: BDAG Lexicon Noun Examples

Lexical form (nominative singular)	Genitive ending to reveal stem	Article to indicate gender	When the word first appears, etc.	A basic gloss (if applicable)

ἄνθρωπος, ου, ὁ (Hom.+; loanw. in rabb.; ἡ ἄνθρωπος [Hdt. 1, 60, 5] does not appear in our lit.) 'human being, man, person'.

ἡμέρα, ας, ἡ (Hom.+; loanw. in rabb.)

πνεῦμα, ατος, τό (πνέω; Aeschyl., Pre-Socr., Hdt.+. On the history of the word s. Rtzst., Mysterienrel.3 308ff).

13.1.4: Noun Definitions

As mentioned before, most Greek nouns do not have just one English word to translate it. A lexicon will categorize the various translation options and provide you with information on what texts translate the word in that manner, will provide examples, and will cite significant secondary sources for the word. The subcategories may be up to four categories deep (1. a. α.[2] א.[3]).

Do not make the mistake of reading the entire entry of a word when you are doing a word study. The first thing you do is look at the entry in its entirety, in particular noting the major categories and subcategories. The following is a condensation of the categories of

---

1. In some lexicons (like Louw-Nida) the lexicon will indicate gender with m, f, or n.

2. This level uses Greek letters.

3. This level uses Hebrew letters.

πνεῦμα, *without the additional information* of each category (this example categorizes three levels deep):

1. **air in movement,** *blowing, breathing*

   a. wind

   b. the breathing out of air, blowing, breath

2. **that which animates or gives life to the body,** *breath, (life-)spirit*

3. **a part of human personality,** *spirit*

   a. when used with σάρξ, the flesh, it denotes the immaterial part 2 Cor 7:1; Col 2:5. *Flesh and spirit*=the whole personality. . . .

   b. as the source and seat of insight, feeling, and will, gener.[1] as the representative part of human inner life. . . .

   c. *spiritual state, state of mind, disposition* ἐν ἀγάπη πνεύματί τε πραΰτητος *with love and a gentle spirit.* . . .

4. **an independent noncorporeal being, in contrast to a being that can be perceived by the physical senses,** *spirit*

   a. God personally

   b. good, or at least not expressly evil *spirits* or *spirit-beings*

   c. *evil spirits*

---

1. The BDAG lexicon uses abbreviations extensively: *gener.* means generally, *w.* means with, *art.* means article, *gen.* means genitive, and *abs.* means absolute. One of the great advantages of having BDAG in a Bible software format is that every abbreviation is hyperlinked to be able to access it quickly. In other forms of the lexicon, you will need to access the list of abbreviations in the box.

5. **God's being as controlling influence, with focus on association with humans, *Spirit, spirit***

   a. the Spirit of God

   b. the Spirit of Christ

   c. Because of its heavenly origin and nature this Spirit is called *(the) Holy Spirit*

      α. w. the art. τὸ πνεῦμα τὸ ἅγιον

      β. without the art.

   d. abs.

      α. w. the art. τὸ πνεῦμα.

      β. without the art. πνεῦμα

   e. The Spirit is more closely defined by a gen. of thing. . . .

   f. Of Christ 'it is written' in Scripture. . . .

   g. The (divine) Pneuma stands in contrast to everything that characterizes this age or the finite world. . . .

      α. in contrast to σάρξ. . . .

      β. in contrast to σῶμα. . . .

      γ. in contrast to γράμμα. . . .

      δ. in contrast to the wisdom of humans 1 Cor 2:13.

6. **the Spirit of God as exhibited in the character or activity of God's people or selected agents, *Spirit, spirit***

   a. πνεῦμα is accompanied by another noun. . . .

   b. Unless frustrated by humans in their natural condition, the Spirit of God produces a spiritual type of conduct. . . .

   c. The Spirit inspires certain people of God. . . .

d. The Spirit of God, being one, shows the variety and richness of its life. . . .

e. One special type of spiritual gift. . . .

f. The Spirit leads and directs Christian missionaries in their journeys. . . .

7. **an activating spirit that is not fr. God,** *spirit*

8. **an independent transcendent personality,** *the Spirit*

Every division in the example above has a lot of information in it, including bibliographic information for those who want to do even deeper word studies. *Most of the time you will not have to read this information, so learn how to spot the important stuff.* Notice, too, how our word example πνεῦμα in many different divisions are translated as "spirit." But each time the word is translated as "spirit" under the different divisions there are different nuances to the meaning of the word. This is why the information provided in a lexicon is so important: it helps you understand the nuances of meaning in translation.

Finally, after you have taken an overview, take the time to find out where BDAG placed your word for the verse you are studying. Please take note, the authors of BDAG were brilliant *but they were not infallible.* You may disagree with the decision BDAG made over the word in question.

Adjective information is similar in the lexicon to nouns. One of the main differences in the first information is that adjectives do not have gender, so feminine and neuter endings will be shown instead.

13.2: BDAG Lexicon Adjective Examples

Lexical form (nominative singular)	Feminine and neuter ending	When the word first appears, etc.	information on the comparative and superlative forms

ἀγαθός, ή, όν, (Hom.+) Comp. ἀμείνων (not in NT, but e.g., PGM 5, 50; 6, 2; Jos., Bell. 5, 19, Ant. 11, 296) 1 Cl 57:2; IEph 13:2; 15:1; βελτίων, also κρείσσων. . . .

13.2.1: Adjective Definitions

Definitions for adjectives will follow the same basic structure as nouns, but be careful to note how the lexicon highlights the two main uses of an adjective (attributive and substantive). The following is a condensation of the categories of ἀγαθός, without the additional information of each category:

1. **pert. to meeting a relatively high standard of quality, of things.**

   a. adj. useful, beneficial καρποί

   b. used as a pure subst.: sg. (Hom. et al.; ins, pap, LXX), ἀγαθόν, οῦ, τό the good

      α. quite gener. τὰ ἀγαθά σου

      β. possessions, treasures

      γ. possessions of a higher order

2. **pert. to meeting a high standard of worth and merit, good**

   a. as adj.

      α. of humans and deities

      β. of things characterized esp. in terms of social significance and worth

   b. as subst., sg. (s. 1b). Opp. (τὸ) κακόν

      α. that which is beneficial or helpful

      β. τὰ ἀ. (ἀληθινὰ ἀ. Orig., C. Cels 7, 21, 10) good deeds

Looking at the above example, notice that when the adjective is attributive, it is noted as "adj." (i.e., adjective). When the word is acting as a substantive it is noted as "subst." (i.e., substantive).

The first paragraph of information for verbs in *BDAG* are often longer because it will provide examples of all tense and verbal forms from the NT and other early Christian literature, as well as provide a citation for that form.

Lexical form (present indicative)	Tense and verbal forms with citations	When the word first appears (and other examples)	A brief definition and/ or gloss

βάλλω fut. βαλῶ; 2 aor. ἔβαλον, 3 pl. ἔβαλον Lk 23:34 (Ps 21:19); Ac 16:23 and ἔβαλαν Ac 16:37 (B-D-F §81, 3; Mlt-H. 208); pf. βέβληκα (on this form s. lit. in LfgrE s.v. βάλλω col. 25). Pass.: 1 fut. βληθήσομαι; 1 aor. ἐβλήθην; pf. βέβλημαι; plpf. ἐβεβλήμην (Hom.+). gener. to put someth. into motion by throwing, used from the time of Hom. either with a suggestion of force or in a gentler sense; opp. of ἁμαρτάνω 'miss the mark'.

While this is a typical first paragraph, some verb entries will also include links to advanced grammars if that verb is listed in them.

Definitions for verbs follow the same structure as other word forms. BDAG will often indicate verb usage based on its relation to its object, and within the sub-sections will often list numerous examples of the word with different subjects or objects. The following is a condensation of the categories of βάλλω, without the additional information of each category:

13.3.1

Verb Definitions

1. **to cause to move from one location to another through use of forceful motion, *throw***

    a. w. simple obj. *scatter seed on the ground*

    b. *throw*

    c. to cause or to let fall down, *let fall*

2. **to force out of or into a place, throw (away), drive out, expel**

3. **to put or place someth. in a location, put, place, apply, lay, bring**

    a. w. simple obj. κόπρια β. *put manure on, apply m.*

    b. w. indication of the place to which τὶ εἴς τι: *put*

    c. other usage ῥίζας β. *send forth roots, take root*

4. **to bring about a change in state or condition,** εἰρήνην, μάχαιραν ἐπὶ τὴν γῆν **bring peace, the sword on earth**

5. **to entrust money to a banker for interest,** *deposit money*

6. **to to move down suddenly and rapidly,** *rush down,* **intr.**

Looking at the above example, notice also that the section will indicate if a verb is working as an intransitive.

The following glossary lists all Greek words introduced in the text-book along with their meaning, part of speech, frequency, and section introduced.

Ἀβραάμ, ὁ	Abraham (pr. noun), ch. 1
ἀγαθός, -ή, -όν	good, useful (adj.), ch. 11
ἀγαπάω	I love, cherish (verb), ch. 8
ἀγάπη, -ης, ἡ	love (noun), ch. 10
ἀγαπητός, -ή, -όν	beloved (adj.), list 5
ἄγγελος, -ου, ὁ	messenger, angel (noun), ch. 4
ἅγιος, -α, -ον	holy; pl. saints (adj.), ch. 6
ἀγοράζω	I buy (verb), list 12
ἀγρός, -οῦ, ὁ	field (noun), list 11
ἄγω	I bring, lead, arrest (verb), list 4
ἀδελφός, -οῦ, ὁ	brother (noun), ch. 2
αἷμα, -ματος, τό	blood (noun), list 1
αἴρω	I raise, take up, take away (verb), ch. 11
αἰτέω	I ask, demand (verb), list 3
αἰών, -ῶνος, ὁ	age, eternity (noun), ch. 9
αἰώνιος, -ος, -ον	eternal (adj.), list 3
ἀκάθαρτος, -ος, -ον	unclean (adj.), list 12
ἀκολουθέω	I follow, accompany (verb), list 1
ἀκούω	I hear (verb), ch. 4
ἀλήθεια, -ας, ἡ	truth, reality, faithfulness (noun), ch. 10
ἀλλά (ἀλλ')	but, yet, except (conj.), ch. 2
ἀλλήλων (-οις, -ους)	one other (of one another, to one another) (pron.), ch. 11
ἄλλος, -η, -ον	other, another (adj.), ch. 8
ἁμαρτάνω	I sin (verb), list 8
ἁμαρτία, -ας, ἡ	sin (noun), ch. 7
ἁμαρτωλός, -ός, -όν	sinner, sinful (adj.), list 7
ἀμήν	amen, truly (particle), ch. 9
ἄν	(conditional, untranslatable particle) -ever; if, would, might (particle), ch. 7
ἀναβαίνω	I go up, come up, rise up, advance (verb), list 2

ἀναγινώσκω	I read (verb), list 12
ἀνάστασις, -εως, ἡ	standing up, resurrection (noun), list 9
ἄνεμος, -ου, ὁ	wind (noun), list 12
ἀνήρ, ἀνδρός, ὁ	man, husband (noun), ch. 3
ἄνθρωπος, -ου, ὁ	man, person (noun), ch. 2
ἀνίστημι	I rise, get up; I raise (verb), ch. 11
ἀνοίγω	I open, unlock, disclose (verb), list 3
ἄξιος, -α, -ον	worthy (adj.), list 9
ἀπαγγέλλω	I report, tell, bring news (verb), list 8
ἅπας, ἅπασα, ἅπαν	all, every (adj.), list 11
ἀπέρχομαι	I depart, go away (verb), ch. 10
ἀπό (ἀπ', ἀφ')	[+gen] (away) from (prep.), ch. 2
ἀποδίδωμι	I give back, pay (verb), list 7
ἀποθνήσκω	I die, am about to die, am freed from (verb), ch. 10
ἀποκρίνομαι	I answer (verb), ch. 4
ἀποκτείνω (ἀποκτέννω)	I kill (verb), list 3
ἀπόλλυμι	I destroy, kill; I perish, die (verb), list 1
ἀπολύω	I release, divorce (verb), list 4
ἀποστέλλω	I send (away) (verb), ch. 9
ἀπόστολος, -ου, ὁ	apostle (noun), list 2
ἅπτω (ἅπτομαί)	I touch, hold, grasp; I light, ignite (verb), list 10
ἄρα	then, therefore (particle), list 6
ἀρνέομαι	I deny (verb), list 11
ἀρνίον, -ου, τό	lamb, small lamb (noun), list 12
ἄρτι	now (adv.), list 11
ἄρτος, -ου, ὁ	bread, loaf, food; burden (noun), list 1
ἀρχή, -ῆς, ἡ	beginning, first; ruler (noun), list 6
ἀρχιερεύς, -έως, ὁ	chief priest, high priest (noun), ch. 9
ἄρχομαι (ἄρχω)	I begin; I rule over (verb), list 2
ἄρχων, -χοντος, ὁ	ruler (noun), list 10
ἀσθενέω	I am weak (verb), list 11
ἀσπάζομαι	I greet, salute, welcome (verb), list 5
αὐτός, αὐτή, τουτό	he, she, it (-self, same); pl. they (pron.), ch. 6
ἀφίημι	I let go, leave, permit, divorce, forgive (verb), ch. 8
ἄχρι (ἄχρις)	(+gen.) until (prep.), list 7

βάλλω	I throw (verb), ch. 9
βαπτίζω	I baptize, wash, dip, immerse (verb), list 3
βασιλεία, -ας, ἡ	kingdom (noun), ch. 7
βασιλεύς, -έως, ὁ	king (noun), ch. 10
βιβλίον, -ου, τό	scroll, papyrus strip (noun), list 11
βλασφημέω	I slander, blaspheme (verb), list 11
βλέπω	I see (verb), ch. 9
βούλομαι	I will, want (verb), list 10
Γαλιλαία, ας, ἡ	Galilee (pr. noun), ch. 1
γάρ	for, so, then (conj.), ch. 1
γενεά, -ᾶς, ἡ	generation (noun), list 8
γεννάω	I bear, beget, produce (verb), list 1
γῆ, -ῆς, ἡ	land, earth (noun), ch. 3
γίνομαι	I become, am, exist, happen, take place, am born, am created (verb), ch. 5
γινώσκω	I know, come to know, realize, learn (verb), ch. 5
γλῶσσα, -ης, ἡ	tongue, language (noun), list 6
γραμματεύς, -έως, ὁ	scribe, secretary (noun), list 4
γραφή, -ῆς, ἡ	written document, scripture (noun), list 6
γράφω	I write (verb), ch. 4
γυνή, -αικός, ἡ	woman, wife (noun), ch. 3
δαιμόνιον, -ου, τό	demon (noun), list 4
Δαυίδ, ὁ	David (pr. noun), ch. 1
δέ	but, and (conj.), ch. 1
δεῖ	it is necessary (verb), ch. 11
δείκνυμι (δείκνυω)	I show, explain (verb), list 12
δεξιός, -ά, -όν	right, right hand, right side (adj.), list 6
δεύτερος, -α, -ον	second (adj.), list 8
δέχομαι	I take, receive (verb), list 5
δέω	I bind, stop (verb), list 8
διά (δι᾽)	(+gen.) through; (+acc.) because of (prep.), ch. 2
διάβολος, -ος, -ον	enemy, adversary; devil (adj.), list 10
διαθήκη, -ης, ἡ	covenant (noun), list 11
διακονέω	I serve, wait on (verb), list 10
διακονία, -ας, ἡ	service, ministry (noun), list 11

διδάσκαλος, -ου, ὁ	teacher (noun), list 5
διδάσκω	I teach (verb), list 1
διδαχή, -ῆς, ἡ	teaching (noun), list 12
δίδωμι	I give (out), entrust, give back, put, grant, allow (verb), ch. 5
διέρχομαι	I go/pass through (verb), list 8
δίκαιος, -α, -ον	right, righteous, just (adj.), list 2
δικαιοσύνη, -ης, ἡ	righteousness, justice (noun), list 1
δικαιόω	I justify, vindicate, pronounce righteous (verb), list 10
διό	therefore, for this reason (conj.), list 6
διώκω	I pursue, persecute (verb), list 8
δοκέω	I think, suppose, seem (verb), list 4
δόξα, -ης, ἡ	glory (noun), ch. 7
δοξάζω	I praise, honor, glorify (verb), list 5
δοῦλος, -ου, ὁ	slave, servant (noun), ch. 9
δύναμαι	I am able, I am powerful, I can (verb), ch. 4
δύναμις, -εως, ἡ	power, ability (noun), ch. 9
δυνατός, -ή, -όν	possible, strong, able (adj.), list 12
δύο	two (adj.), ch. 9
δώδεκα (indecl.)	twelve (adj.), list 3
ἐάν	if (ever), when (ever), although (+subj.) (conj.), ch. 3
ἑαυτοῦ, -ῆς, -οῦ	himself/herself/itself; our-your-themselves (pron.), ch. 6
ἐγγίζω	I bring near, come near (verb), list 9
ἐγγύς	(+gen.) near (prep.), list 12
ἐγείρω	I raise up, wake (verb), ch. 8
ἐγώ (pl. ἡμεῖς)	I; we (pron.), ch. 6
ἔθνος, -ους, τό	(sg.) nation; (pl.) Gentiles (noun), ch. 7
εἰ	if (particle), ch. 2
εἰμί	I am (verb), ch. 5
εἰρήνη, -ης, ἡ	peace, health (noun), list 1
εἰς	(+acc.) into, in; to, toward; among (prep.), ch. 1
εἷς, μία, ἕν	one (adj.), ch. 6
εἰσέρχομαι	I enter, come in(to), go in(to) (verb), ch. 5
εἴτε	(even) if; whether/or, or, either/or (conj.), list 4
ἐκ (ἐξ)	(+gen.) from, out of, of, by (prep.), ch. 1
ἕκαστος, -η, -ον	each, every (adj.), list 2

ἐκβάλλω	I cast out, send out, drive out (verb), list 2
ἐκεῖ	there, in that place (adv.), ch. 11
ἐκεῖθεν	from there (adv.), list 10
ἐκεῖνος, -η, -ο	that, [pl.] those (pron.), ch. 6
ἐκκλησία, -ας, ἡ	assembly, church, congregation (noun), ch. 10
ἐκπορεύομαι	I go, come out (verb), list 11
ἐλπίζω	I hope (verb), list 12
ἐλπίς, -ίδος, ἡ	hope (noun), list 6
ἐμαυτοῦ -ῆς	of myself, my own (pron.), list 10
ἐμός, -ή, -όν	my, mine (adj.), list 3
ἔμπροσθεν	(+gen.) before, in front of (prep.), list 7
ἐν	(+dat.) in, on, by (prep.), ch. 1
ἐντολή, -ῆς, ἡ	commandment, law (noun), list 4
ἐνώπιον	(+gen.) before, in front of (prep.), list 1
ἐξέρχομαι	I go out (verb), ch. 5
ἔξεστι(ν)	it is right, possible (verb), list 12
ἐξουσία, -ας, ἡ	authority, power (noun), ch. 11
ἔξω	(+gen.) out, outside; [adv.] without (adv., improper prep.), list 4
ἐπαγγελία, -ας, ἡ	promise (noun), list 6
ἐπερωτάω	I ask (for), question, demand (verb), list 5
ἐπί (ἐπ', ἐφ')	(+gen.) on, over, when; (+dat.) on the basis of, at; (+acc.) on, to, against, for (prep.), ch. 1
ἐπιγινώσκω	I know (verb), list 8
ἐπιθυμία, ἡ	desire, lust (noun), list 10
ἐπικαλέω (ἐπικαλέομαι)	I call on (verb), list 12
ἐπιστρέφω	I turn back, return (verb), list 11
ἐπιτίθημι	I lay on, place, put, add (verb), list 10
ἑπτά (indecl.)	seven (adj.), list 2
ἐργάζομαι	I work (verb), list 9
ἔργον, -ου, τό	work, deed, action (noun), ch. 7
ἔρημος, -ος, -ον	desolate, wilderness, desert (adj.), list 7
ἔρχομαι	I come, go (verb), ch. 5
ἐρωτάω	I ask, request, entreat (verb), list 4
ἐσθίω	I eat (verb), ch. 5
ἔσομαι	I shall be (future of εἰμί) (verb), list 3

ἔσχατος, -η, -ον	last, least, end (adj.), list 6
ἕτερος, -α, -ον	other, another, different (adj.), list 1
ἔτι	yet, still (adv.), list 1
ἑτοιμάζω	I prepare (verb), list 9
ἔτος, -ους, τό	year (noun), list 7
εὐαγγελίζω (mid. εὐαγγελίζομαι)	I bring good news, preach, announce (verb), list 6
εὐαγγέλιον, -ου, τό	good news, gospel (noun), list 3
εὐθέως	immediately, at once, suddenly (adv.), list 11
εὐθύς (εὐθέως)	immediately (adv); straight (adj) (adv.), list 5
εὐλογέω	I bless (verb), list 9
εὑρίσκω	I find (verb), ch. 5
εὐχαριστέω	I give thanks (verb), list 10
ἐχθρός, -ά, -όν	hostile, enemy (adj.), list 12
ἔχω	I have (verb), ch. 4
ἕως	(conj.) until; (prep.) [+gen] as far as (conj.), ch. 7
ζάω	I live (verb), ch. 8
ζητέω	I seek, desire (verb), ch. 10
ζωή, -ῆς, ἡ	life (noun), ch. 9
ἤ	or, than; (ἤ . . . ἤ either . . . or) (particle), ch. 3
ἤδη	now, already (adv.), list 5
ἥλιος, -ου, ὁ	sun (noun), list 12
ἡμέρα, -ας, ἡ	day (noun), ch. 2
Ἡρῴδης, ου, ὁ	Herod (pr. noun), list 8
θάλασσα, -ης, ἡ	sea, lake (noun), list 1
θάνατος, -ου, ὁ	death (noun), ch. 9
θαυμάζω	I marvel, wonder (verb), list 8
θέλημα, -ματος, τό	will, desire, wish (noun), list 4
θέλω	I want, wish, will, desire (verb), ch. 4
θεός, -οῦ, ὁ	God, god (noun), ch. 1
θεραπεύω	I serve, heal (verb), list 8
θεωρέω	I look at, behold, see, observe (verb), list 5
θηρίον, -ου, τό	wild animal (noun), list 7
θλῖψις, -ψεως, ἡ	affliction, trouble, tribulation, oppression (noun), list 8
θρόνος, -ου, ὁ	throne, seat (noun), list 4

θύρα, -ας, ἡ	door (noun), list 10
Ἰάκωβος, -ου, ὁ	Jacob; James (pr. noun), list 9
ἴδιος, -α, -ον	one's own; his/her/its (adj.), ch. 10
ἰδού	look!, Behold! (interj.), ch. 7
ἱερεύς, -έως, ὁ	priest (noun), list 12
ἱερόν, -οῦ, τό	temple (noun), list 3
Ἱεροσόλυμα, τά or ἡ	Jerusalem (pr. noun), ch. 1
Ἱερουσαλήμ, ἡ	Jerusalem (pr. noun), ch. 1
Ἰησοῦς, -οῦ, ὁ	Jesus, Joshua (pr. noun), ch. 1
ἱκανός, -ή, -όν	sufficient, able, worthy (adj.), list 10
ἱμάτιον, -ου, τό	garment, cloak, clothing (noun), list 5
ἵνα	in order that, that (conj.), ch. 2
Ἰουδαία, -ας, ἡ	Judea (pr. noun), list 8
Ἰουδαῖος, -α, -ον	(adj.) Jewish; (noun) Jew, Judean (adj.), ch. 7
Ἰούδας, α, ὁ	Judas/Judah (pr. noun), list 8
ἴσθι	you be! (Imperative of εἰμί) (verb), list 8
Ἰσραήλ, ὁ	Israel (noun), list 4
ἵστημι	I stand, set, place; I cause to stand (verb), ch. 5
Ἰωάννης, -ου, ὁ	John (pr. noun), ch. 1
Ἰωσήφ, ὁ	Joseph (pr. noun), list 11
καθαρίζω	I cleanse (verb), list 12
κάθημαι	I sit (down), live (verb), list 1
καθίζω	I sit, set, place (verb), list 7
καθώς	as, even as, just as (conj.), ch. 7
καί	and, even, also (conj.), ch. 1
καινός, -ή, -όν	new (adj.), list 9
καιρός, -ου, ὁ	(appointed) time, season (noun), list 2
κακός, -ή, -όν	evil, bad, wrong, harm (adj.), list 6
καλέω	I call, name, invite (verb), ch. 4
καλός, -ή, -όν	good, beautiful (adj.), ch. 11
καλῶς	well, rightly (adv.), list 10
καρδία, -ας, ἡ	heart (noun), ch. 8
καρπός, -ου, ὁ	fruit, crop, result (noun), list 4
κατά (κατ᾽, καθ᾽)	(+gen.) down from, against; (+acc.) according to, throughout, during (prep.), ch. 3

καταβαίνω	I come down, go down (verb), list 2
κατοικέω	I settle, dwell, inhabit (verb), list 8
καυχάομαι	I boast, glory (verb), list 10
κεφαλή, -ῆς, ἡ	head (noun), list 3
κηρύσσω	I proclaim, preach (verb), list 5
κλαίω	I weep, cry (verb), list 9
κόσμος, -ου, ὁ	world, universe (noun), ch. 4
κράζω	I call out, cry out (verb), list 6
κρατέω	I grasp, am strong, take possession (verb), list 7
κρίνω	I judge, decide, prefer (verb), ch. 10
κρίσις -εως, ἡ	judgment, decision (noun), list 7
κύριος, -οῦ, ὁ	lord, Lord (noun), ch. 1
λαλέω	to sound, talk, speak (verb), ch. 4
λαμβάνω	I take, receive (verb), ch. 5
λαός, -ου, ὁ	people, crowd (noun), ch. 8
λέγω	I say, speak (verb), ch. 5
λίθος, -ου, ὁ	stone (noun), list 5
λογίζομαι	I count, think, calculate (verb), list 9
λόγος, -ου, ὁ	word, matter (noun), ch. 2
λοιπός, -ή, -όν	(noun) rest; (adj.) remaining; (adv.) henceforth, finally (adj.), list 6
λύω	I loosen, release (verb), ch. 4
μαθητής, -οῦ, ὁ	disciple, student (noun), ch. 3
μακάριος, -α, -ον	blessed, happy (adj.), list 6
μᾶλλον	more, rather (adv.), list 2
μαρτυρέω	I bear witness, testify (verb), list 3
μαρτυρία, -ας, ἡ	testimony (noun), list 10
μάρτυς, -υρος, ὁ	witness (noun), list 11
μέγας, -η, -α	large, great (adj.), ch. 6
μείζων (μείζον)	greater, larger (comparative of μέγας) (adj.), list 7
μέλλω	I am about to, intend (verb), ch. 10
μέλος, -ους, τό	body part; musical part, melody (noun), list 11
μέν	on the one hand, indeed [or left untranslated] (particle), ch. 5
μένω	I remain, live, abide, stay (verb), ch. 10
μέρος, -ους, τό	part (noun), list 9
μέσος, -η, -ον	middle; (prep +gen.) in the middle; (adv) among (adj.), list 5

μετά (μετ', μεθ')	(+gen.) with; (+acc.) after (prep.), ch. 3
μετανοέω	I repent (verb), list 11
μή	not, no; lest (conj.), ch. 1
μηδέ	nor, and not, but not (conj.), list 5
μηδείς, μηδεμία, μηδέν	no one, nothing (adj.), list 1
μήτε	and not; neither . . . nor (conj.), list 11
μήτηρ, μητρός, ἡ	mother (noun), list 2
μικρός, -ά, -όν	small, little; a little, a short time (adj.), list 7
μισέω	I hate (verb), list 9
μνημεῖον, -ου, τό	tomb, monument (noun), list 9
μόνος, -η, -ον	alone, only (adj.), ch. 10
Μωϋσῆς, -έως, ὁ	Moses (pr. noun), ch. 1
ναί	yes (particle), list 11
ναός, -ου, ὁ	temple; palace (noun), list 8
νεκρός, -ά, -όν	dead (adj.), ch. 9
νόμος, -ου, ὁ	law (noun), ch. 3
νῦν	now (adv.); the present (noun) (adv.), ch. 7
νύξ, νυκτός, ἡ	night (noun), list 5
ὁ, ἡ, τό	the (article), ch. 1
ὁδός, -οῦ, ἡ	way, road, journey; conduct (noun), ch. 11
οἶδα	I know, understand (verb), ch. 5
οἰκία, -ας, ἡ	house, home (noun), list 1
οἰκοδομέω	I build (verb), list 9
οἶκος, -ου, ὁ	house, home (noun), ch. 10
οἶνος, -ου, ὁ	wine (noun), list 11
ὀλίγος, -η, -ον	little, few (adj.), list 9
ὅλος, -η, -ον	(adj.) whole, complete; (adv.) entirely (adj.), ch. 10
ὅμοιος, -α, -ον	like, similar (adj.), list 8
ὁμοίως	likewise (adv.), list 12
ὄνομα, -ματος, τό	name, reputation (noun), ch. 3
ὀπίσω	(+gen.) after (prep.); back (adv.) (prep.), list 11
ὅπου (ποῦ)	where, whereas (conj.), list 2
ὅπως	how, (so) that, in order that (conj.), list 6
ὁράω	I see, notice, experience (verb), ch. 5
ὀργή, -ῆς, ἡ	wrath; anger (noun), list 11

ὄρος, -ους, τό	mountain, high hill (noun), list 4
ὅς, ἥ, ὅ	who, which, what (pron.), ch. 6
ὅσος, -α, -ον	as great as, as many as, as much, how much (pron.), ch. 10
ὅστις, ἥτις, ὅτι	whoever/whichever/whatever; everyone, which (pron.), ch. 8
ὅταν	whenever (conj.), ch. 9
ὅτε	when (conj.), ch. 11
ὅτι	because, that, since (conj.), ch. 1
οὐ, οὐκ, οὐχ	not (particle), ch. 1
οὐαί	woe! how terrible? (interj.), list 7
οὐδέ	and not, not even, neither, nor (conj.), ch. 7
οὐδείς, οὐδεμία, οὐδέν	no one; nothing (adj.), ch. 6
οὐκέτι	no longer (adv.), list 7
οὖν	therefore, then, accordingly (conj.), ch. 2
οὐρανός, -οῦ, ὁ	heaven, sky (noun), ch. 2
οὖς, ὠτός, τό	ear (noun), list 11
οὔτε	neither (conj.), list 2
οὗτος, αὕτη, τοῦτο	this (one); pl. these (pron.), ch. 6
οὕτως	thus, so, in this manner (adv.), ch. 3
οὐχί	not, no (particle), list 6
ὀφείλω	I am obligated, I owe (verb), list 11
ὀφθαλμός, -οῦ, ὁ	eye, sight (noun), ch. 11
ὄχλος, -ου, ὁ	crowd, multitude (noun), ch. 7
παιδίον, -ου, τό	child, infant (noun), list 6
πάλιν	again (adv.), ch. 8
πάντοτε	always (adv.), list 9
παρά (παρ’)	(+gen.) from; (+dat.) beside, in the presence of, with; (+acc.) alongside of, other than (prep.), ch. 4
παραβολή, -ῆς, ἡ	parable (noun), list 6
παραγγέλλω	I command (verb), list 12
παραγίνομαι	I come, I appear (verb), list 10
παραδίδωμι	I entrust, hand over, betray (verb), ch. 9
παρακαλέω	I call, urge, exhort, comfort, beseech (verb), ch. 10
παραλαμβάνω	I take along, accept, receive (verb), list 7
παρίστημι (παριστάνω)	I present, offer; (intrans.) I stand by (verb), list 9
παρρησία, -ας, ἡ	boldness (noun), list 12

πᾶς, πᾶσα, πᾶν	every, each; [pl.] all (adj.), ch. 6
πάσχω	I suffer (verb), list 9
πατήρ, πατρός, ὁ	father (noun), ch. 2
Παῦλος, -ου, ὁ	Paul (pr. noun), ch. 1
πείθω	I persuade, believe, trust (verb), list 6
πειράζω	I tempt, test (verb), list 10
πέμπω	I send (verb), list 2
πέντε (indecl.)	five (adj.), list 10
περί	(+gen.) about, concerning; (+acc.) around (prep.), ch. 3
περιπατέω	I walk (around), live (verb), list 1
περισσεύω	I abound (verb), list 10
περιτομή, -ῆς, ἡ	circumcision (noun), list 11
Πέτρος, -ου, ὁ	Peter (pr. noun), ch. 1
Πιλᾶτος, -ου, ὁ	Pilate (pr. noun), ch. 1
πίνω	I drink (verb), list 3
πίπτω	I fall (verb), list 1
πιστεύω	I believe (in), have faith, trust (verb), ch. 4
πίστις, -εως, ἡ	faith, belief, trust (noun), ch. 3
πιστός, -ή, -όν	faithful, believing; reliable (adj.), list 4
πλανάω	I deceive (verb), list 10
πλείων, -ων, -ον	larger, more, greater (comparative of πόλυς) (adj.), list 6
πλῆθος, -ους, τό	multitude (noun), list 12
πλήν	(+gen.) only, except (prep.); but, nevertheless (conj.) (prep.), list 12
πληρόω	I fill, fulfill, complete (verb), list 2
πλοῖον, -ου, τό	boat, ship (noun), list 4
πνεῦμα, -ματος, τό	wind, spirit (noun), ch. 2
ποιέω	I do, make (verb), ch. 4
ποῖος, -α, -ον	what kind of, which (pron.), list 11
πόλις, -εως, ἡ	city (noun), ch. 8
πολύς, πολλή, πολύ	much, [pl.] many; (adv.) often (adj.), ch. 6
πονηρός, -ά, -όν	evil, bad, wicked (adj.), list 3
πορεύομαι	I go, proceed, live (verb), ch. 4
ποτήριον, -ου, τό	cup (noun), list 12
ποῦ	where? (particle), list 7
πούς, ποδός, ὁ	foot (noun), list 1

πράσσω	I do, I accomplish (verb), list 10
πρεσβύτερος, -α, -ον	older; elder (adj.), list 4
πρό	(+gen.) before, above (prep.), list 7
πρόβατον, -ου, τό	sheep (noun), list 10
πρός	(+gen.) for; (+dat.) at; (+acc.) to, against (prep.), ch. 1
προσέρχομαι	I come to (verb), list 2
προσευχή, -ῆς, ἡ	prayer (noun), list 11
προσεύχομαι	I pray (verb), list 2
προσκυνέω	I worship; I do obeisance (verb), list 5
προσφέρω	I bring, I offer (verb), list 7
πρόσωπον, -ου, τό	face, appearance, presence (noun), list 3
προφήτης, -ου, ὁ	prophet (noun), ch. 8
πρῶτος, -η, -ον	first, earlier, foremost (adj.), ch. 8
πτωχός, -ή, -όν	poor (adj.), list 11
πῦρ, πυρός, τό	fire (noun), list 3
πῶς	how? (particle), ch. 11
ῥῆμα, -ματος, τό	word, thing (noun), list 4
σάββατον, -ου, τό	sabbath, week (noun), list 4
σάρξ, σαρκός, ἡ	flesh, body (noun), ch. 8
Σατανᾶς, -ᾶ, ὁ	Satan (noun), list 11
σεαυτοῦ -ῆς	of yourself (sing.) (pron.), list 8
σημεῖον, -ου, τό	sign, miracle (noun), list 3
σήμερον	today (adv.), list 9
Σίμων, Σίμωνος, ὁ	Simon (pr. noun), ch. 1
σκότος, -ους, τό	darkness (noun), list 12
σοφία, -ας, ἡ	wisdom (noun), list 6
σπείρω	I sow (verb), list 6
σπέρμα, -ματος, τό	seed, offspring (noun), list 8
σταυρόω	I crucify (verb), list 7
στόμα, -ματος, τό	mouth (noun), list 3
σύ (pl. ὑμεῖς)	you (sg.); y'all (pl.) (pron.), ch. 6
σύν	(+dat.) with (prep.), ch. 9
συνάγω	I gather together, invite (verb), list 5
συναγωγή, -ῆς, ἡ	synagogue, meeting, gathering (noun), list 5
συνείδησις, -εως, ἡ	conscience (noun), list 12

συνέρχομαι	I come/go together (verb), list 12
σῴζω (σώζω)	I save, heal, deliver, rescue (verb), ch. 11
σῶμα, -ματος, τό	body (noun), ch. 8
σωτηρία, -ας, ἡ	salvation, deliverance (noun), list 7
τέ	and (so), so [consec: both . . . and] (conj.), ch. 3
τέκνον, -ου, τό	child, descendent (noun), list 1
τέλος, -ους, τό	end, goal; tribute (noun), list 9
τέσσαρες	four (adj.), list 9
τηρέω	I keep, guard, observe (verb), list 3
τίθημι	I put, place (verb), ch. 11
τιμή, -ῆς, ἡ	honor (noun), list 9
τις, τι	someone, anyone; something, certain one (pron.), ch. 6
τίς, τί	who? which? what? why? (pron.), ch. 6
τοιοῦτος, -αύτη, -οῦτο(ν)	such, of such kind (pron.), list 5
τόπος, -ου, ὁ	place, position; opportunity (noun), list 1
τότε	then (adv.), ch. 7
τρεῖς, τρεῖς, τρία	three (adj.), list 4
τρίτος, -η, -ον	third (adj.), list 5
τυφλός, -ή, -όν	blind (adj.), list 6
ὕδωρ, ὕδατος, τό	water (noun), list 3
υἱός, -οῦ, ὁ	son, descendant; child (noun), ch. 2
ὑπάγω	I depart, go away; I draw off (verb), list 2
ὑπάρχω	I am, exist; I possess (verb), list 5
ὑπέρ	(+gen.) in behalf of; (+acc.) above (prep.), ch. 7
ὑπό (ὑπ', ὑφ')	(+gen.) by; (+acc.) under (prep.), ch. 3
ὑπομονή, -ῆς, ἡ	endurance; staying (noun), list 12
ὑποστρέφω	I return (verb), list 11
ὑποτάσσω	I subject; I submit (verb), list 10
φαίνω	I appear, shine (verb), list 12
φανερόω	I reveal, make known (verb), list 7
Φαρισαῖος, -ου, ὁ	Pharisee (pr. noun), ch. 1
φέρω	I bear, carry, produce, bring (verb), list 4
φημί	I say, affirm (verb), list 4
Φίλιππος, -ου, ὁ	Philip (pr. noun), list 11
φοβέω (mid. φοβέομαι)	I fear (verb), list 1

φόβος, -ου, ὁ	fear, terror; reverence (noun), list 7
φυλακή, -ῆς, ἡ	guard, watch, prison (noun), list 7
φυλάσσω	I guard, keep (verb), list 12
φυλή, -ῆς, ἡ	tribe (noun), list 12
φωνέω	I call, shout (verb), list 8
φωνή, -ῆς, ἡ	sound (noun), ch. 9
φῶς, φωτός, τό	light (noun), list 3
χαίρω	I rejoice (verb), list 3
χαρά, -ᾶς, ἡ	joy, delight, gladness (noun), list 5
χάρις, -ιτος, ἡ	grace, favor (noun), ch. 8
χείρ, χειρός, ἡ	hand; arm; finger (noun), ch. 4
χρεία, -ας, ἡ	need (noun), list 7
Χριστός, -οῦ, ὁ	Christ (pr. noun), ch. 1
χρόνος, -ου, ὁ	time (noun), list 6
χωρίς	(+gen.) without (prep.); separately (adv.) (prep.), list 9
ψυχή, -ῆς, ἡ	soul, life, self (noun), ch. 11
ὧδε	here; in this way, so, thus (adv.), list 5
ὥρα, -ας, ἡ	hour; occasion, moment (noun), ch. 11
ὡς	as, while (conj.), ch. 2
ὥσπερ	as, just as (particle), list 11
ὥστε	therefore, so that, in order that (conj.), list 2

Red lines indicate clause breaks, with the thicker red line indicating sentences; blue underlines indicate the main verb or each clause; blue boxes indicate the main verb of the independent clause; and green lines indicate the bracketed sentence.

APPENDIX F:
1 JOHN 1:1–4
SYNTAX SHEET

Ὃ ἦν ἀπ᾽ ἀρχῆς, / ὃ ἀκηκόαμεν, / ὃ ἑωράκαμεν τοῖς ὀφθαλμοῖς ἡμῶν, / ὃ ἐθεασάμεθα / καὶ αἱ χεῖρες ἡμῶν ἐψηλάφησαν περὶ τοῦ λόγου τῆς ζωῆς — καὶ ἡ ζωὴ ἐφανερώθη, / καὶ ἑωράκαμεν καὶ μαρτυροῦμεν καὶ ἀπαγγέλλομεν ὑμῖν τὴν ζωὴν τὴν αἰώνιον / ἥτις ἦν πρὸς τὸν πατέρα / καὶ ἐφανερώθη ἡμῖν — ὃ ἑωράκαμεν καὶ ἀκηκόαμεν ἀπαγγέλλομεν καὶ ὑμῖν, / ἵνα καὶ ὑμεῖς κοινωνίαν ἔχητε μεθ᾽ ἡμῶν. / καὶ ἡ κοινωνία δὲ ἡ ἡμετέρα μετὰ τοῦ πατρὸς καὶ μετὰ τοῦ υἱοῦ αὐτοῦ Ἰησοῦ Χριστοῦ. / καὶ ταῦτα γράφομεν ἡμεῖς, / ἵνα ἡ χαρὰ ἡμῶν ᾖ πεπληρωμένη.

that which was from the beginning — what we have heard — what we have seen with our eyes — what we have beheld — and our hands have touched concerning the word of life — and the life was revealed — we have seen — and — we testify — and we proclaim to you eternal life — which was from the father — and was revealed to us — what we have seen — and heard — we proclaim also to you — in order that you also may have fellowship — with us — And also our fellowship (is) with the father — and with his son Jesus Christ — We are writing these things to you — in order that our joy may be complete

Index